T0344726

SHORTY'S YARNS

Western Livestock Journal

VOLUME 11, NUMBER 1   LOS ANGELES, CALIFORNIA   NOVEMBER 24, 1932

THE LONG HORN SPEAKS

The old long horn looked at the prize winning steer
And grumbled, "What sort of a thing is this here?
He ain't got no laigs and his body is big,
I sort of suspicion he's crossed with a pig.
Now, me! I can run, I can gore, I can kick,
But that feller's too clumsy for all them tricks.

They're breedin' sech critters and callin' 'em Steers!
Why the horns that he's got ain't as long as my ears.
I cain't figger what he'd have done in my day.
They wouldn't have stuffed me with grain and with hay;
Nor have polished my horns and have fixed up my hoofs,
And slept me on beddin' in under the roofs

Who'd have curried his hide and have fuzzed up his tail?
Not none of them riders that drove the long trail.
They'd have found mighty quick jest how fur he could jump
When they jerked a few doubles of rope off his rump.
And to me it occurs he would not look so slick
With his tail full of burrs and his hide full of ticks.

I wonder jest what that fat feller would think
If he lived on short grass and went miles fer a drink,
And wintered outdoors in the sleet and the snow.
He wouldn't look much like he does at the show.
I wouldn't be like him; no, not if I could.
I cain't figger out why they think he's so good.

His little short laigs and his white baby face –
I would finish him off in a fight or a race.
They've his whole fam'ly hist'ry in writin', and still
He ain't fit fer nothin' exceptin' to kill.
And all of them judges that thinks they're so wise,
They look at that critter and give him first prize."

SHORTY'S YARNS

Western Stories and Poems of
BRUCE KISKADDON

Illustrations by
KATHERINE FIELD

Edited and with an introduction by
BILL SIEMS

Utah State University Press
Logan, Utah

Utah State University Press
Logan Utah 84322–7800

Book design by Dawn Holladay.

Manufactured in the United States of America.
Printed on acid-free paper.

Library of Congress Cataloging-in-Publication Data

Kiskaddon, Bruce, 1878-1950.
  Shorty's yarns : western stories and poems of Bruce Kiskaddon / illustrations by Katherine
Field; edited and with an introduction by Bill Siems.
     p. cm.
  ISBN 0-87421-579-X (acid-free paper) -- ISBN 0-87421-580-3 (pbk. : acid-free paper)
  1. West (U.S.)--Literary collections. 2. Ranch life--Literary collections. 3. Cowboys--Literary
collections. I. Field, Katherine, 1908- II. Siems, Bill, 1945- III. Title.
  PS3521.I764A6 2004
  818'.52--dc22
                                    2004001967

Contents

LIST OF ILLUSTRATIONS & POEMS

Kiskaddon's portrait and signature, from
the title page of the editor's copy of
Rhymes of the Ranges and Other Poems
(1947).

Introduction ~ An Uncommon Waddy

Writing of his life on the range, Bruce Kiskaddon always presented himself as a common waddy, a hired man on horseback. But to the readers of his poems and stories in the *Western Livestock Journal* during the 1930s and '40s he was a star—"the best cowboy poet that ever wrote a cowboy poem."[1] On a monthly schedule he cast nuggets of experience into meter and rhyme and spun loosely autobiographical yarns with the dry, understated humor so valued in cowboy culture. His settings were the arid Colorado, New Mexico, and Arizona locales he knew and loved. The time was his young manhood, the two decades on either side of 1900 when barbed wire took the last of the open range, often told from a 1930s present to frame an old man's reminiscences or to speak of the survival or demise of old ways. His Depression-wracked readers were ranching at a time when scientific breeding, feedlots, and corporate organization were on the rise. Modern agribusiness was crowding out both the tough range cattle that had fed on whatever they could find and the tough but inefficient extended families of owners, cow bosses, and waddies that had been the social and economic fabric of the West. Nostalgia ran high as ranchers struggled to adapt old knowledge and values to the accelerating pace of change. Through the 1930s the *Western Livestock Journal* served the needs of its audience well, with a solid diet of practical market, feeding, and breeding information, leavened with reminiscences and gossip appealing to the old-timers. Kiskaddon was their most compelling reminiscent writer, for his voice spoke directly to the hearts of his readers through the medium of shared experience.

> That's why I'm giving you warning—there's something I could not tell:
> The joys as clear as the morning—the tortures akin to hell.
> They never will reach outsiders, who were raised in the town's confines;
> But they're here for the hard old riders, who can read them between the lines.
> (From "Between the Lines")[2]

He spoke with an amused detachment from ambition, with a wry, uncomplaining tolerance for the foibles of humans and animals, and with a worker's willingness to do whatever needed to be done.

> He looked upon life as a sort of a joke.
> He didn't want money, but he never was broke.
> But when things got in earnest he shore could talk sense,
> And he could shoe hosses, mend wagons and fence.
> (From "The Drifter")[3]

Most importantly for his rural readers struggling through the Depression, Kiskaddon spoke up for the lowly, and had a survivor's resolve to face the future squarely, even though gripped by sorrow for a loved, unrecoverable past.

I liked the way that we used to do, when cattle was plenty and folks was few . . .
The waddy that came on a company hoss was treated the same as the owner and boss . . .
Them good old days is past and gone. The time and the world and the change goes on,
And you cain't do things like you used to do when cattle was plenty and folks was few.
(From "The Old Time Christmas")[4]

Fifty years after his death, Kiskaddon's poetry remains alive in new anthologies and oral tradition, but his prose has been virtually forgotten. This is unfortunate, for his stories are worth saving. Less polished and more broadly humorous than the poems, filled with spectacular misspellings to mimic western ranch speech, the stories are a loosely tied string of old-timers' yarns, in which Kiskaddon himself appears as the character "Shorty." As a common waddy with a small man's feistiness and a young man's mischief, Shorty encounters the wicked world with a succession of companions: Bill, high-headed and a bit of an outlaw; Rildy Briggs, untamable and unstoppable young cowgirl; and Ike, an old-fashioned dandy and "a very fortunate person." More or less in the background is "the Boss"—actually a series of bosses—generally affectionately respected as long as he remains democratic in his dealings with the waddies. Buffoonery is provided by a succession of pompous characters, from townspeople who look down their noses on wild, unwashed waddies to professors from the East who have read books on how ranches should be run. Although the actors at first seem straight from stock, they often have realistically quirky human behavior. Many otherwise predictably funny stories have unexpected turns of events where love, death and other serious matters suddenly crop up. Aside from a few adaptations of familiar rangeland jokes, the stories have the feeling of actual events presented through composite characters assembled from real remembered people whose names have been changed simply to "protect the innocent." From the right sort of old-timer, such tales are irresistible:

Well, it wasn't so excitin', Like a buckin' hoss or fightin', Or a rattle snake a bitin',
But when all was said and done;
All your life you never tire, Of the yarns told by some liar, That you really did admire,
As he set there in the sun.
(From "Augerin")[5]

Kiskaddon's stories are not well known, so perhaps I should relate how they came to light. Searching for Kiskaddon poems in a library volume of the *Western Livestock Journal*, I was delighted by a chance encounter with "The Fortune Teller Sends Ike Fishing," an amusing tale of Ike and Shorty which clearly had a precursor and promised a sequel. The existence of stories by Kiskaddon had been totally unknown to me, and I began to search for more. My excitement grew as additional stories turned up, but my greatest surprise was finding the autobiographical sketch comprising chapter 1 of this volume, accompanied by the grainy halftone photograph of a hat-shaded Kiskaddon in spectacles that appears on the title page. It then became my purpose to discover as many stories as possible by combing through all the volumes I could find of *Western Livestock*

Journal. Eventually the search covered issues from 1924 through Kiskaddon's death in December 1950 and beyond, and turned up sixty-four articles published from August 1932 through October 1939.

One of the reasons that Kiskaddon's poems have been remembered when the stories have not, why they were clipped from the *Western Livestock Journal* and pasted in ranch family albums or saved from the monthly calendars published by the Los Angeles Union Stockyards, is that many of the poems are beautifully illustrated with line drawings created in ink by Katherine Field.[6] Field was a New Mexico rancher with little more formal training for her art than Kiskaddon had for his. Although the poems were usually created first and sent to Field to be illustrated, these collaborations often fit together so well that it is remarkable the results were obtained without face to face communication.[7] However it was done, Field and Kiskaddon were sufficiently attuned to produce a truly collaborative result, with poem and drawing so intertwined that the removal of one diminishes the other. Field's drawings are sometimes mistaken for the work of Will James, by whom she was clearly influenced, but she surpasses him in her ability to create a real sense of place and weather with a few well-chosen strokes. Her renditions of horses and horse behavior are especially fine. The search through library archives for Kiskaddon's stories also turned up Katherine Field drawings which are not well known and which have become separated from the poems they originally illustrated. To show some of these rejoined pairs, this volume uses illustrated poems to introduce each of the chapter divisions of the stories. To my knowledge only the illustrations for "After the Fall Roundup," "Thinkin'," and "All Dressed Up" have previously been reprinted with their poems since their original publication in the *Western Livestock Journal* or the Los Angeles Union Stockyards calendars.

The high regard for Kiskaddon and Field in the ranching world, coupled with fragmentary knowledge of their personal and artistic lives, has surrounded them with an aura on its way to becoming legend.[8] But knowledge is preferable to romance, and I am grateful to have had communications with members of the families of Kiskaddon and Field, who have shared their memories and stories. Based on discussions in the spring and summer of 2003 with Katherine Field's daughter, Dorothy Chapin, and with Bruce Kiskaddon's granddaughter, Lynn Held, plus a brief examination of Held's extensive collection of Kiskaddon memorabilia, I have been able to add some detail to the sketches of the lives of Kiskaddon and Field. These biographical sketches are only a starting point, with more to be gained from the Kiskaddon memorabilia and deeper interviews with Held and Chapin. The family memories and artifacts of Kiskaddon and Field should be preserved in a public repository, and I hope that publication of this collection will help catalyze that preservation.

Those who enjoy the poems and stories of Bruce Kiskaddon and the drawings of Katherine Field are indebted to three men, without whose backing much of their work would never have been created. Kiskaddon and Field were working people with other jobs throughout their creative lives. Like other unsalaried artists with day jobs, they needed sufficient financial reward to justify pouring extra time and energy into creative work, no matter how much they loved it. Nelson R. Crow was the founder, editor, and publisher of the *Western Livestock Journal* and one of Kiskaddon's earliest promoters.[9] John A. McNaughton was general manager and vice president of the Los Angeles Union Stockyards and the initiator of a long-running series of monthly advertising calendars that published even more of the illustrated poems than did the *Western Livestock Journal*.[10] Frank M. King was the associate editor of the *Western Livestock Journal* who controlled the Longhorn and Mavericks sections in which nearly all the Kiskaddon material appeared. King knew Katherine Field's family, looked upon her as his protégée, and almost certainly brought her into the publishing projects.[11]

Finally, there would probably be nothing at all to read without the intervention of Kiskaddon's friend and former boss, Tap Duncan:

> During the summer of 1922 I was working for G. T. (Tap) Duncan in northwestern Arizona. Sometimes I would parody songs to suit local happenings or write verses and different jingles about what took place on the work. Duncan insisted that I try writing some Western Verse. "Just what really happens," he said. I have done so and there has been an ever increasing demand for them.[12]

Kiskaddon's implication that he first wrote poetry in 1922 is at least misleading, for there is strong evidence that he started earlier. The Held collection contains newspaper clippings which clearly suggest that he wrote poetry long before 1922, and a 1919 letter in the collection, from Kiskaddon to his mother, contains a well-crafted poem. John Lomax's 1919 book *Songs of the Cattle Trail and Cow Camp* contains a close version of "When You're Thrown," a poem that appeared in Kiskaddon's first book in 1924, but which must have been composed before 1919 and had probably appeared in a newspaper, perhaps after entering oral tradition.[13] It may be that Kiskaddon first formed the serious intention to write poetry in 1922, and discounted his earlier efforts. This leaves open the possibility that Duncan's encouragement occurred during an earlier period of association, perhaps around 1915.[14]

Bruce Harvey Kiskaddon was born in Foxburg, Pennsylvania, on November 25, 1878, the second of four children of James S. and Caroline Kepler Kiskaddon.[15] By the time he was ten years old his family had moved to southwest Missouri, where he had his first experiences with horses and cattle.[16] Early in the 1890s the family moved again to Trinidad in southeastern Colorado, on the Atlantic side of the Continental Divide. It was during his teenage years around Trinidad that Kiskaddon got his first real ranch experience, particularly in breaking and otherwise working with horses. He had been a small child, and grew into a small man, under 5'5" in height and weighing 140 pounds as an older man. He was always energetic and resilient, but in his younger days had the short temper that sometimes goes with being undersized. In the decade from 1896 to 1905 he drifted from ranch to ranch in southeastern Colorado, northeastern New Mexico, and Arizona. It was this period that produced the memories from which most of his stories and poems were fashioned.

Following a serious injury in 1906 Kiskaddon "went to the cities," a statement upon which he did not elaborate in his autoiographical sketch.[17] Newspaper clippings in the Held collection imply that it was at about this time that he began to work as a bellhop in a succession of hotels across the country, including one in Boston. In a fit of wanderlust he traveled to Australia about 1912, and ended up back in the saddle on the big cattle stations of West Queensland. In "The Fortune Teller Sends Ike Fishing" he has Madame Egypta tell Shorty that he will never be rich but that he will never come to want, that he will live most of his life in big cities, and that he will be married three times. The first two "predictions" seem to fit Kiskaddon, so it may be that the third does also. If he was married multiple times, perhaps his departure for Australia was the result of some marital disarray.[18]

Kiskaddon returned to the United States after August 1914 when the outbreak of World War I brought hard times to Australia, and during the next two years he held a succession of jobs including, probably, a stay with Tap Duncan at the Diamond Bar, hotel work, and possibly bit parts in the movies. He was living in southern California, where he had relatives, when the United States entered World War I.[19] When the country entered the war on April 6, 1917, Kiskaddon lied about his age of thirty-eight in order to enlist in the army, and spent most of the next two years as a mule skinner for the USA, including sixteen months in Europe.

After being mustered out in June 1919 he again went to the cities, but returned to the northern Arizona ranges in 1922 for a two-year stint with his friend Tap Duncan. This watershed experience convinced him by November 1924, at nearly forty-six years of age, that he was no longer young and also, through Duncan's encouragement, that he could have a late-blooming literary career. So Kiskaddon moved to the Los Angeles area, probably Hollywood, and self-published *Rhymes of the Ranges*, a sixty-page paperback containing thirty-one poems. *Rhymes of the Ranges* included four of Kiskaddon's best: "When They've Finished Shippin' Cattle in the Fall," "The Old Night Hawk," "The Time to Decide," and "Between the Lines." He must have distributed this book through his network of friends, which included riders who worked in the moving picture industry.[20] In fact by 1924, Los Angeles, with its year-round temperate climate and its jobs in the movies and at the Union Stockyards, had accumulated a community of several hundred aging former cowhands.[21]

Here Kiskaddon's trail becomes faint, although he is listed in the 1927 Los Angeles directory as a salesman, living in Hollywood on Hyperion Avenue just off Sunset Boulevard. In 1928 he self-published a second slim volume of poems, *Just as Is*.[22]

Printed in a paper-wrapped format similar to his first book, its twenty-eight poems include thirteen reprinted (several in abbreviated form) from *Rhymes of the Ranges* and fifteen new poems unrelated to range life, the best of which are "Your Dog" and "The Old Master." An interesting composition, "True Love," describes the love between a father and a daughter "from four to eight years old," who has now grown to a woman and gone away. *Rhymes of the Ranges* is a rare book, but *Just as Is* is nearly nonexistent. Aside from copies in the Library of Congress, at Brown University, and in the Held collection, it seems to have vanished entirely.

On May 7, 1930, Kiskaddon married Margaret Amelia "Mellie" Larsen, born September 20, 1891, in Copenhagen, Denmark.[23] Mellie was an attractive, tiny, blond woman who had already been married and widowed twice. She had a grown daughter Mildred, about twenty-one, and a son Gene, about six years old, both of whom lived with the newlyweds and became de facto stepchildren of Kiskaddon, although he did not formally adopt them and they did not take his name. According to family tradition, Bruce met Mellie through hotel work, where he was bell captain and she was an elevator operator.

A May 17, 1931, reunion near Hollywood of over two hundred cowhands who had been on the range prior to January 1, 1901, apparently did not draw Kiskaddon, although in the fall of 1932 he joined the Chuck Wagon Trailers, the organization formed at this first reunion.[24] He does not appear in the Los Angeles directory again until 1934 when he is listed as a bellman, married to Nellie [Mellie] M. Kiskaddon, and living at 1706 W 53rd St., west of the South Central neighborhood. Frank King described Mellie as Kiskaddon's "little blond BOSS,"[25] and she is probably the woman who appears in a poem that follows an old waddy's distress at being unable to squeeze into his old cowboy clothes to attend a Chuck Wagon Trailers spring roundup:

But his woman she really surprised him at that
Fer she got him new boots and a new Stetson hat.
He got in the front seat but she drove the car.
You know how old fellers with younger wives are.

When he got to the round up he met all the boys
And he had him a day such as old folks enjoys.
He looked 'em all over and right then he knew
They had all wore the clothes that their wives told them to.
(From "His Old Clothes")[26]

Information supplied to Hal Cannon by Richard Crow, son of Nelson Crow, confirms that Kiskaddon was working as a bellhop in downtown Los Angeles in the 1928–1932 period, and that he continued to do so after he sprang to prominence in the pages of the *Western Livestock Journal*.[27]

Katherine Field was born November 26, 1908, on her parents' ranch in northwest Socorro County, west central New Mexico, the youngest of nine daughters.[28] Her father, Nelson A. Field, known as "Navaho" for his friendship to the Indians through many years, had come to the area to work as a cowhand in 1886 and married Katherine's mother Ida in 1887. Katherine, "Katie" to her family, had infantile paralysis at age four, and from that time on had to use braces and crutches when traveling on foot. Nevertheless she rode easily while working her own cattle on the range and in roundups. By age twenty-one she owned her own ranch, a gift from her father, and the old Bar-V-Slash brand. While other Field daughters had talents of various kinds, Katie's gift for drawing with pen and ink was extraordinary. She especially loved horses, and became marvelously adept at bringing them to life on paper. She was an unusually quiet and watchful person, and it is apparent that she deeply observed and absorbed the moods of the range land and taught herself to bring them forth in her drawings.[29] Although Field was largely self-taught, she received some instruction from Will Shuster of Santa Fe, and participated in group shows at the Museum of New Mexico in Santa Fe in the late '20s and early '30s.[30] Her first published drawing may have been "Longing" in *The Cattleman*, July 1927, accompanied by a poem of her own composition.

Nelson Field was one of the many friends Frank M. King claimed among old-timers in the southwest, and it was due to King's promotion that Field's daughter's art became known among the twelve thousand or so ranch families that subscribed to the *Western Livestock Journal* and received the Los Angeles Union Stockyards calendars during the 1930s. As Katherine Field's fame grew, Frank King several times reported in Mavericks columns that she was working on book illustrations for various authors, but other than Kiskaddon's 1935 *Western Poems* and 1947 *Rhymes of the Ranges and Other Poems*, the only book examples of her work I have been able to find are in Jack Culley's *Cattle, Horses, & Men of the Western Range*, and only one illustration is unique to that work, the other nine being reprints of Kiskaddon poem illustrations.[31]

In 1935 Katherine married John Guerro, a Navajo who had worked for her father in 1934, and by the end of 1942 they had two children, six-year-old John and three-year-old Dorothy Katherine.[32] Nelson Field had gone bankrupt in the early '30s, largely by extending credit through his trading post to Navajo people plunged into desperate poverty by the Depression, and that crisis was compounded by Ida's growing frailty and the onset of dementia in Nelson.[33] The other daughters had moved away from the Field ranch, and through the late '30s and early '40s John and Katie struggled to hold on to the debt-ridden ranch. Somehow Katie found time for drawing, out of love of her art and because the ranch family needed the cash income from poem illustrations. Eventually the failing health of her parents and her children's need for schooling forced Katie to move to Albuquerque while John worked at the ranch during the week and came to town on weekends. Finally the care of children and parents became too pressing, and she was forced to take a leave of absence from illustration. From the beginning of 1943 through the end of 1948 Kiskaddon's poems were illustrated by Amber Dunkerley, a skilled worker, but lacking the Field magic. By the late '40s John and

Katie had gotten the ranch out of debt and were even able to run a better grade of stock. In 1949 Field resumed her collaboration with Kiskaddon, but it was sadly short-lived. Kiskaddon died in December 1950, to be followed in death within half a year by Field herself on June 28, 1951, a victim of cancer at age forty-two.

On August 25, 1932, the *Western Livestock Journal* published its first Longhorn section, a project of associate editor Frank M. King under the auspices of Nelson Crow. The "Longhorn" included King's Mavericks gossip column, but had much additional space for fiction and history of the old-time range by a variety of authors. The Longhorn was inaugurated with a front page Kiskaddon poem, "Cow Sense," illustrated by Katherine Field, and a Kiskaddon story, "It Was a Draw!," built from standard range repartee much like the "Arkansas Traveler" exchanges between the stranger and the farmer. The responses to Kiskaddon and Field were overwhelmingly positive, and additional Kiskaddon stories and illustrated poems soon followed. By October the *Journal*'s subscription coupons were claiming that readers felt Kiskaddon's poems alone were worth many times the $1 cost of a year's fifty-two issues.[34] By November Frank King announced that he and editor Nelson Crow intended to see to the publication of a book of Kiskaddon's poems, all illustrated by Katherine Field.[35] Appearing at the fall roundup of the Chuck Wagon Trailers, Kiskaddon was hailed as "the ace of the deck of the thrilling cowboy poets."[36]

By the beginning of 1933 the illustrated poems were an advertised monthly feature of the Longhorn, and the Los Angeles Union Stockyards had started issuing the monthly series of illustrated poems that would continue unbroken for twenty-seven years, with reissued poems being used after Kiskaddon's death. At first the Stockyards and *Livestock Journal* illustrated poems were separate series, but by June of 1933 the two publishers were sharing poems and making nearly simultaneous issues. Over the years the Union Stockyards was the more faithful publisher, for the *Western Livestock Journal* printed an average of eleven poems per year from 1933 through 1947, but then published only ten poems in the last three years of Kiskaddon's life.

As Kiskaddon's fame grew he was often called upon to recite his poems before large groups, especially for the spring and fall Chuck Wagon Trailers roundups and the annual Great Western Livestock Show in Los Angeles.[37] He wrote special poems for Chuck Wagon Trailers roundups, including "The Chuck Wagon" and "His Old Clothes," and in the spring of 1933 he was chosen as one of five directors of this social organization of old-time cowhands.[38] Sometimes Kiskaddon and Mellie would chauffer Frank King (who did not drive) and King's wife Sophie to a CWT roundup.[39] Because the Chuck Wagon Trailers were frequently visited by cowboy entertainers such as the Arizona Wranglers, Powder River Jack Lee, and the famous Curley Fletcher, rodeo rider and author of "Strawberry Roan" and "Ridge Runnin' Roan," it is certain that Kiskaddon knew these people, at least somewhat.[40] In fact, the tight Los Angeles old waddy social world overlapped both the group of cowboy movie riders and the emerging practitioners of high speed cowboy songs in harmony, such as the Beverly Hillbillies, and it is reasonable to suppose that Kiskaddon knew some people in both groups.[41] Kiskaddon's poems also began to be reprinted in other publications, such as *The Westerner* (Denver) and *The Cattleman* (Fort Worth).

Scattered through volume 11 of *Western Livestock Journal* (November 1932– October 1933) were six unembellished Kiskaddon reminiscences, gathered here in chapter 2. But when the first greatly enlarged, glossy monthly feature issue was unveiled in January 1934, Kiskaddon changed his format and launched his series of fictionalized "Bill stories" with "Concernin' Bill." "Concernin' Bill" is mostly a range joke about a cowboy's brains, but before long the stories become more elaborate. Kiskaddon unveils himself as Shorty, and then in quick succession he introduces his untamable cowgirl heroine, Rildy Briggs, along with Eph, Zeb, the Millinary Lady, the Cigar Gal, the Medicine Man, the Mask Marble, and a host of others. Finally sending Bill off to fight in the Spanish-American War after twenty-two mostly lighthearted episodes, Shorty carries Rildy, Eph, and Zeb into a new set of entanglements with a pair of professors (or "perfessors" if you prefer), one of whom Shorty and company dub "Ann Elizer." Involving water rights and land grabs as they do, the professor stories are a little less rollicking than the Bill stories, but it all turns out well for the waddies in the end.

In "Shorty Goes Home for Armistice Day" there is a two-paragraph fast-forward from 1898 to 1936 that is so much like Kiskaddon's life it leaves no doubt he is describing his own return to Trinidad, Colorado, and how he catches up with Bill and Eph, whom he finds at the jail but not in the roles he expects. After stepping back to 1899 for an unadorned reminiscence in "Shorty Meets Some Missourians," Shorty then heads to Arizona for a fateful encounter with Ike and a whole new set of characters, from which unravels another long series of yarns. Each of these Arizona tales ends with a judgment either that "Isaac is a very fortunate person," or "Ike is a fool for luck." As Kiskaddon nears the end of his career as a prose writer, Shorty again becomes enmeshed in water and land issues and the stories become darker in tone as the Boss moves toward firing Ike. "Hell among the Yearlin's" is a strange composition, the only one of Kiskaddon's stories that has any bitterness to it, and it makes me wonder if some crisis in Kiskaddon's own life was involved in its creation, perhaps some disagreement with management at *Western Livestock Journal*. After Ike moves on to start an independent life, two more stories in 1939 finish off the yarns. "Shorty's Boss Buys Purebred Bulls" is a prose sequel to "The Longhorn Speaks" and a fitting ending to the stories of an old-time range rider from the longhorn days. The last article is a sweet, simple nonfiction account of a driving trip in which Bruce and Mellie visit Tap Duncan and his family in Kingman, Arizona. Of all the possible reasons Kiskaddon's prose writing came to an end, it seems most likely that he simply reached the end of all the stories he cared to tell about his friends from the old days and then stopped.

Kiskaddon was at his peak of prominence from 1934 through 1939. In December 1935 the *Western Livestock Journal* published *Western Poems*, comprised of the first three years of his collaborations with Katherine Field. This is the book that had been proposed by Frank M. King and Nelson Crow in 1932. The little paperback book of forty poems sold very well at $1 per copy, advertised only through the *Journal* and possibly the Stockyards calendars. During 1937 Kiskaddon and Field were quite busy, for besides the usual *Journal* and Stockyards poems they produced an additional thirteen illustrated poems for use in the advertisements of the Holaday & Hampton Livestock Commission Company. For most of these poems Kiskaddon used the pseudonym "The Holaday & Hampton Poet." In 1938 he probably wrote a half dozen unsigned advertising jingles for Gorman & Monheim, commission livestock agents.[42] While this was a poor use of a fine poet, it was doubtless good for his pocketbook.

Apparently Kiskaddon never made enough money from his writing or believed the accolades enough to give up his day job at the hotel. The Los Angeles directory of 1940, the last issued, still listed him as a bellman living at the W 53rd address. There are people who do not want stardom, even if it is thrust upon them, and Kiskaddon may have been one of these. Imagining Kiskaddon the author, the poet, dressed in a little bellhop's monkey suit is an invitation to pity him for the irony and injustice of such misplacement, but it might be a mistake to accept that romantic interpretation of his situation. I have seen a remarkable photograph in the Held collection, taken some time in the '30s, of Kiskaddon in his bell captain's uniform. The inward look of sturdy self-possession on his face as he strides toward the camera would have deflected pity from even the most sanguinary of bleeding hearts. Honest labor, no matter how unglamorous, is worthy of respect. Kiskaddon had a waddy's willingness to work, whatever his job, and would not have felt demeaned by it. True, you can read sadness on the bell captain's face. You can imagine this man occasionally drinking to excess, as Kiskaddon did, and you can believe that, like the Old Night Hawk, he has seen his dreams and ambitions fail, but you cannot pity him. You are looking at a man of strength and integrity who has made his bargain.

> Yes, I've lived my life and I've took a chance,
> Regardless of law or vow.
> I've played the game and I've had my dance,
> And I'm payin' the fiddler now.
>
> (From "The Old Night Hawk")[43]

No doubt he was as good a bellhop as he was a cowboy and a writer, and would have been one that hotel guests enjoyed and therefore tipped generously.

During this same 1934–1939 period Frank M. King gradually decreased his booster's praise of Kiskaddon and Field. Strangely, King's columns had only a single brief notice of the publication of *Western Poems*, the book he had agitated for three years earlier. While Nelson Crow provided a preface for the book, and Weaton Hale Brewer, a San Francisco advertising executive, provided a glowing introduction, Frank King's name appears nowhere in the book. Earlier in 1935 King had self-published the first of his own four books, *Wranglin' the Past*, and he had been promoting his own product relentlessly in the *Livestock Journal*. Perhaps there was some jealousy that prevented Frank King from celebrating Kiskaddon's book wholeheartedly. As much as King boosted Kiskaddon in the early days, there seemed always to be some reserve between the two. King was a tenacious advocate of old-time cowboy culture, but he took himself rather seriously and never seemed to have the slightest doubt, as he shot from the hip, over any position he adopted. Kiskaddon was a different sort, deeply reflective, self-effacing in his humor, and with a basic aversion to bluster.

> A shy shrinkin' man makes me tired;
> I hate men that bluster and bluff.
> The feller I've always admired
> Was the man that knew when to get tough.
>   (From "When to Get Tough")[44]

King was fifteen years Kiskaddon's senior, and a man who applied the word "friend" liberally in his voluminous writings, yet only once in all his references to Kiskaddon does he call him "friend"—after Kiskaddon had provided two substitute Mavericks columns in September and October of 1935 when King was desperately ill with an infection. Still, when Kiskaddon assembled and self-published *Rhymes of the Ranges and Other Poems* in 1947, the book he meant to be his legacy, Frank M. King provided a generous foreword:

> All this experience is reflected in his western poems, because he has had actual experience in the themes he puts into verse. He had no college professor teach him anything. He is a natural born poet and his poems show he knows his business. The best cowhand poems I ever read.[45]

The 1947 *Rhymes of the Ranges* is still the most complete book of Kiskaddon's poetry, although it unfortunately has only one Katherine Field drawing to go with its 159 poems. Many of his best poems are collected in the book, and it is remarkable when viewing his whole output to realize how little his quality changed in the course of his career. He never wrote himself out, in part because he had the wisdom to move on after he had his say, and avoided overgrazing the ranges of his inspiration.

Through 1947 Kiskaddon's poems continued to appear in the *Western Livestock Journal* at the pace of ten or twelve per year, but the publication itself was changing, especially after the end of World War II. The monthly feature issue kept increasing in size, with more and more advertisements for feed supplements and purebred bulls, more cattlemen pictured in businessman's garb, fewer in wide-brim western hats. Less and less of the magazine was devoted to the social lives of the livestock raisers. The Chuck

Wagon Trailers disappeared from its pages, and finally even Frank M. King began to seem irrelevant. The Longhorn and Mavericks sections became indistinguishable as King turned into a one-issue journalist, loudly (and no doubt correctly) proclaiming the continued injustice of the treatment of the Indians, a message that could not have been pleasing to many postwar stockmen basking in the glow of unaccustomed high prices and newfound prosperity.

After Kiskaddon's death from pneumonia on December 7, 1950, only a brief obituary appeared in a Mavericks section of *Western Livestock Journal*, a minimal response considering the role he had played in helping the publication expand in the Depression-ridden 1930s. But the *Journal* also apparently took no notice when Frank M. King died a few years later, or even when Nelson Crow passed on—it had moved beyond the personal to the purely economic. Kiskaddon's obituary in the December 8, 1950, *Los Angeles Times* said he was the father of Val Stassan (the name adopted by Mellie's son Gene) and Mrs. Mildred Van Der Linden, neither of whom was the mysterious little girl between four and eight years old who had grown up and moved away. It also said that he was the beloved husband of Mellie. Mellie was indeed prostrate with a grief from which she did not fully recover, although she lived another thirty-four years.

Bruce Kiskaddon never quite faded away, because the children and grandchildren of the Depression-era parents who saved the Union Stockyards calendars and clipped poems from *Western Livestock Journal* read and memorized some of the old poems in the scrapbooks. In 1985, the year after Mellie Kiskaddon died, Waddie Mitchell stood up at the first Cowboy Poetry Gathering in Elko, Nevada, and recited a Kiskaddon poem. Later that year Hal Cannon published an anthology of cowboy poetry and gave Kiskaddon a prominent place, and two years after that he edited a new anthology devoted entirely to Kiskaddon.[46] Mason and Janice Coggin made a nearly complete collection of the Union Stockyards calendars, and from their collection published another Kiskaddon anthology, including many rarer items.[47] Perhaps their valuable collection will end up in some public repository. Since the passing of Mason Coggin, Jana Marck and Walt "Bimbo" Cheney have carried on a program of republishing the calendar poems.[48] Hopefully they will continue, for the calendar poems that never appeared in the *Western Livestock Journal* are really the most difficult Kiskaddon poems to find, since apparently no public library holds them.

Not long ago on a hunch I called the cemetery closest to the Kiskaddon house on W 53rd St. in Los Angeles, the Angelus Rosedale Cemetery, Mortuary and Crematorium, and asked about Bruce. They told me he had been cremated there and his ashes delivered to his funeral service rather than to their mausoleum. So he is not under a headstone and hopefully not in a jar on a shelf somewhere. Kiskaddon had loved to wander, and I want to imagine that Mellie drove him again in their old car to a high butte with a long view and left him there, where he could be on the move again.

Nobody will know which way I go,
They'll only know I'm gone.

(From "I'm Hittin' the Trail Tonite")[49]

Acknowledgments

The biographical introduction would have been far sketchier without the good fortune of hearing memories and family stories from Lynn Held, granddaughter of Bruce Kiskaddon, and from Dorothy Chapin, daughter of Katie Field. Lynn Held also allowed me to examine her large collection of Kiskaddon memorabilia, an experience which transformed my thinking about her grandfather. The treatment here of Kiskaddon family history also benefitted from the tenacious genealogical research of Melanie Held, Lynn Held's daughter-in-law. In addition to his knowledgeable and supportive commentary on the manuscript, I am indebted to Hal Cannon for his anthologies of cowboy poetry, which first made me aware of Kiskaddon, and especially for his thought-provoking introduction to *Rhymes of the Ranges: A New Collection of the Poems of Bruce Kiskaddon*, which gave me my initial picture of the man. Cannon's opening sentence, "There's no darker place than at the edge of the spotlight," is still for me a powerful epigraph on Kiskaddon's life.

Western Livestock Journal, original publisher of the Kiskaddon stories and many of the poems reprinted in this volume, is now based in Denver and is in its eighty-third continuous year as a weekly newspaper for livestock producers. As ownership and operation have been passed down through generations of descendents of its founder, Nelson Crow, the publication has been restructured and reinvented numerous times in a remarkable run of service to an industry that has experienced repeated upheavals. Elusive early volumes of *Western Livestock Journal* were ably tracked down by the library staff of my home institution, Washington State University, particularly by the detective work of David Smestad. The staff of Utah State University Press has made a first-time editor's experience one of pleasure, and I am especially grateful to executive editor John R. Alley for recognizing the value of the Shorty stories. David Stanley of Westminster College, Salt Lake City, provided a generous and useful review of the manuscript. Stanley is also co-editor of *Cowboy Poets & Cowboy Poetry*, an excellent overview which helped me see Kiskaddon in context.

Over the years many good friends have fed my enthusiasm for cowboy poetry and song and indulged my obsession with Kiskaddon. I am particularly grateful to friends Ted Hensold, the better half of the "Educated Fellers"; Ron Kane and Meghan Merker, keepers of the true flame of old-time music; Dick Warwick, a fine contemporary cowboy poet who is Kiskaddon-like in his self-effacement; the late Dewey Wichman, master entertainer and joyous spirit; George Thompson and Sharon "Silver" Glenn, ranchers, poets, musicians, horse people, and examplars of all I admire in modern ranchers of the West; and

Tom Martin, who in his combined roles as business manager at my chemistry day job and fellow western history enthusiast (and proofreader of the Shorty stories) has helped me reconcile my disjointed set of passions. Special thanks go to rancher-poet Jon Bowerman, who fifteen yeas ago was graciously and unstintingly supportive of a greenhorn city dweller who had the temerity to recite "The Old Night Hawk" to a group of cowboy poets.

My deepest gratitude is to all my family members, whose love and support have been life's framework and who have also made specific contributions to this book. My parents Ernie and Bill Siems provided a generous liberal education that did not force an indecisive offspring into a final choice between science and history, even in his sixth decade. My stepdaughters Marcelle Heimdal and Zoë Heimdal have been enthusiastic supporters of the Shorty project, the former as an on-the-spot detective agency in Los Angeles and the latter as a talented web and print graphic design resource. Most of all I am indebted to my life partner—music partner, thoughtful reader, and designer of the graphic elements of this volume—Dawn Holladay, who has created the space in our lives where Shorty could come and live.

A Note on the Text

The chapter organization is not Kiskaddon's and was adopted for ease of reading. The order of the stories has been changed in some instances from their serial appearance in the *Western Livestock Journal*. The autobiography has been placed first because it provides background for all the stories. Some changes were made to partially straighten out references ahead and back to other stories, although it has not been possible to completely eliminate gaps and inconsistencies. In at least one instance there seems to be a missing story and in another there are two versions of the same story. Kiskaddon's method of writing and the editorial practices of the *Livestock Journal* are not known, so it is not possible to determine how the inconsistencies occurred or how the author would have wished to resolve them.

The original articles or copies were scanned, converted to text with optical character reading software, and then hand-corrected. Kiskaddon intentionally exaggerated his misspellings to recreate the speech of an uneducated waddy, and he was also quite inconsistent in punctuation, capitalization, and paragraphing. These idiosyncrasies appear unchanged in the text that follows, with the exception of a few errors that were obviously unintended or which obscure the meaning of a passage. In these cases the altered text is enclosed in [square brackets]. Although some editorial notes explain obscure Shorty-isms, the reader is often left to sound out words like "towerist" (tourist) and "statchu" (statue).

AFTER THE FALL ROUNDUP

Now the summer work is over and the wagon's pullin' in,
And we've said good bye to fellers that we mightn't see agin,
Fer a cowboy don't write letters so we mighty soon lose track
Of the boys that stops and works a while and never does come back.

When yore clothes is soter tattered and yore hat brim sags and flops,
And yore boots is wore and battered, them that had the fancy tops,
When the owners and the bosses and the hands is most all in,
And the[m] strings of summer hosses is slowed up and lookin' thin.

When them thin clouds start a trailin' through the soft and pleasant sky,
And you watch old buzzard sailin' soter useless way up high.
And it makes the toughest cow boy soter study after all,
When he's draggin' with the wagon to the home ranch in the fall.

Fer he caint help but remember that most cow boys don't git old
And he'll get to one November when he caint stand work and cold;
He shore knows that he'll be sorry when he gits like you and me,
Jest an old man tellin' stories 'bout how good he used to be.

I

Autobiography

Answering the requests of many readers of Western Livestock Journal, *Bruce Kiskaddon, famous cowboy poet, writes his autobiography.*[1] *His book "Western Poems" has had tremendous sale. There is hardly a cattlemen's meeting but what someone adds to the occasion by reciting a Bruce Kiskaddon poem. Probably his "Little Blue Roan" is the most popular. Now we'll let Bruce tell his own story.* —The Editor, *WLJ, May 31, 1938.*

My first work with cattle was down in southwest Missouri. I was twelve years old. Four of us, all about the same age, were day herding a bunch of cows on what unfenced country there was around that place. We had quite a lot of room and at night we put them in an eighty acre pasture. We four kids worked at it all summer. We rode little Indian horses and went home at night. Not much cow punching, that's a fact, but it was big business to us. The talk of opening the Indian territory for settlement had started,[2] and already the open country was beginning to be occupied by boomers' camps. People were coming from everywhere to be ready for the opening. They were a mixed up lot. Some honest folks and a few mighty tough hangers-on. Two things I always remember. One was a poker game. They had tied up the sides of a tent and got to playing on a tarp on a bed. The place was crowded and many men from other camps had set in. There was more money stacked there than us kids had ever seen. The man that owned the bed and tent had to go and sleep at a neighbor's wagon. He said, "We started that game yesterday and it was just a little game, and Lord, it's growed till it's plum beyont us now."

The other one was a scare I got. My Father sometimes allowed me to ride a horse he had instead of my pony. Older folks shook their heads. I was riding a horse that was too much for me and besides there were a lot of fellows that would take a horse like that away from a kid and ride him out of the country. There was a lot of truth in what they said. I was undersized. In fact, I weighed about sixty-five pounds.

One day I had been hunting strays and was coming back on a hillside road that was only used in muddy weather when the lower road was impassable. I rounded a turn and right ahead of me met two men on horses that had been ridden till they were ready to drop. I knew what breed of cat they were at a glance. I jerked a knot in my reins. A horse like I was on meant everything to one of them. As I turned off the road they yelled at me to stop, but I turned the horse off the side hill and gave him the quirt. He took down through the rocks and jack oaks and I had to go leather with both hands to stay on top. They fired a shot at me but I could not have stopped if I wanted to and I sure didn't want to. I got to the lower road and managed to get the horse slowed down. I knew what I had met. Those fellows were trying to get away from the law.

A couple of years later we went to Trinidad, Colorado.[3] I was too small to work in a mine or in the railroad shops and that was about all there was to do in that town. I was not being raised for an ornament, anyone could look at me and see that, and I sure wasn't being raised for a pet.

My first job was in a furniture store. One day we had loaded a one horse wagon and the driver got on the seat. I was to sit beside him and hold a dresser mirror. I took it off the load but I turned it with the face toward the horse. He had on an open bridle. When he looked up and saw that other horse coming down on him upside down, he tore out and wrapped that load of furniture around one of the few [telephone] poles [they] had in Trinidad. I never disappointed him. I lit on top of him, mirror and all. I didn't get hurt but the driver of the wagon and the furniture were all in need of repairs and the horse had lamed himself. That ended my mercantile career.

J. M. John, who had some ranches down the river and a small spread on the dry Cimarron,[4] was good enough to give me a job. I was a sort of chore boy on the start. He had a lot of patience with me and finally loaned me a saddle. No rattle trap outfit either. A good one. I was very small for my age and had a mean temper, and used mighty poor judgment a lot of times, but he kept me on the outfit. I had two good points. I could stand all sorts of weather and I would work like a nigger. I was easy on horses and had a lot of endurance. From then on I drifted around from one small outfit to the other. At Bowen's ranch I met up with a man by the name of Johnson. He was half Cherokee Indian. He was breaking horses and he and I went into pardnership. I had learned by then to hog it out with most cold back horses but knew little of real breaking.

Johnson was about forty years old and what I learned from him about handling raw horses helped me all through my life on the range. I also worked for a man named E. B. Templin who raised large horses and broke them to work. He was a splendid horseman and made good money. One of my bosses was J. S. Gresham who was afterwards sheriff of Los Animas county, Colorado. He was buying and shipping horses when I worked for him.[5] The summer of nineteen two I worked for Nels Nelson who had a small spread between Limon Junction and Deer Trail.[6] That was the first I had ever seen them dip cattle. I just stopped there and stayed much longer than I had intended to. I had bought a swell fork saddle from Mueller in Denver and it was the only one in that part of the country then.

The next summer I remember I was back in the southern part of Colorado. We had gone down on the lower Picket-wire for some cattle. We had to gather them. One night we corraled a big bunch of cows and calves in a rincon[7] and went to stay all night at Leonard Richardson's place on the other side of the river. That night it rained hard on some of the canyons above and when we woke up the river was over its banks. The water was so deep in that corral that the calves would soon be swimming. We caught our horses and were ready to cross when two little kids rode up on a pair of little three year old hackamore colts. It was Johnny Cordova and Tommy Carter. Leonard Richardson and Charlie Carson, a J. J.[8] man, rode in and I followed. I heard somebody yell at another one to come back. I looked back and that little Tommy had put that colt into the river. He was hanging to the back whangs of his saddle and coming right along. Tommy was about twelve years old. We got the gate open and the cattle took to the water pretty well. They seemed to know they were cornered. The trip back was a tough one for the river was coming up fast and the current was swift, but we never lost any cattle. Tommy came back with us. I never saw him again for over twenty years and when I did he was working as a riding actor in Hollywood.[9]

The country I learned in was a "tie hard" country. Sometimes a Dally man would drift in, and most of the hands dallied a little if working in a corral. But in the main they were short rope men and most of them rode double rig.[10]

A couple of years later I got hurt and thought I would never be able to ride again and went to the cities.[11] But seven years later[12] I drifted down to Australia. I got up into West Queensland and somehow I got to riding again. I worked for a British company that had three stations, as they call ranches. One was twelve thousand acres, one was fifty thousand, and the other was ninety thousand acres. That was the station where I worked longest. It was odd to me for they rode flat saddles with knee grips and carried long whips. They worked their cattle in chutes and "yards," as they called corrals. A round up was a "Muster" and the remuda was the "Draft." They called their cinches "Girths." But let me state they were good stockmen and horsemen and most of them had the nerve of the devil. There were lots of bad snakes there. One morning I was riding a saddle with one "girth." My horse bucked with me. I was getting along all right for those bush saddles are good to ride a bucker in, but the "girth" broke. I lit on my back with the saddle between my knees. A big drover laughed and said. "You cawn't say as the yankee bloke didn't stick to his flamin' pig skin," meaning the saddle.

They were a fine set of fellows to work with and I stayed a year longer than I meant to, then the war in Europe started.[13] Most of my friends enlisted and times got hard, so I came up to the states again. I went to work in the cities again[14] till the sixth of April, 1917. Then I lied five years about my age[15] and enlisted. I was in the army twenty-six months and was sixteen months over seas. When I came back[16] I never expected to go outdoors again, but in 1922, I went out for a two-weeks visit with G. T. Duncan.[17] He had a spread sixty miles from Kingman, Arizona. The crew was busy, so I went out to help on one work. Well, I kept making one more work and one more work. It was late in November of 1924 that I finally decided my two weeks was up and came back to town.[18] Duncan, "Tap" as his friends call him, was a character. One night in the fall, it was cold and raining, and he took his bed into an old shed where we camped. I went to take my bed in and a belated rattle snake buzzed at me. I warned him about it. "I know it," he said, "but I got here first and if he don't like it let him get to h— out of here." Well the rest of us slept outside but old Tap was snoring loud in twenty minutes.

That was my last job with a cow outfit. My eyes were bothering me and I was getting gray. In short I found out I wasn't young any more. Punching cattle in a rough country is not an old man's job. That is if he really gets in and makes a hand. As you get older a bucking horse can outguess you mighty quick. You are not so active if you get a horse jerked down, or if one falls with you it stoves you up a heap worse than it did years ago. And you don't go down a rope to many big calves before you get that all gone feeling, especially if you are about five feet five.

But I still like the smell of a camp fire and like to hear the creak of saddle leather and the rattle of spurs. And I like the smell of cows. Yes even if I can tell there have been cows in the drinking water, it don't bother me much if the mixture ain't too strong.

This article don't deal much with the tragedies and romances of the range countries I was in, but it is just a little sketch of what happened to me.

Startin' Out

When you have to start out on a cold winter day,
The wind blowin' cold and the sky is dull gray.
You blow on the bit till you take out the frost,
Then you put on the bridle and saddle yore hoss.

He squats and he shivvers. He blows through his nose.
The blanket is stiff for the sweat is shore froze.
Then you pick up yore saddle and swing it up high,
Till the stirrups and cinches and latigoes fly.

The pony he flinches and draws down his rump.
There's a chance he might kick, and he's likely to jump.
He rolls his eye at you and shivvers like jelly
When you pull that old frozen cinch up on his belly.

It is cold on his back and yore freezin' yore feet,
And you'll likely find out when you light on yore seat,
That you ain't got no tropical place fer to set.
It is likely the saddle aint none overhet.

But a cow boy don't pay no attention to weather.
He gits out of his bed and gits into the leather.
In the winter it's mighty onpleasant to ride,
But that's jest the time when he's needed outside.

2
Startin' Out

Rough Hands [1]

A rough hand is a heap of help pervidin he has sence with it. No boss wants a feller that is allus tryin' to make a good hoss buck and holdin' up the crowd in the mornin' to see him put on a wild ridin' exhibition, and most owners would a heap ruther hear a waddy talk about how to shoe and how to keep a hoss in shape and learn him the work than about how high he can kick him in the shoulder when he's buckin'.

A real forked hand is wuth plenty all the time but he ort to use jedgement with it. A wrangler that charges a bunch of shod saddle horses in a narrow place and gits some of their heels tromped or a good hoss kicked and lamed is a loss. Fer hands don't train hosses and bring them twenty or thirty mile to a work jest to have 'em lamed up in the remuda.

Then take on a drive there is allus the fellers that bunch up and ride along visitin' and readin' their saddle horns till the herd takes on a whale of a spread, and then takes down their ropes and runs their hosses and chases weak cattle or fat steers neither of which aint so good. And the feller on day herd that is either pullin' up bresh with his rope to see how much his hoss will pull or else makin' or fixin' at sumpthin' till the cattle scatter and then gittin' out and raisin the Devil.

The hand that allus has his rope ready when it is calf brandin' time or that is there to pull 'em out of a bog or doctor screw worms, or can take an ole moss back out of the bresh or a rough mountain is a real man and no foolin'. But the feller that sets in a winter camp and bakes his boots at the fire when he ort to be out choppin' ice so the critters can drink is like enough to be the one to git out along in the afternoon and bust some ole lame steer on the froze ground to look at his foot when him and all the world knows he's jest tender from bein' up around the rim rocks.

I ain't sayin' but what I've tried to show off some times and I've lamed up hosses and crippled and even killed stock when I could have got around doin' it but I am plum ashamed of it and the bosses was better about it than I would have been if I had been in their place. But I will say that I mostly tried to take care of things and not to do damage and I allus figgered that the boys and the cook and boss would a heap ruther a feller drug in a little wood and was willin' to help cook a little if need be than to put on a wild west show when there wasn't no use in it. Lots of boys that is top hands is settin' on the fence some wheres or hangin' round town or [mebbyso] chuck ridin' and don't know why they caint work twicet fer the same outfit. But if they would take a couple of drinks to sorter give 'em a broad view of things and generally speakin' set down and git wise to theirselves they could figger out why some awkward hands that caint ride fer sour apples or throw a rope into the crick is allus workin' and they aint.

The rough hand with sense is a find fer any boss but the rough hand without no sense is as about as much use as a fly wheel on a curry comb or a bull dog in a sheep camp.

Hair Cuttin' [2]

Mind how we used to clean up after the work was made and most of the boys had pulled into the home ranch with the wagon?

Yessir. We sunned blankets, washed clothes and got right busy. By the time we was all sudsed out and shaved it was about time to do some hair cuttin'. Some times there was a chair or two around the bunk house, but most of the boys would ruther set on a box because it seemed a heap more nat'rl and then, too, any cow puncher that really could cut hair had learnt on a box, and a chair sort of cramped his style. And some of them boys could shore cut hair.

We got out the old comb and worked it on a tight string till we had most of the gum out of it and then we got a whet stone and sharped up the best pair of shears that was around the place. After that all we had to do was to set 'em on the old store box and take to it.

To be sure the shears might pull some and the old comb might be a little shy of teeth in spots but that wasn't our fault and it didn't worry us none. I don't know what you would call the style of hair cuts we got, but any how they wasn't no pansy pompadores among 'em.

Then, too, we had sort of a clearin' house balance. All the little fellers that had sent off fer clothes mostly found when they got 'em that they was so big that if they went out in a high wind them shirts and pants would have whupped 'em to death, but that was all right fer they jest fitted the big fellers and the big fellers found out that the first time they washed their clothes they shrunk till they fitted the little fellers. It was only the medium sized boys that was out of luck.

When we got all slicked up there was generally a country dance timed-fer about then, and fer a day or two after we rode ten or fifteen mile to sit an' watch some gal chaw gum, or if she was right high chinned she had an old organ and she sung, "In the Glomin'," and "After the Ball," while she tromped and pawed the organ. After that it was time fer three or four months more work.

Folks today would reckon it was a purty slow time, but we allowed we shore was cuttin' a fat hog them times and was a whole lot happier than them that knows a heap better.

Wild Dogs ³

During the winter of nineteen hundred there was a bunch of dogs did considerable damage to calves in the part of the country where we lived. They were dogs of all sizes and breeds. One was very big. Several dogs from ranches joined them. As a rule they killed any honest dog that came in their way.

There was a strip of ground between two deep arroyos that was honey-combed with clay caves and some of these came out between the two watercourses, and here they denned up. They were as well protected as a prairie dog town. Only one of them was foolish enough to get into a trap. We then tried poison and that thinned them out pretty fast; two big dogs and a couple of small ones still kept it up. One day late in March I rode into a big arroyo and jumped three of them. One was the big fellow. The wind must have kept them from hearing me for we were right amongst each other before we knew it. I cut down and up on the big fellow, the first shot went short, but the next one wallowed him and by that time I had rolled off and leaded him plenty.

He was as big as a Saint Bernard and in fine condition. That was the finish for them, and in the remaining four years that I was in that section of the country they never showed up again. Small calves were their favorite dish, and several times they tore down meat that was up outside of houses or camps.

Likely many of my fellow readers have had similar experiences. If you have, please write it to *Western Livestock Journal*.

In the near future I will tell you how a clever buckaroo got a big lobo that had fooled all the trappers in the region.

Wolves ⁴

This is not a trapper talkin'. I never could catch anything in a trap but a pole cat, and, come to think of it, I have pinched my fingers a time or two. Some years ago two boys went onto a mesa to trap wolves. Later we asked an old trapper if they got anything. "Yes," he said, "one of 'em ketched pnewmony an' died an tother one ketched a train for home." That's about how the average feller gets a wolf.

The winter of nineteen one I was left at home alone for six weeks.⁵ Twice during that time the old dog came into the house growling and the next morning I found wolf tracks. I always left a door open for him. They never bothered anything that I knew of. Wolves went through that country but didn't seem to stop or kill. The next winter I was crossing the valley to get to my dad's home and I met a wolf right in the fenced lanes. There was snow and I could see him plain. He passed within twenty yards of me on the other side of the fence and didn't seem to take any notice of me. The next winter Joe Morgan and I were at a place on the Chicosa arroyo, working for Jim Gresham. I took Joe's pet hoss and went to chop a water hole open while he made breakfast one morning. It was just light enough to see when I got there and there were some coyotes around a carcass, but closer was a big lober. Why they go near a carcass I don't know, for they kill their own meat.

Well, I dropped my ax and charged him. He was awkward on the getaway for some reason and the little hoss was rarin' to go. We stepped right up to him and I had a loop built but I had to guide the hoss for he wasn't follerin' wuth a durn. The wolf took a dodge in a cactus patch and when he did the little hoss just run off with me for a ways and when I got him bent, that wolf was somewhere else. Anyhow, I chopped ice.

The toughest wolf I ever knew was in northern Arizona. He ranged over a lot of country. Indian Jeff got a couple of wolves and so did another Indian, but this old boy kept right on killin' calves. Charlie Duncan took a peeve at this wolf and put on a rifle for him. Charlie and I worked together that summer and every time we heard him bawl the kill cry it made us cuss. The varmint was too smart for us. It lasted all winter and into the next summer, that feud. It got to be a sort of a steady idea of Charlie's. Till, one day we came back to camp at Horse Flat tanks where we had been two days before and the wolf had gone into the ashes of our fire and dug out pieces of jerky and bacon rind and biscuit. That settled it. Charlie took to buildin' little fires over a trap and mashin' them down a little with a pan and puttin' bits of grub in them. I reckon it was about the third fire that he fell for and, as the feller says, he sure got his foot in it. He was the biggest one I ever saw. I always thought a lot about wolves. They ain't all the same and no wolf is the same all the time, but there aint time and room to talk about them in a paper, so I beg Mr. King's pardon for this long-winded yarn.

Reptiles [6]

Most all fellers that has worked on the outside has a lot of rattle snake and centipede and tirantula yarns that they have told so often that they git so they believe them their selves. Now I don't claim to be no snake expert but I aim to try and sort the snake yarns that are true from amongst them that aint and tell 'em. I hope all you boys will reckon I got the bunch clean and classified up all right. There's a heap bigger stories than these but then theres a heap better snake men than me because one time I went to try and help sober a feller up and he could tell me about a lot of snakes I couldn't even see. So I figured I wasn't much of a snake man.

The worst snake scare I got was when I was a kid. I went out to fix some paster fence and run out of wire. I had an old ax along and I went to cut down a few buck horn [cactus] and drag into the break till next day and jest as I hit one cactus a rattler whizzed and a piece of cactus flew off and hit me in the laig. I dropped the ax and fell back on the seat of my overalls to die right now but when I grabbed fer the bit place I found there was a cactus pod there and I revived.

Another time me and another boy about my size stopped over night at a place and the man that was holdin' it down had raised some melons. Well when the sun had been down long enough that we allowed the melons had cooled we all went to the patch. The big feller was ahead and he weighed about two hundred pounds and he jumped a rattler. Not one of them that piles up and waits but one of them little devils that comes a ramblin' rattlin' and a snappin' all at once. I was the fust one out from there and I says to the other boy that I don't like them kind of snakes. "Snakes Hell!" he says. "I was runnin' to keep from being tromped to death by that big feller."

One time a bunch of us boys camped at an old corral and shed where they had fed meal cake the winter before. It was a nasty rainy night and one feller drug his bed into the place where they had kept the meal cake. A little later we went to go in and a rattler whizzed. We couldn't find him and hadn't no light but matches so we bedded down under the open shed. The feller that was already in there allowed if they didn't like his company they could do the next best thing. The rest of us, well, we wasn't quite that tough.

One hot morning a bunch of us woke up and one of the hands had a daddy long leg spider on his neck. We told him it was a tirantula. That old boy snuck around soft and careful fer about five minutes to keep from insultin' that spider and when it got around where he could see it he like to chased every body out of camp.

There was a cook got bit with a centipede one night when he was walkin' around camp in a pair of slippers. It was a big centipede and it looked he had clinched and then half raised and grabbed again for he made a Y shaped bight. He corded his leg and the blood popped out on all them little places where the centipede had tracked. I had a good sized bottle of permangenate of potash and I just rubbed the crystals into the places. It sure made him shake that laig. His laig swelled bad and he was lame fer a day or two but he went right on at work. I shook a scorpion out of my pants one mornin' before I put them on. I prefer doin' it previous to doin' it afterwards. It's safer.

Old Time Country School Days [7]

The kids has more fun now than they used to and has a lot more clothes and pitcher shows and things. They don't have as many sisters and brothers and as many lickin's as we did and they don't have to go and build a fire in an old school house and thaw out on a winter mornin', but I reckon they miss out on a lot of things at that.

One time we had a teacher down in the Missouri hills and she come from a big town. She asked more fool questions and knowed less than anybody in the settlement. Not barrin' one old cuss that argyed the world was flat. She seen some hogs that had their tails froze off the winter before and wanted to know why their tails was cut off and one big boy told her that they got such big gobs of gumbo mud on their tails that it stretched the hide on their face till they couldn't get their eyes shut and the flies put them blind. And she believed it.

There was two old houn' dogs that we always took to school and I reckon they knew about as much as most of us at that. One mornin' we run a cotton tail rabbit into a rock pile and dug him out. We got him by the hint leg and he wasn't hurt none and we put him in the school marm's desk. When school took up she raised up the lid and see that rabbit a squattin' in there and she allowed it was a rat and she sure give up a yell. We opened the door and poked him out and he got out of doors and took to the timbers with both houn's after him. The school marm told the directors it was the biggest rat she ever see and that he had a tail over a foot long. Which we figgered was some tail for a rabbit.

Come Christmas we penned her out and made her treat and the directors allowed we hadn't done no harm so she sort of throwed in with us. Yessir she even rode a mule to a country dance and helped doctor a couple of sick babies that winter and we reckoned she ort to settle right there for life but she was too durn good lookin' and a town feller married her the next summer, but if she had got a couple more winters in the hills she would sure have joined up with us hill billies and no mistake.

Yessir one recess they was two boys a fightin' and she run out to part 'em and slipped and slid on a patch of ice in front of the door. She slid plum out from under her petticoats and we saw that she wore the old red flannels same as our Maws did and we figgered her in fer one of us right now. That stopped the fight fer she took our mind off fightin' and no mistake.

I often wonder where she went but us kids sure did like her fer she was the only school marm we ever had that was young and good lookin' and laffed more at a joke than us kids did. I reckon a lot of old fellers has went to that same sort of school house and bent down hickory trees and et pork sausage and corn bread and lived to a good age afterwards.

The Traveling School Master [8]

West Queensland is a funny place for an American to get into, or it was about twenty years ago when I was working there. They work different from us and their cow talk aint like ours and their way of thinkin' and livin' is all different.

A pasture is a "poddick" and a round-up is a "muster" and the range is a "run" and the home ranch is the "homestead" and a fence rider is a "boundary rider". They rode flat saddles and carried long whips and nearly every "station hand" and "drover" had a tin pot on his saddle to boil himself a pot of tea with his lunch.

But what seemed odd to me was the travelin' school master. This feller takes a team and a buckboard and makes the rounds in a certain section of the country and gets around every two or three months. He sometimes has to wait a few days if his pupils are visitin' on a near-by "station" as they call a ranch, or if some boy is out helpin' on a muster.

He waits till he ketches all the kids on any station and then he examines them to see what they know, and after that he leaves them some more books and takes the ones that they are through with and drives on. They can never tell within a few weeks when he will land on a place because he has to wait sometimes in a place and then again the roads may be pretty bad after rains for that country can sure git boggy in wet weather and bridges jest aint. So you see the travelin' school master has to be a pretty good bush-man hisself to git bye.

Funny thing the kids all seem to like him and it is plum surprisin' how much they learn and the most of them are mighty proud to tally up with him on what they learn while he is away. When he leaves it is not uncommon for one or two kids on those big leases to ride five or six miles to open and close a "poddick" gate for him while his team "is still a bit brash." For he has to use what he can for hosses. There is no feedin' in that country and sometimes a hoss gits away on him and the hoss they stake him to may not have had much harness work.

Yes sir, him and them kids is pardners from the word go and when I think how a lot of them bush raised kids check up their affairs with him and act like real little men and women, it makes me ashamed of the way some kids that get a real break act in this country. BUT, the government don't put nobody but a one hundred per cent man and gentleman on that job.

It Was a Draw! [9]

Joe Morgan and Anse Craig were turrible fellers to tell big windys and to ask fool questions, but they both made their braggs that they never told a yarn that they couldn't explain, and never asked a question they couldn't answer.

One night over at Flat Lakes they tangled in camp. Anse he started it. "Speakin' of speed," sez he, "I mind one time I was workin' fur the Circle Diamond outfit and jumped a antelope. I was on my top hoss and 'bout a mile from there I ketched him and jest as I snubbed him up short my shadder ketched up and cum alongside."

"How'd ya figger?" he sez, lookin' at Joe. "Taint nothin'," sez Joe. "You was goin' too fast fer yer shadder to follow." "Reckon that's about right," sez Anse.

"Speekin' of speed," sez Joe, "One time up in Utah a mighty fast old shep dog jumped a cotton tail rabbit, which went round a haystack and dive in. Old Shep thinks he's still runnin' and the fourth time round old Shep ketched hisself by the tail."

Joe looks at Anse and Anse sez: "He natcherly run his own tail off and was around to ketch it fore in hit the ground." Joe he nods and then Anse sez:

"Speekin' of Muskeeters, 'stead of speed, when I was up in Montanny, they had Muskeeters that would set around on the trees and bark, and a great many of 'em would weigh a pound."

When that one hit Joe, he set up and slid like a cuttin' pony, but he was stayin' with it. He bites off a chaw and spits and sez:

"I reckon that's about right. They couldn't set on the trees 'thout settin' on the bark. And take enough of 'em and they'd weigh a pound. A great many of 'em."

Then Joe asks Anse how a groun' squirrel digs his hole and don't throw out no dirt.

"Dunno," sez Anse, "How does he?"

"He starts at the bottom and digs up," sez Joe.

"How does he get down thar?" asks Anse.

"Dunno," sez Joe. "That's your question, you answer it."

'Bout then two outside men come in and by the time we helped 'em unpack their beds and throw their hosses to the remuda, Joe's and [Anse's] high power talk got all busted up.

THE COW BOY'S SHIRT TAIL

There is one thing people inquire about;
They ask why a cow puncher's shirt tail comes out.
Most any rough hand that you happen across —
If he's skinnin' a beef, if he's shoin' a hoss;
If he's ridin' a broncho or flankin' a calf —
Well, his shirt tail is out, or at least the last half.

If you've seen some old waddy jest bustin' his neck
To escape from some critter that's got on the peck,
You've discovered two things, jest between you and I,
That a cow boy can run and a shirt tail can fly.
He knowed what he'd get if he happened to fail,
So he shore didn't stop to arrange his shirt tail.

Now workin' wild stock where the brush is right thick,
Where the cattle is sudden and the cow boys is quick;
If you notice a man and a hoss disappear,
That is, if you view the event from the rear,
The thing that you always will keep on your mind,
Is that cow puncher's shirt tail a floppin' behind.

Them "Levi P. Strauss" is built small in the seat
And a cowpuncher's frame doesn't carry much meat.
He can eat a big breakfast and long before night
He's so empty and hongry that nothin' fits tight.
And besides, he gits rassled and tussled around
Till the best behaved shirt tail won't hardly stay down.

Yes, I know it's a fact and beyond any doubt
That a cowpuncher's shirt tail will keep comin' out.
It's the work that they do and the clothes that they wear,
And it's partly perhaps that a cow boy don't care;
So I've had to explain to folks, time and again,
Their shirt tails come out 'cause they caint keep them in.

3

Introducing Bill

Concernin' Bill[1]

Speakin' of Bill, the first time I ever see him is at a little mountain town up in Colorado when we was both a heap younger than what we are now.

I was lookin' into a mirror, which same don't give no favorable opinion of myself, so I takes to lookin' at a large pitcher on the wall. It was a large lady in Mae West clothes and she is settin' by a table and holdin' up a big glass of beer.

There was the pitcher of a goat mixed up in the affair but things was sorter hazy at the time and time ain't improved things none as regards the goat. I hears argyment at the other end of the bar and a feller is sayin' that this here country is so mountainous that there ain't no room to do nothin'.

Then I hears Bill say, "You're shore wrong there, this country is stood up on end like, and you got four sides and the top to use whuras in a level country you only got the top. As fer it bein' rough I mostly been able to git what I went after around here." "Yeh," sez the other feller, "and leave most of youre clothes and a lot of youre hide on the bresh." "Clothes don't make the man," sez Bill. "No but they go a long ways toward keepin' him frum freezin' to death in the winters they've got up in these parts," sez the other feller.

Well I goes out and forks my hoss and starts up to where I am workin' and who ketches up with me but Bill and we git right friendly. About three miles up the creek we find a hand that has been throwed and kicked in the head and his brains is oozin' out. We finds his hoss and there is a big spur track acrost the saddle so we figger it is a accident. We goes back to town and gits a buckboard and the doctor. When the doctor gits there he looks at the feller and sez, "That's his brains." "Shore is," I sez. "Can you two fellers swear that this man was a cow puncher?" asks the doctor. Bill sez he can and I remarks that he was in a work I was on about two weeks ago. The doctor takes our names and high tails it fer town and don't wait fer nothin'.

About two months later Bill and me is in town and we meet this doctor and he won't have nothin' to do with us, so after a few drinks we goes up to him and tells him to name what he's sore about. "Well," sez he, "you mind that feller you found up on the south fork of the crick with his brains kicked out? Well I went and reported to the medical world that I had made the amazin' discovery that a cow puncher had brains, and I give you two rannies fer witnesses. They wrote to some of the natives here and them natives wrote back that you two fellers was the biggest liars in these parts and so my amazin' discovery won't go down in history."

There's a heap more I can tell you about Bill but we ain't got room here on account of paper only havin' two sides.

Bill's Injun Trouble [2]

There is one Injun affair that aint never got into print as I know of, but I know it happened because I was there and done seen it.

Yes it was my old friend Bill that I have mentioned before in the colums of this here cow paper. I hadn't seen Bill fer a spell havin' been down in the lower country, but I was like "Betsy from Pike" in the old song. I was "Full of that strong alkali" so I drug it fer the high country again where there was good water and lots of work in the summer time.

I got into the little town where we used to hold out and sez hello to the bartender and soter relaxes as folks sez these times. And takes to waitin' fer Bill between drinks. Well I am in a friendly frame of mind when I see Bill comin'. He is ridin' a raw bronc that he can jest about turn with the hackamore. I don't rush out to meet him like some politician, this not bein' good manners in them parts. He knows where I'll be if I'm in town, so he looks fer a place to tie. I ort to gone out and let him tie onto my saddle horn but I was in a state of mind where a feller overlooks any triflin' matters.

Bill caint tie to no porch posts fer the bronc might set back and bust 'em and there is a few old buggy and wagon teams tied to the only two hitchin' racks in town and if the bronc tares down a rack it is goin' to bust up things bad. Bill don't think to go and turn him in the corral back of the livery stable, but he gits one of his big idees.

Next to the saloon is the pool room with a seegar stand, and out on the board porch is a seegar statchu of a Injun. In one hand he is holding out a bunch of seegars and in the other a tommy hock all raised like he was goin' to knock you in the head. I soter figgered he was supposed to be jest darin' any feller to try and swipe his tobacker. This Injun Chief is stood up on a high pedestool that has rollers onder it like one of them fancy bed steads. I see right off that Bill has got a couple of drinks some place before he lit in town fer he has that look he allus had when he didn't care a cuss fer nothin'. He looks the lay out over and then he cheeks the bronc and gits down and gits his hoss as close as he can to the seegar Injun and ties his rope right around the middle. Then he comes up to where I am and we cuss each other out right friendly and go inside and take a few and find out what we have been a doin' fer the last year and then some. We are jest to the pint where Bill tells me about how a married woman that I admired a heap is now divorced and livin' happy ever after, when the citizen that runs the seegar place busts into the bar room and starts to throw sand on his back about that hoss bein' tied to that seegar statchu.

Bein' in a peaceful humor me and Bill starts out to move the hoss. But this here peevish cuss gits in front of us and to make a showin' he rushes over and soter pints his finger at the bronc. Well the hoss jumps back and jerks the rope and that Injun chief on the rollin' pedestool goes right toward him and the bronc don't know whether the Injun aims to feed him tobacker or brain him with the tommy hock and he aint waitin' to see. There has been some talk about who led Geronimo out of Mexico but there was no doubt about who led this Injun out from there. It was Bill's hoss. He shore went frum there a runnin' and a kickin'. The seegar statchu follerin' about three feet behind when it aint swingin' in circles. The pedestool busted loose fust and then the arms, laigs and tommy hock and wodden feathers and tobacker soter scattered out and the bronk fogged it down the street with jest the main chunk a draggin'. A public sperited buckboard team broke loose and jined and a old lady did a sprint that I aint seen beat yit. Some chickens was prospectin' around out in the road but they all go out from there leavin' a few feathers which settled down with the dust. The hoss goes round a corner and the chunk he is draggin' ketches on the post of the rickety old bob wire fence. Bustin' the post and turnin' the hoss fer a grunt knocker. Bill and me is follerin', not runnin' very straight but purty fast considerin' the load we was carryin'. We gits to the hoss before he gits up and gethers enough wind to run agin, but we jest gits the rope when he blows his stopper agin and drags and wallers me and Bill all around, him bein' in the state of mind where he caint tell us frum the seegar statchoo.

The citizens begins to show their heads here and there and finally comes the town marshall, him bein' the last to arrive at the trouble, as is customary. Well Bill had to pay fer that Injun and we allus figgered the price was purty steep. But then we wasn't art collectors and I bet Bill is the fust and only actual cow puncher that ever bought a statchoo. That was the only Injun upraisin' me and Bill was ever mixed up with, but it goes to show the turrible treachery of the Injun character. A Injun chief won't do to tie to.

Bill Meets a Funeral [3]

Now speakin' of funerals it makes me think of one that me and Bill met up with. You see it's like this. Me and Bill has took time off to go to town and is jest washed and shaved, when the old man sez to us that we needn't saddle up fer he has jest ketched up his buckboard team that's been runnin' out quite a spell and he figgers it will be a good idee fer me and Bill to hitch them up to a old spring wagon and work them to town and back so that they will be soter smoothed down fer his buckboard work.

We agrees and then the old man sez fer us to tie on a whole passel of dry hides that's been hangin' around the place and leave them at the hide house when we git to town.

The old man shore don't overlook nothin' I sez to Bill. "He shore does," sez Bill, "or you wouldn't a worked fer him as much as you have." I could a told Bill a few things but it ain't no use so I jest helps him git the hides piled into the back of the old spring wagon and tied on fer keeps.

Ever body on the place thinks of sumpthin' he wants frum town seein' we're goin' with a wagon and the cook comes out with two pair of shoes in a gunny sack which he wants half soled. We gits hitched and the team ain't so good. Bill is drivin'. The nigh hoss tries to start but the off hoss starts a neckin' party by rairin' up and puttin his haid over the nigh hoss but I strings him out by throwin' the sack of shoes and hittin' him alongside of the haid and he leaves frum there right now. I figgered the shoes could go to town some other time.

Well nothin' much happened till we got to town where we sees a saloon that sez "First Chance" on the sign and we stops and has a couple to soter ile us up and then starts on to git rid of them hides and put the team in a livery stable. The town had a opry house and a bank and generly speakin' was a town. We jest got to the main corner when around come a funeral. They was two hosses to the hearse and they had soter bushes of feathers stuck on their bridles and the two fellers on the seat had on plug hats and white gloves and frock coats. The hearse team takes one look at our load of hides and sets right up on the britchin. Our team hadn't never seen men dressed like them was and settin' up so high and they whirled 'round and high tailed it before we could do a thing. They busted loose frum the spring wagon which upsot and throwed me and Bill out on the hard walk in front of the bank and then they got onto the paved walk accrost the street where they had about as much luck as a couple of billy goats on a dance floor and they slipped down and got all tangled up.

The hearse hosses is lookin' into the winder of a store accross the street but the funeral is still right side up and some men is hangin' onto the team. A cow waddy and a mule skinner is settin' on our team holdin' them down. A feller that knows me sez, "Shorty, what are you settin' in front of the bank fer?" "Because they's money in it," sez Bill. I feel like I was knocked loose frum most all of ever thing I ever had. I wasn't used to bein' slung onto pavement and then a passel of dry hides and a spring wagon rolled onto me.

Bill is on his feet and cussin' and I am jest goin' to arise when I looks up and there stands the purtiest little lady with big blue eyes, and I'd a thought she was a angel if I hadn't seen her step up on the curb. They's a milliner store accrost the street and I figgers this is the milliner lady shore enough. You bet I leans right back agin that load of hides and takes to gruntin' like a bloated steer.

"Is they any thing I can do fer you?" sez this lovely little lady. I pertends to have trouble speakin' and I sez, "Lady," I sez, "I'm soter shook inward like and if they was a quiet place where I could set fer a spell I reckon I'd be all right." "Come right over to the store," she sez and she heps me up and puts her arm around me and leads me over to the store. I looks back at Bill and when I ketched his eye I see jealousy and anger there plum appearant.

That don't bother me none and I lays down on a lounge in the back of the store and leaves Bill to fix the wreck while the milliner lady gives me a fancy bottle to smell of which she sez is salts. I thanks her fer the bottle and smells of the salts but don't take none. But then the milliner lady is another story so I reckon I had better stop with jest me and Bill and the funeral.

Bill Doctors the Chimleys [4]

There was a dance at the little town hall and all was invited by the committee. Me and Bill didn't go together because I was some ways from there and didn't know whether I could go or not, and Bill bein' sore didn't wait fer me and went with two fellers that had jest come into the country.

I got there when the dance was in full swing and I see there was a soter hostile feelin' of some kind. And it didn't take long to figger out that it was Bill and them other two rannies that was at the bottom of it. They was shore lit up and was a makin' a lot of wise cracks and doin' a lot of onnecessary jiggin' on the corners and a swingin' gals by the waist that had allus been swung jest by the hands.

They wanted me to have a drink, so I went out and took one or two jest to be peaceful and friendly like. But anyhow it got me to where I could git the idee of the way them other three boys was feelin'. Twarn't no use to try and jine up with 'em fer they had too much head start on me, but after that it was soter funny to watch.

They was three men on the committee and they was three waddys makin' the ruckus so I figgered all things bein' free and ekul, it was a good idee to give ever body concerned their haid and let 'em buck. But them three hay shakers that was givin' the "bailie"[5] had another idee and the next thing I see was the old village marshall a showin' his badge to the boys and invitin' 'em to vamoose. The other two rannies was fer startin' somethin' but Bill he augered[6] 'em out of it and they all went out peaceful. Then the wife of one of them committee fellers sez she is glad they went and that the folks that is ranchin' in the valley don't want ignurant cow hands a comin' in and messin' up their social doins and she wishes them as hadn't already went would go now. That soter got onder my hide, fer I seen right now how most of them hay shakers felt about us cow folks.

Well I went outside and I heered one old feller say that his brother had sent him a sack of walnuts all the way from Missoury and he took a couple of his friends over to his wagon and give 'em each a pocket full and then they went to another wagon and fishes out a jug and all drinked and sez to each other that the committee is shore 'nough three smart fellers and plum gentlemen. They didn't see me aytall and I was glad they

didn't fer it give me a chance to hit up their jug. After a couple of drinks and a few min-
utes thought I ketched a right peart idee. I got my hoss where I could grab him right
quick and then I went over back of the boardin' house and got a big slop bucket off'n
the back porch. I dumped out what slop was in it, knocked the ice out of it and poured
it plum full of them walnuts.

There was a lamp burnin' at the bottom of the town hall stairs which I blowed out
right now. The door was open and they was a doin' the "Over the waves" waltz. I gits
close to the top of the stairs and then I slings that bucket of walnuts all over the top steps
and the top landin' and waved the old slop bucket by the bail and lets her go in amongst
'em fer good measure, and yells like a wild man and then I runs out and rides hell fer
leather twoard the feed lot where Bill is feedin' beef about five miles frum there. When I
gits to his shack I don't find nobody and I am plum anxious about Bill and them other
two rannies and also I feel a leetle bit lonesome in case the committee or some of the town
marshall's friends might come a visitin' out there. Course they ain't nothin' they can prove
but they might be a heap of things they can do if they happens to be several of 'em.

I see them two strange rannies has throwed their beds in the shack so I crawls into
Bill's hot roll and I am waked up some time later when them three boys rides up. The
next day we fills up the feed racks good and plenty and have jest knocked off work early
when the boss drives up in his buckboard. I aint said nothin' about the night before to
the boys and they aint said nothin' to me fer we each figgers that the other feller has let
go awful easy.

The boss he goes into the house and purty soon we all eases in to git the powders[7]
what ever they're a goin' to be. We all lights a smoke and then he sez, "Boys," he sez,
"They was soter a ruckus down to town last night. I aint blamin' nobody nor takin'
sides. Bill and these here two Texas boys done right by leavin' the dance peaceful when
they was asked to, although they hadn't ort to raised so much sand while they was there.
But, they never done right when they took the ladders from the alfalfa stacks and clum
up on the houses of all them committee fellers and the town marshall and plugged them
chemleys full of gunny sacks and hoss blankets and sech. Them men and their famblys
come home along twoard mornin' and tried to light a fire. They never knowed what
was wrong and they tore the stove pipes down and ev'ry thing and they had to put the
women and kids to bed whilst they clum up on top of the house and oncorked their
chimbleys. One man froze his foot and another one a ear and Zeb Thompson cut his
hand all to the Dickens on the stove pipe." The other boys looks sad like but I caint
help from bustin' out laffin' right now. The boss lets me have my laugh out and then
he sez to me. "Look a hyar Shorty, you aint got no call to laff none. You went and took
that sack of walnuts out from Lige Bascom's wagon and poured 'em into the boardin' house
slop bucket and slung 'em all over the top steps and the landin' of the town hall. And
when you slung the bucket into the crowd you like to broke my sister in law's laig. The

crowd all run out to git you and they tromped on them walnuts and fell and slip all over their selves and quite a passel of 'em fell down stairs. The town marshall hit his tail bone on the steps and is jest about parlized. Him and his woman had to stay at a neighbors on account his chimbly was plugged and they wasn't no warm place to doctor him."

The boss fills his pipe again and sez. "Now I figger to send you young sprouts to build a ground tank at the place over between the hog backs and I am sendin' them two old fellers out to feed the beef and watch the line camp. If these here Texas boys wants to do tankin' work I reckon they might jine in." That plan took us all as bein' agreeable and the boss went out to go home. Bill looks out at the winder. "Look!" he sez, "The boss is took vilent with a spell." He starts out but one of them big long Texans grabs him. "Never mind," sez Tex. "He aint used to laffin' so hard and he's soter doubled up like. It was right good of him to keep us all in these parts after the ruckus. Howsomever I was a watchin' that sister inlaw of hisn and I reckon he wouldn't have felt so kind twoard us if Shorty hadn't of hit her in the laig with that there boardin' house slop bucket."

City Folks Go Bear Huntin'[8]

Bill and me was sent to the upper ranch in the hills to pack in some salt fer the cattle up on that fork of the creek. They had hauled the salt as far as old man Harbin's place by wagon, but from there on we had to pack it. When we gits to Harbin's place it looked like Barnum and Baily's circus was there, fer they was four tents and a whole passel of towerists with fishin' poles that had little spools and cranks on 'em and old Harbin has give it out that he is a guide, and the next day them folks is goin' to pay him to show 'em where to ketch all the trout they can carry and also fer the privilege of campin' on his land.

The boss keeps a packin' outfit cached at Harbin's place and furnishes the salt fer Harbin's cattle and his too, fer which Harbin stakes us to pack animals to git up onto the range. We overhauled the outfit and them towerists was all around us a lookin' and askin' questions. I slips out and gits to a place where there is some soft ground below the corral and I goes to work and fixes a few tracks that looks like shorenough bear tracks and I has to laugh, fer I aint done like that sence us kids used to set in the dust and fix tracks and brands and ask the old fellers if we had made 'em right. Well, purty soon I takes them Jaspers and shows 'em them bear tracks and right now they wakes up and we find that they have enough Winchesters and shot guns and six shooters to lick the Arkansas cavalry and the Missouri Militia. Bill sez that all town folks goes armed if they git where there ain't no sidewalks.

They invites us over to supper and we sez we'll be there. Well, Bill tells his idee to me and it aint bad aytall. We goes and fills our pockets with corn before we goes over to their camp. And when we leaves it is plum dark, so we scatters that corn around jest outside the fire light, then we goes and gits some more corn and lays a thin trail of it frum the gate of the old man's hog pen up to where we had scattered the other corn. I had gone to sleep, when Bill wakes me, and it is right late. We takes a couple more handfuls of corn and goes to the pen where them three hogs is, and Bill keeps a cluckin' to 'em and we throws 'em a sprinkle of corn at the gate of the pen and lets 'em out. They starts right off follerin' that feed and a rootin' and snufflin' and growlin' and gruntin' and they sounded like all the bears in them parts was there with their relations.

Bill he sez, Shorty, we better git behind a rock pile that was handy, and it wasn't long before I knowed Bill was right. We waited fer a spell and the hogs was a follerin' that feed trail right along, and then it shore sounded like the battle of Bull Run, fer all the shootin' irons in that camp was a goin' off and I heered the old man Harbin's winder glass bust somewhere in the house and a hog a squealin' over at the towerist camp, and some big slugs of lead come clost enough so me and Bill heerd 'em too.

Old Harbin come out with a lantern and everybody was a hollerin' to each other, and they found one dead hog and the other had vamoosed frum there plum pronto. They builds up the fire and seein' we had no way fer to scald the hog right then, we skun him an dressed him and hung him up. The towerists thought it was a lot of fun, but me and Bill seen the way the Old Man Harbin's eyes looked and the way his whiskers sorter worked whenever he looked at us, and we figgered we better git that salt packed in and git away frum there before them towerists did.

Bill Plays Ghost [9]

When me and Bill pulls into the home ranch we finds two fellers fixin' the fences and the house and barn and corrals. One was a Englishman named Ed and the other was a Irishman named Mike. They had been sailors all their life and was jest travlin' around to see what dry land was like. They was good hands at that soter work and they talked so funny that me and Bill had to laff at them all the time and they laffed at us and reckoned we was plum funny. But in a couple of days we got to know them and they had seen a heap of the world and was good fellers.

Sunday they sez they aim to go into the galley and bile up and wash their kit. Which we finds means goin' into the kitchen and washin' their clothes. After dinner Ed he walks up to the boss and sez, "Skipper," he sez, "me maty wants to go ashore fer a spell. He'll be back afore long, and could he cruise over to the village on that big mule as has been adrift in the paster this week? She looks like a safe craft and we have her docked in by the barn."

The boss winks at us boys and sez he reckons so, and me and Bill eases down where we can see the fun and mebby help if they git tangled too bad with Old Jack the mule. They goes into the corral. "Give us the heavin' line mate," sez Mike and Ed hands him my rope. Mike coils it careful like and leaves a little cat loop in the end. Then he heaves it coils and all right at Old Jack and durned if he don't git him with the loop and two coils right round the neck. "Tow him up to the bitts and make fast!" yells Ed. "Now fer the steerin' gear," sez Mike, and Ed comes out of the shed with a work bridle that has two hitch reins snapped onto the bit. They gits the bridle onto Old Jack and Ed runs over and grabs my saddle blankets. I am about to kick but Bill sez not to stop the show. "Here's the battin'," he sez. "Git over on the sta'b'rd side and see I lay her trim. Don't go astern, the beggar might kick. Cross his bows and keep forrud, that's it. Now hold hard on her bowlines while I heave the crows nest top side. Aye, that's the style, now pass me the riggin's under her keel and I'll lash her fast." They did a pretty good job of saddlin' if they did go at it awkward. "Board her from the port side," sez Ed. "Grab the bowsprit and cock yer foot into the ladder round." Up Mike goes and finds a hoggin' string tied in the front whangs.[10] "What's this lanyard fer?" he asks. "To flog with I reckon," sez Ed, "and a fine idee too." "All right cast her off," sez Mike and Ed onties old Jack from the post. "Now flog aft with yer lanyard!" he yells. "Pull hard on yer sta'b'rd line, she's onder way, that's right, she's comin' about. Ease off and haul the port line; now slack away and let her drift. I'll pilot ye out the bloomin' gate!" And Old Jack walks off with Mike on his back.

After Mike is gone Ed tells us that Mike don't fear nothin' but ghosts, but he is tur-rible afraid of ghosts and he wants we should skeer that Irishman out of a year's growth. So we gits a tarp and cuts eye holes in it and gits a beef skull with the horns on and wires it onto the tarp fer a head. Then Bill ties two beef bones onto his stirrups fer laigs and gits a big bone to hold in each hand fer arms and then we gits Old Snowflake, a plum gentle old white hoss and waits fer dark. Ed is goin' to hide behind some bresh in the draw and after Mike gits past he aims to take after him and we know if he don't skeer Mike he'll shore skeer the mule. When it's time we saddle up but Old Snowflake won't let Bill mount him in a rig like that so we blindfolds the old hoss and Bill climbs on him.

We has another laff fer Bill looks ten foot high, and his head is a skull with horns on and his bone laigs most nigh drags the ground. I pulls off the blind, and boy howdy! Old Snowflake squats and snorts and then he lights into buckin' like I never see a hoss his age buck before. And pore Bill aint got a Chinaman's chance to ride him wropped up like he is. "Ahoy there!" yells Ed. "Haul hard on yer bow lines! Oh me oath he's on his beam ends he'll capsize. Bear a hand mate, Bill's overboard and afoul of the wreck-age he'll be stove in afore we can cut him clear! Oh Lord Bill's sunk and the beast is adrift with the riggin's!" I caint do nothin' fer laffin' to see Bill bucked off and that tarp fast to the saddle and Bill and them bones a flyin' all roads. Ed gits him onwropped from the tarp and he aint hurt much only his feelin's.

Purty soon Mike comes in feelin' good and has a jug which he sez he lashed fast to the bowsprit of his saddle. Well, we all took a bracer and felt better. Next mornin' at breakfast Ed tells the yarn with all the trimmin's and the boss and the cook jest roars. "I didn't know," sez Mike, "that a cowboy was supposed to go overboard fer jist a bit of a squall like that."

After breakfast Bill packs his bed hoss and saddles up. The boss hates to see him go but he fixes up his check and tells him to come back when he's tired of the high country. The two sailors is there to open the gate fer him and Ed yells "Good luck Maty, sorry yer jumpin' ship at this port but we may run across ye later." Then he sez to the boss, "He's a fine lad, skipper, but he needs a bit of rest and overhaulin' fer he walks and sets like he got a bit stove up astern in the wreck last night."

THAT LETTER

I rode to that box a settin' on a post beside the trail,
That our outfit used fur gettin' all their messages and mail.
There I got a little letter and the envelope was pink,
It shore set me feelin' better but it soter made me think.
Yes the feelin' was surprisin' onderneath my stetson hat.
I could feel my hair a risin' like the bristles of a cat.

Well I tore that letter open and I read it through and through.
All the time I was a hopin' I would savvy what to do.
Men is quick upon the trigger, come to tangle ups and fights,
But a woman, you caint figger what she means by what she writes.
It was purty and invitin' like a sunny day in spring,
She had done a heap of writin' but she hadn't said a thing.

Now, when men folks start to writin' you can mostly onderstand,
And the stuff that thay're a sightin' stands out plain jest like a brand.
They don't never do no playin', they've a sort of sudden way,
For they start right in by sayin' what they started out to say.
Men is given to expressin' what they mean, right then and there,
But a woman keeps you guessin' till your mind goes everywhere.

Fer a spell I'd do some thinkin' then I'd start again and read;
I kept frownin' and a blinkin' till at last I got her lead.
In that letter there was lurkin' jest one simple plain idee.
When I got my mind a workin' it was plain enough to see.
Fer she said her and her mother, come a Saturday next week
Would be over with her brother to the dance on Turkey Creek.

On the start, you see, I never had no notion what she meant,
She had fixed it up right clever in the way the letter went.
Man! I shore did whoop and beller when the idee hit me fair,
She would come without no feller and she aimed to meet me there.
It shore made me like her better fer that bashful gal of mine,
Went and built that whole durned letter, jest to write that single line.

4

BILL AND RILDY BRIGGS

Bill's Joke Goes Wrong [1]

Sunday mornin', two weeks after Bill has strung out fer the high country, we was eatin' breakfast, and the Boss's wife she speaks up and sez: "I don't reckon Bill has gone up to the high country. The way him and Rildy Briggs made sheep's eyes at each other down at the school house dance I bet he bent that old sorrel hoss off the road fur enough to go into Lige Briggs' place and tell Rildy good bye."

That there's a smart idee I sez and old Lige aint losin any chuck rider that will work like Bill, and Bill he's fool enough to hang around all summer and work like a nigger jest to be where Rildy's at. Then the Missus she lights in to a talk about what she thinks of the Briggs tribe but the Boss he makes her be still.

Well, I sez, I reckon it won't do no harm to git on my Sunday hoss and lope over there and find out. "If he's a workin' fer Lige Briggs," sez the Boss, "leave him stay there." And I sez all right. After about two hours ride I comes in sight of Briggs's place which is between two ridges on a crick. He has fenced in paster on each side so you have to go through a lane to git there no matter which side you come frum. I sees a clowd of dust a comin in from the other side of the crick and I know that it is Zeke Briggs. Lige's wuthless brother. He used to come most every Sunday and stay till the middle of Monday and bring his wife and six kids. They would eat all they could hold and git the team up and then borry some grain fer hoss feed and what groceries they could and then go back home fer what was left of the next week. Next I looks down at the place and there is Bill and the two oldest kids gittin an old red range stray out of the meadow where they raised winter feed. They got him into the corral and Bill gits an old slicker. One of the kids gits an old canteen and puts rocks into it. I can see it all, fer by now I have rode up and got down on the ground and am a lookin' through the fence at the show. Bill takes his old hoss and puts the steer into the chute pen and them kids and him run him into the chute and bars him in tight. Then Bill wires that old canteen of rocks and the old slicker onto the steer's tail plenty tight. They turn him out and the way that old bay steer goes up the lane a squallin' and bellerin' is shore plenty fast. Right then over the ridge above the ranch comes Zeke Briggs and his wife and six kids. When the team meets that steer they take out fer home and upset the wagon and

31

spread [Zeke][2] and his brood all over the lane. They have the front wheels of the wagon and are still ahead of the steer when they all top the ridge. Bill's old pack horse is in the paster right close to the gate and I hazes him into the corral and we ropes him and makes fer the bunk house. All Lige Briggs's fambly has started up there on foot and a runnin' to make a work and tally up on Zeke Briggs's fambly, to see how they come out on the wreck and Bill and me has a sneakin' idee that we better be gone when they git back. We throws the old bed and war bag on and hitches her and makes fer the open country in a high lope. Then Bill he speaks fer the fust time. "I don't know where you come frum," he sez, "but I'm shore glad you got here."

When we are eatin' supper at the home ranch that night, The Boss's wife wants to know if she wins the coat she seen in the catalogue, and the Boss sez he reckons she does. Then she tells us how she bet him a new pair of boots agin the coat that I would bring Bill back with me. "He never had nothin' to do with it," sez Bill: and then he ups and tells them the whole story. Bill don't seem to think it's so funny but nobody else can git a full breath fer the next ten minutes. When The Boss's wife gits so she kin talk she sez, "It's a even break to bet on anything onder the sun when you two boys is around. Thanks fer the coat Shorty."

Bill Has Luck [3]

Me and Bill is makin' a little trip to town between works. I have wrote the millinery lady three letters and she has wrote me one which sez to come and see her when I am in town. Bill he wants me to give him a knock down to this here lady and I tell him she ain't that soter lady that takes up with the average drinkin', swearin' cow hand, but seein' he's a friend of mine I'll make him used to her.

When we gits to town the train is jest pulled in and a lot of towerists is out on the platform to git some see and fresh air. Bill and me rides over to the deppo to do a little lookin' our self, and there is a good lookin' feller with a big moustache and a tailor made suit a tellin' the folks all about it. This feller has on the finest pair of cowboy boots I ever see and they are all shined up and you can tell they ain't never had no wear from spurs and stirrups; but what takes our eye is his hat. He has a big beaver Stetson, as big as a side show tent and I bet it cost twenty-five bucks if it cost a dime. He is so busy wearin' an' a wavin' this here hat while he is explainin' all the whys and whereases to the towerists that it is all he can do to find time to twist his moustache.

We are shore puzzled as to what sort of hombre he is fer he ain't no cow man. He is all pink and white and hain't had no more weather and hard work and bad water than a canary bird in a city home. Bill sez, "Shorty," he sez, "I need a hat. Back my play." The train don't stop long and Bill has to work fast and he does. He walks over to the stranger with his old brush battered hat in his hand and smiles real pleasant like and sez,

"Some hat you got there, stranger. Jest look at the difference 'tween your hat and mine." And he grabs that there handsome hat and hands the feller his, and before you know it Bill has put the hat on and is climbin' onto his hoss. I does my play right now. I hollers at Bill to give the man his hat and calls him a thief and takes after him on old Jug, but he outruns me on Chunky. I gallops right back to the deppo and tells the man that I know this here waddy and that I also know the town marshal and to give me his address and I'll see he gits his hat or that this here thievin' cuss goes to jail, fer western folks is honest and don't aim to be disgraced. That gent he hands me a card with his name and address all printed out on it a purpose jest fer him individual, which is a right smart idee seein' mebby he caint write good and that it shore saves time. The train pulls out and he boards it and leaves Bill's old hat layin' on the platform. I takes the hat and goes over to the livery barn and in about five minutes in comes Bill.

We puts our hosses away and then we express Bill's old hat to the stranger's address C.O.D. Also we send him a telegram on the train that his hat has been sent, so he won't worry no more till he gits Bill's old hat. I go up to Jake's place to have a couple of drinks and soter compose my mind so as to interduce Bill proper to the Millinary Lady and some little time gets away from me before I know it, and in walks Bill, and he has been to the barber shop and got all slicked up and his boots shined and nothin' will do but what I take him to meet the lady right now. Well, she admires that hat right first off and Bill takes it off and puts in on her haid and bein' millinary minded she talks hat a plenty. The hat looks grand and after all the perfume the barber has put on Bill's haid it even smells grand. I ain't no place, fer I am jest a little bow laigged, seedy lookin' waddy, so I don't say nothin', but I leaks out frum[4] there and makes fer Jakes place again. Purty soon Bill he comes in and takes one with me and then we go up to the hotel where we stop when we are in town, and signs up fer a room.

In a little side room back frum the office there seems to be a card game on and we takes a look. A mighty slick lookin' feller is dealin' and he seems to have a little argyment now and then with another town feller that is a stranger to him. The game is to take and pick the ace frum amongst three cards after he has dealed them face down. We all make a few small bets and win or lose a little and it seems to be a little game and all friendly, but Bill he sneaks me away fer a couple of minutes and wises me up about what is goin' to happen. "Never give a sucker a break," sez Bill. "That's their game, and it works both ways if they git some feller that ain't a sucker."

Well, I gives Bill mighty nigh all my roll, and we goes back. Right soon after that the dealer goes away and leaves his cards, and this here other town feller marks the ace with his thumb nail till the dealer could feel it if he couldn't see it. When he comes back a freighter wins a little bet. So does a mule skinner, and the town feller he does too, and then he starts to hoorah this dealer about bein' afraid to back his game. The dealer sez he will take all he will put up and the feller only has three dollars, and the dealer sez he's a piker and that all of us is pikers and if we think he is afraid of his game to come on. Right now Bill comes in and throws down his money and mine too and asks the dealer to lay 'em out. The dealer covers the bet and deals, and there is that marked card layin' in the middle. Bill slaps his hands down on all three cards. "It's the one on the left," he sez. "'Taint this un 'taint this un," he sez. And he turns the marked card, which aint the ace, and he turns the card on the right, which aint the ace. Here's yore money, Bill, I sez, jest as he turns the cards and gethers up the dough and throws it into the front of my shirt which is onbuttoned. This ketches 'em off stride and the capper and the dealer jines up to argy, but before they git goin' the mule skinner grabs Bill's hand and turns it over. That aint no ace neither. "Say!" yells the mule skinner, "This here game is crooked and I lost ten bucks!" An he grabs up his chair, but before he can swing it them two gents is gone to no place. Me and Bill goes up to our room and cuts the money. And suppose, I sez, that them fellers had been good enough to have left the ace on the table figgerin' you would shore take the marked card? "In that case," sez Bill, "I still had a even break, fer I knowed the marked card wasn't the ace."

I goes over to the barn and tends to the hosses and then to the barber shop and gits all slicked up and jest as I am goin' up to see the millinary lady I meets her and Bill comin' down the street. They tells me they are a goin' to the theyater show which is at the opry house that night. They has the gal frum the hotel cigar stand with them and she sez she wants to go fer a hoss back ride in the moonlight, and Bill he speaks up real big-hearted like and sez he'll let us have old Chunky if we want to go, and the gal is all tickled about that she is goin' to ride a cow hoss on a big saddle. And I know and so does Bill that a hoss back ride is about as much fun fer a cowboy as diggin' a ditch is fer a section hand. Well, 'twasn't so bad. The cigar gal wasn't as little and cute as the Millinary Lady, but she was a heap better at tellin' funny stories and was a lot more romantic like. So me and her agreed to turn the Millinary Lady over to Bill and that I an' her would keep company when I come to town.

Bill Goes to Turkey Creek Dance [5]

One night little Sammy Jackson rides into camp and gives it out that there is goin' to be a dance at his dad's ranch over on Turkey Creek and it is timed so that the wagon will be in easy ridin' distance of there that night. Course me and Bill went along with the rest of the boys and things was a goin' fine till Rildy Briggs comes in with a feller that was a stranger to most of us. Bill, he shore looks at 'em jealous fer he ain't fergot Rildy, and that feller is a big good lookin' man and all dressed up in store clothes.

To make it wuss she don't speak to Bill but gives him a soter high chinned look. I sizes this hombre up an sees that he is plenty tall, and wide with it and has a gun under his glad rags in a shoulder holster. I don't like him. Not any. Old Miss Jackson tells me that his name is Barnes and that he is werkin' on the ranch fer Rildy's dad. The boys was all peaceful and keepin' in line except two or three kids that was a leetle too young to shave and jest old enough to want to show off a heap. Barnes he goes a lot out of his way to declare hisself and allow that he aint skeerd of nobody and that there is goin' to be order there or he'll know why.

Nobody liked that fer we had all allowed we could jest about take care of ourselves, and that passel of kids was plum harmless. It wasn't very long till little Johnny Curtain comes fallin' in at the door drunk and bumps agin a couple that is dancin', and right now this Barnes grabs him by the slack of the pants and slings him out at the door, and declares hisself agin. Bill is goin' to take it up but I get him stopped. We goes outside and I see Bill is talkin' to the kids and that Barnes and Rildy is settin' in a winder with their backs stickin' out in the dark. Sammy comes out and hands Bill his dad's old six shooter and I begin to be skeerd, but Bill he steps up quiet like with the gun in his left hand and what does he do but hit Barnes a turrible punch over the kidney with his right hand and at the same time he fires the gun into the ground with his left.

Rildy gives a scream and Barnes he hollers that he is shot and falls into the room, and keeps hollerin' fer help and fer a doctor. Next he is givin' out dyin' messages fer his folks. And when I asks him if he aint got no farewell word fer Rildy he sez he is married, and right then the wagon boss was on the job, and jerks Barnes' coat and vest off and seperates his pants and shirt and starts lookin' fer the bullet hole. Barnes has on a pair of big broad galluses which we stripped down and we also took off his six gun.

We was havin' a heap of fun till them fool kids ups and tells what Bill done, and say that Barnes feller wasn't dyin' no more. He bellers out a string of cuss words and plows right into Bill like a mad bull and you bet Bill is right there to tear up sand with him. Barnes' shirt tail is out and his galluses is a floppin' wild and all the folks that don't git out of the way gits knocked over and tromped down till they clinch and go to the floor togather, and the house shakes like a wagon box on a rocky road. Rildy rushes up and tries to kick Bill but she fouls her foot in one of them galluses and falls down and they both go a rollin' over her till she yells like a mashed cat. Bill's overalls is shrunk and tight and the seat busts open with the strain and his red flannin onder drawers shos up mighty plain and old Miss Jackson yells that he has been knifed. Her not havin' good eyesight and havin' got her specs knocked off in the fracas. 'Bout that time both men is on their feet agin and it's any body's fight till Rildy grabs a big specimen rock that is used to prop the door open and slams it at the back of Bill's head, but jest then Bill dodges frum a lick and the stone goes apast his head and hits Barnes between the eyes and knocks him stiff as a plank.

After that them two fellers is pulled apart by the crowd and the wagon Boss grabs Rildy 'round the waist and hollers fer the fiddlers to strike up the music, fer he sez that Rildy is a heap better at dancin' than she is at throwin' rocks, and he makes so much fun fer everybody that the dance goes on peaceable agin, but you kin see by the looks of that Barnes feller that he figgers mebby Rildy busted him with that rock a purpose. And you can see too that Rildy has gone plum foolish over the wagon boss, which makes Bill and Barnes so jealous minded that they goes outside and makes up and talks about the onsartinness an foolishness of women folks in general.

Bill Takes the Mules to Pre[a]chin' [6]

The wagon boss didn't make sech a hit with Rildy Briggs as a feller might think, because when we gits back frum the work the Boss's wife she tells us that Rildy has took up with a young preacher that comes and preaches in the valley sometimes, and that he is goin' to have meetin' in the school house on Sunday night. Bill he allows we ort to go and see what soter hombre this preacher is, and I agrees, fer from the way Bill acts I figgers there is goin' to be a little action before it is all over.

Sunday night we saddles up to go but Bill stalls around till the boss and his wife goes and then he takes his saddle offen the hoss and leads out the old mule team, Jack and Judy. He saddles old Judy and tells me to saddle Jack. I ain't stuck on ridin' that old work mule but knowin it's part of Bill's game I does it. We git to preachin' while they are singin' and they are shore goin' like a revival, and above all the bellerin' you can hear some feller singin' bass. We looks in at the winder and boy howdy! If there ain't that preacher. Better than six foot tall and two hundred pound if he weighed a ounce, all bone and muscle too and he is not so young but middle aged and right at his best. You could see in a minute the crowd was with him.

We light off and I tie Jack to the hitchin' rack and Bill takes Judy around to the other side of the school house and we gits into a back seat jest as the singin' is over and the preacher starts to pray. I gits Bill's idea and like to bust out a laffin' right now fer if them mules caint see each other they will keep a brayin' as long as they can hear each other. The preacher is jest started to pray and a old brother hollers "Amen!" "Yaw Hee Yaw Hee!" hollers old Judy. One old sister hollers "Glory !" and Old Jack brays out "Yaw Hee Yaw Hee!" "Oh Lord we lifts our voices," sez the preacher and right then both mules cut loose with a bray that a deef and dumb could have heerd a mile away. Rildy she slips back to us and whispers that she is a goin' to tie the mules togather so's they'll be quiet and she goes outside. I gives Bill a shove and winks fer him to foller fer I figger the play is Bill's fer the preacher has the bull by the tail and caint turn loose seein' he's all fouled up with his prayin' right about then. Bill he don't move so I starts to go but Bill he pulls me back onto the seat. Well we don't hear the mules no more and purty soon Rildy comes in and sets down lookin' very polite and mannerful.

But all the same it looks like Bill has got the preacher down fer everybody is tickled and some of the young folks has got to where they don't try to keep frum laffin', but the preacher he jest laffs too and then he sez he guesses he better preach about a mule and he shore does. He preaches about a feller named Absalom that lived back in Bible times and he went and made a war and tried to steal the country away frum his dad. Seems like this Absalom was a brat that had been spoilt in the raisin'. He was a good lookin' cuss and wore long hair and rode a mule, and once when there was a big fight on, this here mule he cold jaws[7] on this Absalom feller and stampedes into the bresh and Absalom got drug off and while he was fouled up by the hair the other outfit come up and speared him to death. That preacher makes it purty strong that Absalom wasn't much of a hand or he wouldn't be ridin' a mule and the laugh was shore on me and Bill but we had to take it.

After meetin' Rildy comes and talks to us till the folks had all sed good night and gone and the preacher fetches his team and buggy to take her home and she even lets Bill help her climb in and we sez good night and goes to get our mules.

The mules is gone and we are loose on foot six miles frum the ranch. That walk wasn't nothin' cheerful and I tells Bill he's a fool fer lettin' that gal git loose alone like that [and] he ort to listen to me. "All right," sez Bill, "I didn't listen to you at the meetin' but I expect to listen to you all the way home.["] But the boss met us with the spring wagon before we got half way because he had found the mules waitin' at the paster gate. He said Rildy had tied them togather all right but she hadn't tied them up to nothin' so they jest nacherly went home.

The next night after supper they shore hurrahed us a heap and fer once the boss's wife takes up fer Rildy and sez she's a plum smart gal, and she reckons that there Absalom sermon was a good one and the preacher come out of that tangle about right. "Wait till he preaches the one about Sampson," sez Bill. "What do you mean?" asks the boss. "Well,["] sez Bill, "he was a feller that got mixed up with a woman 'stead of a mule and he wore long hair too. 'Pears like them long haired fellers didn't have much luck back in Bible times."

The Preacher Loses His Team [8]

It was give out that there would be preachin' at the school house a Sunday and Bill didn't aim to be bluffed out so he sez to me that he is goin' over if I'll go along and he aims to go in and set right there even if the preacher is there with his gal. Now this gal Rildy Briggs couldn't mind her own affairs no more'n a pet hen fer she had done jest as she durn pleased ever since she was a long yearlin' and we heered that she had done and took the Preacher's buggy team and gone a visitin fer a couple of days at a time and left him a settin' at her Dad's ranch till she got back. I knowed that meant trouble fer he had the purtiest and spryest little roan team that was ever in them parts and say how he took care of them.

Well when we got to the school house the folks was pretty well gathered fer meetin' and the preacher wasn't there yet, but we soon see him a comin' and Rildy was in the buggy and she was drivin'. Her kid brother and sister was a ridin' along behind on a pair of old willer tailed ponies. When they gets close Rildy starts showin' off and whips up the team and holds 'em in to make 'em step high. Jest then her kid brother jumps an old mare that's runnin' loose around there and throws a loop around her rump to spook her. The loop snaps off her rump all right but her tail is full of burrs and the rope ketches and holds. Boy Howdy! That button has his rope tied fast[9] and the way the old mare jerks his dinky makeshift saddle off aint no ways slow. The kid lets a yell out of him and the old mare cuts apast the Preacher's team with that saddle a flyin around on the end of the rope and the team leaves frum there right now. Before the preacher can grab the lines they've left the road and jumped a little arroyo. That is the team jumped it and the buggy stayed right there and Rildy and the preacher dove right over the dashboard head first and lands out on the other side. The team takes the buggy tongue and tails in behind the kid's pony but right then the old mare cuts across in front of 'em and that saddle and rope tangles all in amongst 'em and down they goes in a pile and the old mare caint pull loose but she shore aint a throwin' off a bit and the way she pulls is turrible.

By that time me and Bill has forked our hosses and got to the wreck and I cuts the rope and stops the wust of the damage but when we untangled that team they was a sight. They was fresh shod and the way they had tore each other up you couldn't believe and the rope had got around the nigh hoss's hint foot and he was lamed up till he could-n't put that foot to the ground. The preacher lands on the scene and Bill sez, "Now if they'd been mules they'd never a done it." I stops Bill short and tells him it aint no time to joke and by so doin' stops trouble fer that parson man is on the peck and no foolin'. The boss tells me and Bill to take the team over to the ranch and take our time about it and doctor 'em up.

The preacher comes home with the boss and his wife and the next mornin' they sends me down to Briggs's fer the preacher's valise. Rildy and the kid is all full of talk and she sez to tell the preacher to come right down there and explain his conduck by not ever speakin' to her and lettin' old man Johnson and his wife fetch her and the kid home. When I gets to the ranch the preacher and one of the hands has got his buggy there with a pair of shafts in it and he has traded his little team to the boss fer a big old work hoss and is all ready to leak out from there as soon as I get there with the valise. I starts to talk to him about his team but I see I'm all wrong. "Don't mention 'em," he sez. "They air plum [spoilt] now. I broke 'em and I've drove 'em fer three years. They was high strung but it's the fust trouble I ever had with 'em. I don't never want to see 'em again. Tell yore friend Bill goodbye fer me. I've already said goodbye to the folks."

I watched him drive the old hoss out of the gate and shore felt sorry fer him. That night at supper the Boss's wife was a doin' a heap of talkin' about Rildy and her doin's and she wasn't fer her no more but she was shore pityin' the preacher to death. When the boss he grins and sez: "Well if he ever comes back to these parts I reckon either me or Bill will have to ask him if he won't preach that there sermon about Sampson like Bill sed in place of the mule sermon about Absalom."

The Boss's wife was about to git mad and then she busts out laffin' and sez mebby Bill is right about wimmin folks bein' a heap dangerouser to men than mules ever dare be.

Bill Leaves for the High Country [10]

When we gits settled down from laffin' about Rildy and the kid brother and the preacher things soter slid along fer a few days and then one evenin' about dark in rides Rildy and has supper, and when the folks asks her to stay all night she allows she might.

The Boss's wife looks at Bill right pleasant like and asks Bill if mebby he caint put up the dishes, and Rildy grins at him but Bill he aint havin none and he says right p'int blank that he's a goin' a visitin' to some folks down on the crick and he goes down to the bunk house and pulls off his shirt and begins to shave. I don't say nothin' but I figger Bill has jest three shirts and so I takes all three of 'em and dips the tails in the water bucket and a flannil shirt don't dry so quick that a feller would want to ride four mile and back with a wet shirt tail when it's freezin' weather. I don't do no dressin' up myself but I jest high tails it over to where them two gals lived on the creek and leaves Bill to figger it out the best he can and I reckon he caint git into none of my clothes and so he's got to set by the bunk house stove and wait fer hisn to dry. It was a doin' him right fer he hain't no call to git so sassy with a pretty gal like Rildy when she come all that way up to the ranch to sorter make up with him. When I gits to where I am a goin' them two gals was pleasant enough but they started to do a heap of askin' why Bill never come along and I see that he had my time beat there, so I had to tell 'em the whole affair and they shore laffed fit to kill.

When I got back to the bunk house it was late and the place smelled like somebody had beat a skunk to death in there. I knowed the boss had trapped and shot a skunk the day before over by the hoss corrall but I reckoned there wasn't no more skunks about. I lit the lamp to see how Bill had took my joke and Bill wasn't there. Bill's bed was gone and when I went out to the corral his saddle was gone. I crawled into my bed and I like to a strangled and I felt a funny lump of sumpthin'. I lit the lamp agin and if that durned Bill hadn't took and put that dead skunk plum in the middle of my bed. I had to hang my bed outside fer over night and I built up a fire and set by the stove till mornin'. The only thing that comforted me was a pair of old overalls that was still warped to the shape of Bill's laigs and a pair of wore out boots he had throwed on top of 'em. It wasn't really airy one of these, but on top of the heap was a wet shirt tail that had been cut off rough and sudden with a sharp pocket knife.

That sorter made me feel even fer I knowed I was settin' comfortable by a warm stove while Bill was a ridin' out fer the high country on a freezin' cold night without no tail in his shirt.

Shorty Is Bill's Secretary [11]

About a month after Bill has vamoosed fer the high country a letter comes to the ranch fer him. I opens it and reads it. The letter is frum the Millinary Lady. She tells him awful sad like that she had never dast tell him she was married, but now seein' as her husband has divorced her and married a gal back East she is at last free though dead broke. The main reason fer her writin' is that the cigar stand gal is turrible sick in the hospital back in Chicago and needs money to save her life. And she hopes Bill will tell me so's me and him can hep her out seein' we are the only folks she can turn to fer hep in this big and hostile West. I reads it over a few times and I reckons sence Bill aint among them present that it is up to me to take it over. So I writes to her like this, I sez:

Deer Miss De Le Ville:

Yore letter is arrove, and me and Shorty is shore broke up about yore hard luck. Because if it hadn't of been fer bad luck me and Shorty wouldn't a had no luck aytall. We was all set to hep you a plenty and we had all the money we had been savin fer years tied up in a big red bamdanny hankercher and it smelt soter mouldy so we put it out on the wash bench back of the bunk house to air out so's it would smell proper fer to hand it to a lady, and along comes a big stork. Them birds you know that finds the babys onder bushes and frum the way this bundle is tied he figgers it is one of hisn and he flies off with it fore we could ketch him. So if you hear of a stork [f]etchin' a passel of mouldy bills to some house instead of a baby you go right over and explain it to 'em and git yore money. We still had one more play left so we got out all our diamond shirt studs and tie pins and cuff buttons and begins to figger what we could raise on 'em. We had sev'al hundred dollars wuth of diamonds spread out on a saddle blanket when a old bull busts the gate and chases us up onto the fence and before we can git down, a flock of crows lights on that saddle blanket and eats up all them beautiful diamonds. To make it wuss that little fool Shorty starts smokin' 'em up with his six shooter and kills the boss's top hoss which it will take the both of us three months to pay fer, so you cain't expect no hep frum us endurin' that time. Then I signs it "Yore Heart Broke Bill" and sends it to her. I waits fer a answer but don't git none.

A couple of weeks later The Boss sends me up to town with the mule team fer a load of stuff. The livery stable man tells me that Bill is in the jail house and has been sence the day before. That he has had a big fight in the millinary store and he has plum wrecked the Millinary lady's feller, and licked two town folks that tried to stop him and blacked the Millinary Lady's eye and by the time the town marshall and two other fellers got him bulldogged they was hats and bunnits and glass and feathers scattered all over the place.

Well I goes to all the places I am supposed to git stuff and gits it and has it set out so's I can git it right soon in the mornin' and then I goes and tends to the team, after which I goes to the jail house to see Bill. He looks pretty good only you can see that him and his cloths has been tore up and messed around consid'able. I sez hello and he shakes hands and sez, "They wasn't much trouble. I tied 'em on the outside of the pack and they froze hard and I kep slappin' the ice offen 'em and purty soon they was dry." What in the Heck you talkin' About? I sez. "Them shirt tails you dipped in the water bucket, you p'izen little half pint reptile," he sez and he gits mad because I laffs. It seems he ain't forgot about them shirts through all the ruckus and they seems to be tangled in his memory plum parminint.

After we had talked keerless fer a spell I asts Bill how come him to git into the jail house. "Well," Bill sez, "It is shore funny and I cain't jest git the idee myself. You see I comes back to these parts figgerin' I might git a job, seein' everthing is snowed onder fer the winter up in the high country, I takes a couple of drinks and goes down to see the Millinary lady. She starts on me about a letter I had writ and I told her I ain't writ no letter. But she gits hostile and tells me to clear out from her place right now. Then that feller of hern comes in frum the back room and takes a stack in the game, and jest about the time I have got him stomped outen his rind, in comes a lot of folks that ain't got no business there aytall and in the mix up I hits the Millinary Lady in the eye accidental and flattens her out. When the fight is over I discovers that among them settin' on me is the town marshal, so you see I fetched up here and I don't give a good durn."

I goes over to see the cigar stand gal and she sez her and the Millinary Lady aint been friends fer some distance and that she was on a three weeks visit back to Missouri when that letter musta been writ. She gits a heap of fun outen it and gives me some cigars to take the boss and sez to put in her word too when I ast him to come up and spring Bill out frum the Jail. Then I talks to the town marshall and he laffs a heap and sez fer me to fetch that letter and the Boss to town with me.

When I gits back to the ranch the boss is soter interested in the affair and I show him the letter that wuz sent to Bill and told him about the answer I sent back. We gits in the spring wagon and goes to town and gits Bill out and the town marshall keeps Miss De Le Ville's letter and sez he aims to give her a talk agin sech tricks on pore ig'rnt cow pokes. I slips over to the little hospittle fer to see the Millinary Lady's feller and tell him how they got Bill all wrong but he's so bunged up he don't seem to care. And when we git home the boss he sez it is mean enough to read a man's mail but when a feller takes the idee to answer it too he'd orta at least tell the man what he writ.

GOING TO SUMMER CAMP

The winter time is over, and the warm wind melts the snow.
He is headin' fer the summer camp where wagons couldn't go.
I'll bet that old boy's happy fer I know the way he feels;
Way up in that high country where there never has been wheels.

He has got his grub and blankets, and his cookin' outfit now,
And later on he'll have to pack some salt in fer the cows.
Before he's through he'll have to make a few trips there and back,
Fer everything that gits to camp goes up there in a pack.

But he'll see the big fat cattle standin' in the grass knee deep.
He will hear the pines and quakin' asps before he goes to sleep.
Them rapid little mountain streams is home sweet home fer trout.
They taste mighty good fer breakfast; he knows how to fish 'em out.

He'll be glad to git to camp and see the cabin once ag'in.
He wonders how it stood the snow and if the roof fell in,
Fer the high country in the summer is the finest place of all,
And he aims to stay until the snow has run him out next fall.

5

Bill Says Goodbye

Bill Turns Pugilist [1]

After Bill had been back fer about a month, I and him goes to town. We puts our hosses up at the Star Livery and then goes to the Elite Restaurant to eat. Bill shore gits a spell about one of the gals that is workin' there, and she tells him that there is goin' to be a opry at the opry house that night. Her and him make a date, and so I goes over and fixes it up fer me to take the cigar-stand gal.

It turns out to be a purty good show with a chorus and a funny man, but the main act is to be a champeen fighter that offers to take on any man in the crowd fer three rounds. When the curtain goes up fer that act the ramrod of the show comes out a leadin' a big feller in a long soter blanket coat and sez that this hombre is a great fighter and that he has fit all the fighters from Alasky to the Arkypelligo, and that the show offers a hundred and fifty bucks fer any man that will be on his feet with him at the end of three rounds. I see Bill start to git up, but jest then a feller come up onto the stage and he has a jersey stockin' cap pulled down over his face and haid so you cain't tell who he is.

Right then this here Arkypelligo champeen backs down and sez he won't fight him on account he's too tough. He sez he is the Mask Marble. The show manager calls fer some feller to come up and fight this Mask Marble. A feller starts to git up from the crowd, but before he can git anywheres Bill is right there and has throwed his hat in the ring and won't take no fer a answer. The manager he sez to Bill: "Lissen here, you pore farmer, do you mean to say that you'd fight this here physical marble? Why, man, he'd kill you. You must be mad!" "Never mind," sez Bill, "I ain't afeared of yore marble man no matter how much physic you've given him, and I wasn't mad till you started jawin' me, but I shore am now." And with that Bill busts the show ramrod one in the nose and knocks him to a settin' posture. By that time I am up there, too, and backin' Bill's play, fer three of the show fellers seems like they all aim to tie into Bill at the same time. I was standin' them off when up comes the town marshal and the Boss tells me to put up my gun fer this is a boxin' match and not a shootin' affair. "Git these fools away frum here," sez the show man. "I got a real fighter to meet this man." But the old town marshal he sez, "Listen here, mister man, if you think Bill ain't no real fighter you'd ort to see half the male population tryin' to arrest him, and besides you didn't seem to have a lot of luck with him yerself."

About that time the boss takes a stack in the game and he sez, "This here hundred and fifty bucks that goes to the winner. You hang that up with the town marshal here and if yore man wins you git it back. If Bill wins he hands it to Bill." The show man he gives the boss a dirty look and says, "Oh the money's safe enough." "That's what I figgered," sez the boss. "And we aim to put it where it ain't so safe." "Well," said the show man, "seein' the way you fellers has acted I am takin' my man out and there won't be no fight." "You jest think there won't," sez the marshal. "This here whole affair is a hornswoggle fixed up amongst yer own gang and yore in the wrong town by gum. You git yer money here. Make good yer word or you go to the jug." "On what charge?" asks the man. "Well, I kin hold ye twenty-four hours afore I tell ye," sez the marshal, "and if endurin' that time I was called out of town on business, these here citizens might git out and have a heap of fun with you."

Well they brings the money and the liveryman and Bill is behind the screens a gittin' ready. When they comes out they goes into the ring, and Bill and The Marble puts on them little prize fightin' gloves. The Marble ain't a-wearin' nothin' but a soter britch clout and moccaisons, but Bill has only shed his coat. "Give me a chaw of tobacker," he sez to the liveryman. "Not in a fight," sez the boss. "Shore," sez Bill. "I gotta have a chaw or I'll lose on a fowl, fer when I git mad I chaw anything I kin git my teeth on." Well, they dings the bell and they goes at it. They fights into a clinch, but Bill gits his fist into the Marble's eye and shoves him back and the Marble holds his eye shet and the tears is a runnin' out of it. But he dances around and soter weaves and ducks in and slams Bill a turrible lick in the solem plexus. It shore fetches a grunt out of Bill, but the Marble backs away lookin' sick and funny. He has one eye shet and is fightin' one hand-ed. Right then Bill he tares into him with a whole shipment of haymakers and the Marble is knocked out.

The liveryman and the boss gits Bill's gloves off and the marshal hands him the money. The crowd goes wild and yells fer a speech. "Make a speech fer me, Shorty," sez Bill, and so I waves my arm high and when the crowd gits quiet I sez: "Ladies and gentlemen and esteemed citizens: Bein' debatized to speak fer Bill I rise to remark that the Mask Marble won't need his mask no more, seein' Bill has changed his map so nobody won't reckernize him no how. I want three cheers fer the boss and fer the town marshal that seen fair play and helped to stage this part of the opry." I shore gits the cheers, and then I gits out and finds Bill. I sez, "How come ye to win so easy? I thought that lick in the solem plexus would a plum ruint ye." "Well," sez Bill, "I was afeared of that solem plexus lick and I had my old forty-five hog leg in a shoulder holster onder my shirt, and when the liveryman was gittin' me ready I has him hang it around my neck so's it's right over the pit of my stummick. Then we ties it around me with a piece of whang he has in his pocket so's it won't bounce around, and when this jasper lams me in the solem plexus it most nigh busts his fists. It shore hurt, but it didn't stop me.

Then, too, whilst I was holdin' up my hands fight fashion, I spit a heap of tobacker juice onto them gloves, and the fust chance I gits I shoves some of it into the Marble's eye. That's why he couldn't see so good. I reckon we'd ort to drag it fer home 'cause these show folks might claim a fowl. They're jest about that crooked."

We stopped at The Palace saloon and gits four quarts of Scotch. One fer the boss, one fer the liveryman, and one fer the marshal. They had called the turn and was waitin' fer us at the stable. "How's yer solem plexus, Bill?" asks the liveryman. "Right porely," sez Bill, and hands each one of them his bottle of pizen. "Wots the other bottle fer?" asks the boss. "That's fer my solem plexus," sez Bill. We started to saddle up right now, and they wants to know what the hurry is, and I sez that it was time all good citizens was gittin' home to bed. And, that besides, that there bunch of dirty crooks might try to claim a fowl or sumpthin'. They got to laffin' till the boss choked on his likker and they had to pound him on the back, but me and Bill high tailed it out of town and left 'em with it. On the way home Bill asks if I knew who took the cigar-gal and waiter lady home. It shore made us feel cheap fer things had got so interestin' that ontil right then we had plum forgot 'em both.

Bill Does a Fan Dance [2]

After Bill got the worst of the school marm joke[3] things went along purty smooth fer a spell. Then, spring and the boss's niece came to the ranch long about the same time. Bill went plum loco about that gal and a feller couldn't blame him fer she was a heap better lookin' than any woman had ort to be fer the peace and well bein' of a community.

Fust off he jest set and looked at her, then he tried to talk sensible to the boss. If you ever heard a rattle weed cow puncher try to talk sense you know what it sounded like. Next thing I knowed he was stayin' around the ranch and lettin' one of the other hands go with me. He got to be a reg'lar alfalfa savage. He couldn't talk about nothin' but feed and ditches and division boxes and hay stacks and irrigatin'. He worked late and airly and jest tried hisself to shovel and dig and find a lot of hard work fer him and everybody else. Now Rildy Briggs and the boss's niece was right sociable and visited back and forth a heap and I reckoned they both hed their nose to the ground fer what they could find out, but they was mighty friendly.

The fust Sunday after the water had been turned into the main ditch I happened to be in at the home ranch and there bein' nothin' said about work I shines my boots and shaves my jaw and make myself look as near human as possible. Then I rides over to the west paster to see if the ground tank is ready fer water in case of rain. On the way back I sees that a lot of tumble weeds has blowed onder the bridge over the main ditch, and I know it is goin' to be some job to get them out, so I goes in and remarks to Bill about them weeds. Bill gits his hoss and shovel right now and of course hunts up the boss to tell him where he's a goin' so's the boss will know what a valuable man Bill is, and then he high tails it fer the bridge.

I have jest turned my horse out and laid down on my bunk when up drives Rildy and her mother. We all goes out to meet 'em and they was both a laffin' fit to bust. They was leadin' Bill's hoss and Rildy sez, "Sumpthin' must 'a happened to pore Bill. We found this hoss with his saddle on and I reckon these is his clothes and hat that we found a layin' up there by the ditch bridge." "Law sakes," sez Rildy's mother. "I told this here youngun to let that hoss and them there clothes alone for she knowed as well as I did that pore Bill was onder that bridge a workin' to get them weeds out before they backed the water up and busted the ditch." But all the same the old lady was havin' her share of the joke. She had a new pipe and her bonnet was fresh starched. The Boss's wife looked at her right admirin' cause she 'peared to be as full of life and ginger as Rildy did. The boss tells me to take Bill his hoss and his clothes, so I goes and gits the old wrangle hoss and saddles him up. I takes a lot of time fer I figgers that if Bill has to hide out in the willers fer a spell, and the flies tickles his hide some, and he mebby gits sun burned a little it might take a lot of this new ambition out of him.

I am jest a goin' to step onto the hoss when we hears Shep and Shag, the two dogs, a makin' a turrible fuss around behind the barn a little ways down in the hoss paster. We runs around the barn to see what it is and fer a minute we caint really tell what is up. It 'pears they are after some soter livin' critter and a lot of willer bresh. And then we makes out what it is. It's Bill and he has made hisself a screen out of two big bunches of willer bresh he's a carryin'. The two dogs is a doin' some team work and Bill is tryin' to keep the bresh between him and them two dogs. I reckon he was a doin' what in these here modern times would be called a soter fan dance. We was all so surprised that we even forgot to call the dogs off. The dogs was workin' plum purficient and Bill's performance was perfect. Fust he's a wavin' one bunch of bresh between him and the dog in front and then he's sweepin' the other one around behind him to purtect his laigs like a houn dog tuckin' his tail onder him, and next thing he is squatted down and draggin' his bresh around him in circles like an old turkey gobbler a scrapin' his wings on the ground. The rest of us might have been struck plum silent but the language Bill is usin' is plum loud and plenty turrible.

About then Rildy goes into action. She bounces onto that old wrangle hoss and makes fer the scrimmage or dance or what ever you want to call it, on the high lope. Them was the days when it was a argyment if it was modest fer a woman to ride straddle with a divided skirt, but Rildy's skirts wasn't botherin' her none fer they was a flyin' high, and her voice carried like a coyote's. She had jerked down my rope and the way she flogged them dogs out frum there with a long loop was a caution to snakes. Then she takes my slicker frum behind the saddle and throws it to Bill.

The Old Lady Briggs is settin on a wagon tongue gaspin' fer breath and the boss is a leanin' agin the front wheel, and the wife and niece is holdin' onto one another tryin' to stand up, but I runs fer the bunk house and gits Bill's six shooter and mine too and runs into the house and hides 'em, fer I know Bill. Bill picks up his clothes and makes fer the bunk house and we all makes fer the house and leaves him alone in his glory. They starts to ask me about it and I sez that after Rildy got on that there hoss I didn't look at nothin' else and the old lady Briggs she slaps my ears and sez that if Rildy was half as modest and decent as Bill she'd be a heap better pleased, but I tells her that he ain't half as good lookin' as Rildy and that makes up fer it, and then we all has a laugh on that. Purty soon we sees Bill ride out at the gate real slow, and he ain't got his own hoss and he's headed fer town. "Well," sez the Boss, "he'll be back soon fer he ain't head-ed fer the high country this time, and I know that in about two days I'll find him in town with a headache and he'll be glad to come back and go to work."

Bill Buys Some Medicine [4]

A couple of days after Bill has took out fer town, the Boss tells me I had better ride in and git me some new boots and tell Bill that they are goin to make a work and that he had better quit his foolishness and git busy fer he wants him to go with me and meet the wagon.

Bill he aint half as drunk as I had figgered he would be. He is with a feller that is wearin' a black frock coat and gray checkered pants and a stove pipe hat. This feller is tall and slim and looks to me like a gambler or sumpthin'. Bill interdooces him as Doctor Stone. I buys a drink and then Doc Stone sez he has to be a goin'. Bill takes me up to the room where he is stayin' and shows me about a half a bushel of different medicines that he has bought from Doc. He sez that most likely Doc has saved his life fer he was all scratched up and blood pizen might a set in frum any of them scratches and besides he was dog bit in four places and that he might have been took off with hydraphoby if he hadn't had the linnyment to a rubbed on them bites. He has a soter linnyment that is supposed to cure every thing and besides he has a lot of stuff that Bill tells me is shore enough Tagger Fat and has a pitcher of the wild striped tagger right on it. Bill sez it caint be bought frum nobody but Doc and that Doc has it sent to him right frum Calcutty, and the only reason them wild natives sends it to him is because he saved the life of a Hindoo Princess when she was took down with a ragin' fever.

That night we goes to the medicine show and a nigger sings and dances and plays a banjo and Doc he makes the speech. He tells all about the bresh and yarbs he makes his linnyment frum. Also the tropical Nile where he gits the stuff to make the pills and then he tells the big story about the tagger fat. Bill he is all fussed up about it, but me, I caint see but what it's all a big bluff. I tells Bill that if Doc knowed all which he claims to know he won't be way out there in a little town a sellin' Medicine off the back end of old man Grimse's dray wagon. Bill he argys that Doc is jest interdoocin' the medicine and later on will set in a big office and rake in the money.

Next day I gits my boots and Bill gits his medicine packed into his and my slickers so he can take it to the ranch and we starts fer headquarters. I makes a few remarks concernin' the Boss's neice but Bill he aint even interested. All he talks about is medicine and doctors.

When we gits back, the two old ranch hands that the Boss hires every summer has landed in, and they were shore glad to see us. Their names was Eph and Zeb and they were shore a hard workin' pair of old hay tossers.

They was right glad to see us, and of course like all that soter fellers they had to look over every thing we had packed home. The Boss had sent fer a dehornin' saw. "What's that there leetle saw fer?" Zeb asts. "That there is a dehornin' saw," sez Bill. "Good Lord," sez Zeb, "them fellers will keep on with this here dehornin' till Gabriel hisself won't have no horn left to blow on Jedgement Day." "What did you pay fer them new boots of yourn?" Eph asts me. I tells him and he sez. "Waal you shore got beat and besides you got 'em a heap too tight. You fellers pays a heap too much fer your hats and boots. Looka here at my shoes, they'll wear a heap longer than them there leetle boots and I sent to Sears Robuck and got 'em fer a dollar and seventy-five cents," and he holds up a big brogan that it wouldn't be safe to put into a wagon box let alone into a stirrup.[5] Of course they smelled out Bill's medicine right off but Bill bowed up and wouldn't tell 'em nothin' about it so on the quiet I tells 'em that it is some stuff the Boss has sent fer to put on lame hosses and to grease saddles and harness, and that Bill is all swelled up because he had to help pack it down frum town.

Next day me and Bill is shoein' hosses and gittin' ready fer the roundup and Eph and Zeb is greasin' harness and fixin' up the wagons and mowin' machine fer the summer hay cuttin'. Bill is nailin' a shoe onto Old Baldy's off hind foot when Eph hollers to the Boss that they are all out of harness grease. "How so?" the Boss hollers. "I put a big can of it in the stable right onder the curry comb box!" "We never found that!" Eph yells. "We was a usin' that stuff that was in the bunk house. Them that had the pitcher of the Tagger on!" Bill is jest startin' a nail and his mouth and eyes pops open and he hits a wild lick and knocks a nail crooked into Old Baldy's foot and Baldy lets go with both feet and takes Bill right in the seat of his overalls. If Bill hadn't been so close he'd a been oncoupled parminint. As it was he got knocked wrong end up agin the side of the blacksmith shop. We gits Bill into the bunk house and pulls the nail out of Baldy's foot. Eph feels bad about the tagger fat bein' used to grease harness and to square hisself he gits the linnyment and goes to rubbin' Bill where he got kicked. Eph's hand is big as a ham and about as rough as a shoein' rasp and he don't lack much of bein' as stout as a wheel mule, so with all that sharp linnyment he is a pourin' on and that stout rubbin' it aint long till

Bill is shore hollerin' fer quits. Next day Bill is black and blue frum the kickin' and blistered frum the treatment, so I saddles up and throws on the old bed and hazes my string out fer the roundup alone. Bill promisin' he'll be along soon as he can ride.

Bill Visits a Married Friend [6]

We hadn't been on the work many days till here comes Bill ridin' into camp one evenin'. He seems to be in a good humor, although he still rode soter light in his saddle and set over on one laig quite a bit.

After supper he goes away frum the fire and sets down by hisself and I knowed he had sumpthin' heavy on his mind that he wanted to get rid of, so I eases over to where he was. We both rolls up a smoke and then Bill he thaws out and begins: "Shorty," he sez, "it's a terrible thing to be married." Well, I sez, it's most generally a man's own fault if he's married, and it's most generally a man's fault if he don't git along with his woman. "How come?" asts Bill. Well, I sez, most every cow waddy I ever met up with tuck right out after every woman he ever seen, and if she got out of sight he run her by the dust, and if that give out he took to cold trackin' her. Then, too, if he don't git her, you can bet it ain't his fault, but if he don't git along with her, it is because he don't know how to pick 'em or else he don't know how to git along with 'em after he's got 'em.

You ain't gone and got spliced have you Bill? "No," sez Bill. "But I've been and seen a feller that has. You heerd me tell about that feller Ed Jones I knowed up in the high country. Ed was shore a top hand, but he got married about five years ago, and I heerd Ed was shore doin' fine, so I reckoned while I was crippled up I'd ride over and visit with him fer a spell. I went over and stayed one night and I come right to the home ranch and got me some hosses and leaked right out fer this wagon. I tell you, Shorty, that five years of bein' married will ruin the best hand that ever set in a saddle.["]

"I been told how to git to Ed's place and so I know when I ride up onto the hogback and look into the valley that I am lookin' right at Ed's spread. It looks right good fer he has a lot of alfalfy and beans and a mighty nice orchard and garden and a bunch of milk cows a grazin' around. I rides in and there seems to be hogs and chickens around, and there is some of that square onderware hung out on the washline, so I reckons there must be a young Ed or Edny about. I rides out and gits off in the corral and figgers I'll look around and see if Ed's saddle is there, in which case I'll know Ed is somewheres close about. I sees a couple saddles, one of 'em looked good, but away back on the manger of a emty stall in the shed I sees Ed's saddle. The same old double rig he rode five years ago. But what a saddle. There was no rope nor slicker on it and the flank cinch was gone and it had been robbed of all the whangs that had ever been on it. There was no sign of saddle blankets and you only had to look once to see that the chickens had been a-settin' on that old hull a heap more than what Ed had.["][7]

"Way down in the field I sees a feller a workin' in a ditch and he shore is a humpin' hisself over a long handled shovel. I mopes down there and what do you s'pose? It's Ed. And what a Ed. He has on a pair of loose faded overalls that is all patched, and big brogan shoes and, Shorty, I hope to die if he didn't have on a straw hat and galluses.[8] He was shore glad to see me and I helped him git the box fixed into the ditch while he told me how well he had done since he got spliced up, fer it seems his wife had been willed the place where they was and they was makin' it pay in good shape. Long about dark a young feller drives up in a wagon and after he puts his team away he saddles up a hoss and goes fer them milk cows. A feller by the name of George that is a workin' fer Ed he goes and gits some buckets and when the boy gits there with his cows Ed tells me it is his cousin Homer. Well, Ed and George and Homer starts a wringin' the milk out of them cows right now. Then they goes to a soter dugout and gits some more milk, and feeds a whole passel of calves and a mob of hogs. By that time it is dark and we goes to the house.[9] The wife and her aunt are there, and the two kids. The kids was both asleep, but somebody had give the oldest one a pup that is onder the front porch and howlin' plenty loud. The biscuits was burnt on the outside and raw in the middle, and the taters had the same complaint. The meat and coffee would sorter do. The women folks blamed it onto the stove—they said it wouldn't draw. Did you ever see a stove that suited a woman? No sir. You can take a old stove frum a ranch house or line camp that forty men has cooked on with grace and ease and let a woman git holt of it and what? Every man that comes along she has him takin' down the pipe and rebuildin' the chimley and fixin' the damper and cleanin' out the soot, and then she sez that none of them didn't fix it so as it would work right. Take some old hoss that has got along with a whole herd of men and as soon as a woman gits a holt of him he takes to runnin' back and turnin' short and upsettin' the old buggy, and halter pullin' and mebbyso balkin'. Why take even a dog that women folks gits to messin' with and he ain't no account. No sir. The only thing that ain't got too much sense to work fer a woman is a man. He's the only anamile that is jest that dumb."

Well, Bill, I sez, seems to me like Rildy Briggs done a heap better job handlin' a couple of dogs than what you did. Bill gits huffy and allows that it was her fault he had that ruckus with them dogs, and I sees right off that I better keep still if I want to hear the rest about Ed. Bill makes another smoke and goes on with his yarn.

"Well," he sez. "That pup onder the porch howls all night and the two kids takes turns howlin' when they wasn't both howlin' at once, and evry now and then half the fambly was up and trompin' around to try and git what the kids wanted. I tried to sleep out onder the shed with my saddle blankets, but they wouldn't hear to it and shet me up in a room where all I could do was to sweat and listen. Nex mornin' Ed and George was up and milkin' cows before the crow jumped and Homer wrangled the paster. He corrals my old hoss and the work stock and puts his saddle hoss in the corral and ties him to the fence with the reins and, of course, the fust hoss that crowds between him and the fence breaks both reins. Ed knowed better than to let the kid do thataway, but seems like he ain't got no idees workin' in his head aytall. The women folks is out and hollerin' fer somebody to chop wood, and so I chops it, which, by the way, I ain't partial to.[10] The breakfast ain't so bad as the supper, but it ain't nothin' to cheer about. I helps Homer hitch up and load a plow and scraper onto a wagon and Ed hitches up a team of mules to furry out his beans, and when they git ready to turn out I ketches out my hoss and opened the gate. I gits my bridle, but the reins is gone. I asts Ed if he knowed where they was. 'Why, you ain't leavin' already?' Ed sez. But I told him I had only stopped to say hello, fer I had to git my hosses and meet the work. George speaks up and sez, 'Why, Homer reckoned you'd be here fer a spell and he took yore reins to tail out his lines so's they would be long enough fer the plow and scraper.' Ed offered to git 'em fer me, but I tells him I'll make out with a couple of hoggin' strings." Why, Bill, I sez, you got a crackerjack headstall and split lietige[11] reins, what more do you want? ["]Shore,["] sez Bill. ["]I left him my old headstall and tuck the hint lietige offen his saddle and split it fer reins jest to git even.[12] My new Navajo saddle blanket is missin'. Them women has throwed it over a chicken coop and drove a nail in each corner to keep it frum blowin' away. When I goes to take it they hollers to me to wait a minute and brings out a couple of gunny sacks to keep the sun offen them young chickens. 'Laws sakes,' sez the aunt, 'we allows you was a goin' to be here fer a spell and wouldn't want that old blanket no way.'["]

Bill, I sez, you didn't steal no diapers fer saddle blankets did you? Bill he allows he didn't, and then he goes on: "Yessir, Shorty, they makes me wait till they fixed me a lunch before they let me go. I tells them so-long and rides away plum glad to be out of that mess. When I gits on top of the hogback I stops and takes a look and there is Ed in the distance follerin' his team and plow. He stops and takes off one brogan and pours the dirt out of it, puts it back on and starts plowin' again. It's shore turrible to be married, and prosperous. About noon I stakes my hoss on a patch of good grass and gits the lunch out of my slicker and it was shore good. Good biscuits and bacon and aigs. It was wropped in the county newspaper and I read that Ed Jones is likely to run fer road supervisor, and I sez to myself, Pore Ed, he better run fer somewheres."

Bill stops talkin' and makes another smoke. The boys is turnin' in. Over in the distance you could hear the night hawk[13] singin' "Oh beat the drums lowly and play the fife slowly." Bill sez, "Shorty, there's goin' to be a dance at the Rock Creek schoolhouse a week frum Saturday night and this work will jest about meet it." But, Bill, I sez, if you go you'll have to dance with them turrible women that you ain't got no use fer.

"I know that as well as you do," sez Bill. "But, what yer goin' to do?"

The Rock Creek Dance [14]

There was a feller on the work reppin' fer some nester outfits[15] and we called him Uncle Jasper. Now it was soter told around that he had two awful good lookin' nieces, and Bill he cottoned right onto the old feller. Seems like he had come along with his brother's fambly frum up north about a year before and he was a shore good cowman. He had one laig a heap shorter than the other one but he seemed to git about purty good any how. Come time fer Jasper to pull out with his throw back,[16] Bill he talks the boss into lettin' him go along to side him. Bill, I sez, don't go. Stay with the outfit and you won't git into no trouble.

"How would I git into trouble?" Bill wants to know. I shore tells him that he ain't went no place that I know of but what he got in trouble and seein' he and the old step and a half feller is good friends he better let it go at that. But no use, Bill he rides off next mornin' with old Jasper. When Bill gits back from that trip he is fuller of talk than a auctioneer. He tells me how he spent the day at the old man's place and that his oldest niece, Mandy Jane, was shore a scrumptious lookin' gal. How he shoed a pet pony fer the gals and that Uncle Jasper had sent off to Sears Roebuck fer a suit of store clothes, and that him and Mandy Jane fixed 'em up. Fix 'em up? I asks. "Shore," sez Bill. "We tuck and cut the one pants laig short so's it would fit right. We was sure smart about it too. We tuck and laid a pair of his old pants over the new ones to git the measure right. Mandy Jane mighty nigh forgot to allow fur the hem but I thought of it and then I cuts the laig off with my old markin' knife. We shore had a good time that day." Well, Bill, I sez, if you done all that and never got into no trouble you have shore improved a heap.

Come time fer the Rock Creek dance, me and Bill was a little behind the rest gittin' started. We gits there and Bill sez: "Why there is Ed Jones mule team and four spring seats in the wagon. The whole outfit must be here. Yessir there's him and Cousin Homer in there and Mandy Jane and her sister and—Why there's Rildy Briggs dancin' with Cousin Homer, and Uncle Jasper is in there in his workin' clothes." I looks in at the winder too and there is Rildy dancin' with a big double jointed tow headed hoosier and Old Jasper is standin' around in his workin' clothes.

I pulls Bill away from the winder. Bill, I sez, how did you lay them pants when you cut the laig off? "Why, come to think of it they was facin' each other," he sez. Then his mouth falls open and he looks wild. "My Gawd!" he sez, "I cut the wrong laig off." Bill, I sez, me and you has come a long ways to this here dance but the best thing we can do now is fur me and you to leak out frum here and say nothin' to nobody. You are bad enough alone but that there Rildy Briggs is down in these parts and you and her never got togather yet but what you stirred up some sort of a ruckus. But he allows I'm all fussed up over nothin' atall and goes a trompin' into that there school house like he was the most welcome human that ever learnt to walk on his hint laigs. We stands by the door till the set is over and then Bill makes fer Mandy Jane. She turns her head and looks the other way. Bill gits red in the face and starts over to Rildy. Bill I sez Stop! Stop! But he pulls loose frum me and goes ahead. Cousin Homer is still leadin' Rildy around by the elbow and they stops and gives Bill a dirty look, still I caint pull him away and he walks right up and sez, "Hello Homer. Hello Rildy, [e]njoyin yerselves?" I give up and backed away. "We was till you come trompin' in here." sez Rildy. "But any feller that gits so low down that he takes to stealin' bridles and cuttin' up his neighbors' clothes jest tryin' to be smart aint got no place in decent comp'ny if you ask me." "I aint askin' you nothin'," Bill sez. "But if I did I bet you could tell me every body's business but your own, and any gal that would steal a feller's clothes jest to see him run around plum neckid—" Bill never got no further fer Rildy slapped him so hard his face twisted. Bill got so white that his lips looked black but he kep frum hittin' Rildy which was a wonder to them that knowed Bill's temper.

But right then cousin Homer butts in. "If I wasn't on the committee that is givin' this dance I'd invite you outside" he sez. "Don't let that stop you. I can lick you right here in the house" sez Bill. "You try it" sez Homer. Man that was like hittin' a dynamite cap with a hammer. Bill he tore in like a ravin' luniac, but what it took to lick that big corn fed boy was a plenty. Every body was a yellin' sumpthin' and I got a hand full of smokin' tobacker ready for any special occasion as might arise and shoe enough, up rushes that there Ed Jones and he is aimin' to git in a haymaker on Bill so I slings the tobacker into his eyes and he grabs his face and begins to paw like a dog that got a mouthful of hot corn mush. George, his hired man makes a rush at me but he was as awkward as a pet bull and I side steps and gives him a shove and he lands over agin the wall amongst a lot of women folks and upset benches. Mandy Jane she starts screamin' and Homer he looks to see what's eatin' on her and that is the end of the fight fer Bill he gits in one of them swings that he fetches up frum the floor and about three feet behind and lands it on pore Homer's jaw, and he goes out as cold as a frunt quarter of Armour's beef. Bill whirls around with his dukes up and his elbow hits Rildy in the neck and down she goes. Some body hollers that Bill has hit a woman and Bill gits out of there. I grabs his hat off the floor and beat him to our horses by about two jumps.

We say nothin' and string out fer camp on a high lope but before we have gone half a mile Bill's hoss steps in a dog hole and goes a rollin' and Bill he lays there with the wind knocked out of him. The old hoss gits up and stands lookin' at us, and purty soon Bill gits up and tries to walk but he is limpin' turrible. "Oh Lord" he sez "[m]y right laig is shore hurt bad but the bones aint busted." We makes it back to camp and the other boys comes a ridin' in about daylight. Bill rolls out of bed and he gits around mighty slow and his face and hands is all skun up. When the remuda comes in he gits out and ropes the gentles['] hoss in his string. The boss watches him a limpin' around and then he busts out laffin' and sez, "Bill, one of two things. Either yore a goin' to die young or else yore a goin' to git awful tough."

Bill and the Medicine Man Get Quarantined [17]

When me and Bill gits back to the home ranch, Bill he goes to the Boss and allows that he has to go back to the high country fer a spell. And right then sumpthin' happens that I have been lookin' fer a long time. The Boss he looks at Bill purty straight and sez, "Bill," he sez "That's a good idee. You aint been none too settled here. It would mebby do you good to work fer some other spread and git new ideas. We'll pay you off and there won't be nothin' here that we'll need you fer that I know of."

I helps Bill git started and I shore feel bad because I know that the boss is the easiest man in the world to work fer but once he is all fed up on a hand that's the end of it from then on out. Me and Bill has a long talk and he drags it.[18] That night the boss's wife she is worried about what Bill will do when the snow gits deep in the high country and I tells her that Bill sez he aims to git a job wood cuttin' or workin' in a saw mill and give up ridin'. [T]he Boss he busts out laffin' and sez: "Don't worry Bill ain't there, not yit. Chop wood! Why you know that Bill won't hardly chop enough wood to do his own cookin' and that if he is in a shack by him self he'll lay in bed all day before he'll chop enough wood to keep warm. Bill can ride a rough string. He's a fust class roper and a good cow man and as good a lookout as anybody, but that is all. You cain't tell where he'll be nor when he'll quit nor what fool notion he'll git. He's stirred up more trouble around here than a pet hen and if somebody else wants to be bothered with him all right I don't." We all felt bad but we knowed the boss and right down in the bottom of our hearts we couldn't blame him.

Things seemed sort of lonesome without Bill but you had to say they was a heap more restful if not so interestin'. Seemed like there'd been a heap of pressure took off some where. One Saturday Eph and Zeb goes to town with the mule team fer a load of freight. Aimin' to come back of a Sunday evenin'. Late that evenin' I rides in and the next mornin' I meets them two hands a gittin' ready to leave. They has a lot to tell me. Bill ain't gone to the high country but has jined up with the Medicine Man and they have both been put in a shack on the edge of town on account the Medicine Man has took down with the Small Pox and Bill is exposed and therefore quarantined with him. I gits a team and buggy frum the livery stable and we goes out to see them. They said we could drive up and holler to them but couldn't go no closter, and that the Medicine Man wasn't so sick but what he could look out of the winder and holler too.

We drives up and hollers and sure enough Bill pokes his head out[.] I asks Bill if the Medicine Man ain't got no small pox linnyment. To cheer him up like I tells him that we are all out of tagger fat and want to grease the harness agin. The Medicine Man looks out of the other winder and Eph and Zeb gaps and swallers and then Eph busts out laffin'[.] "Wall If 'Taint Wash Higgins!" He hollers, "Hi Wash!" Zeb yells, "Mind when we went to the Coon Foot school house togather down in Barry County,

Missouri? I ain't seen ye sence you was run out of that country fer hog stealin' ten year ago!" "Say Wash!" Eph asts "Did ye render that there tagger fat outen them hawgs ye stoled frum my old man?" The Medicine Man ducks and even at that distance you can see that Bill is effected visible. The feller that is watchin' them comes out frum another shack close by and sez fer us to git out frum there and about then the Doctor drives up and tells us to vamoose.

I tells the Doctor if there's anything I can do fer Bill to let me know but he sez that so fur there ain't nothin' can be done and he allows that Bill will learn a heap more before he gits clear of that there Medicine Man than if he had gone through the medical school. I gets to the ranch along in the afternoon and the two hands has only been there a little while. Them and the boss has had a big laugh about Bill and his new pardner. But I don't feel much like it was so funny. The sun is jest settin' back of the mountains and all them colors is showin' and it put me in mind of pore old Bill fer he always did like to stand in the bunk house door and watch the sun hit the tops of them mountains with the snow on them and then he'd always whistle a sort of sad tune he knowed. And to think he was penned up with a onery hawg thief indefinite and nothin' to look foreward to 'cept mebbyso the Small Pox.

Bill Adjusts Matrimonial Affairs [19]

Shortly after we had been up to see Bill and the Medicine man when they were quarrentined, Old Lady Briggs drives in and tells us that Johnny Martin and Joe Baines has had a awful fight and was both beat up sumpthin' terrible. The Boss's wife sez that there is one thing they caint blame on Bill anyhow. "Is he still in quarrentine?" The boss asks. "No," sez old lady Briggs. "He never took the small pox and he's breakin' hosses fer some of them people over on the river. Last I heard they was camped at the 'dobe corrals." "Well," sez the boss, "If he was runnin' loose at the time he had a hand in it."

That soter set me thinkin' and one day right soon after I manages to git over apast the 'dobe corrals and see Bill. I gits in about noon and Bill is jest toppin' a colt off. He does it good like Bill does any thing once you git him at it. After dinner I gits him away frum the other two boys and asks him about the fight. "Well," sez Bill, "I reckon it wasn't none of my business but you know Johnny Martin is a bachelor and all he mostly thinks about is irrigatin' that little ranch and garden patch of hisn. He was like that till he took to runnin' around with that gal at the Bon Ton restaraunt. He run around with her and bought her presents till he spent all his spare time and cash on her and then she sees he is a picked goose and takes up with Joe Baines and makes a fool of him. Joe don't take his wife no place nor give her nothin' and seein' she's a cousin of mine I don't like to see her at home in a old wore out dress workin' on the ranch and in the house too and that old man of hern runnin' around with that gal and buyin' stuff fer her. I had jest got away frum the quarrentine when I found it out. Johnny and Joe was both tryin' to raise the biggest melon on the crick and that give me a idee. My cousin has showed me Joe's melon and she is as prowd of it as if it meant sumpthin' to her. That night I goes down to Johnn[y]'s place and gits his irrigatin' boots where he leaves them by the shed and puts them on. Then I walks right up the ditch bank and gits Joe's melon and carries it down to Johnn[y]'s and puts it onder the fur corner of a hay stack; bein' shore to mess the hay up so anybody can see it's been fooled with. Johnn[y] he goes to town to sell some stuff and Joe misses his prize melon. 'Course he knows Johnn[y] is bowed up about losin' out with that fool gal, and when he sees them tracks he gits leery right now. He finds the tracks, the melon and the boots jest like I reckoned he would. He stops Johnn[y] on the way home frum town and course Johnn[y] don't know what's the matter but before it is all over they has one whale of a fight and Johnny knocks the stuffin' out of Joe and Johnn[y]'s team runs off and busts his wagon all to smash. Before them two fellers was through they both talk a heap too much and Joe's wife she gits wise and now Joe's wife does the goin' to town. I am shore glad you come along, Shorty," he sez, " 'Cause I've been jest bustin' to tell somebody about it and you are the only one I dast to tell it to."

Bill rolled up a smoke and then he looked at me soter beat like and sez: "Shorty, do you reckon there's them that's so crooked that they cain't be beat nohow." "Meanin' who?" I asks. "That there medicine man," sez Bill. What's he done now besides sell fake medicine and steal hawgs in his younger days? I asks. "Well," Bill sez, "you see it was like this. He wanted fifty dollars fer his formerly." His what? "His formerly," sez Bill. "You see when folks builds medicine they have to have a formerly to go by so they git the right amount of the right stuff in the medicine and the Medicine Man reckons that fer fifty dollars he'll sell me his formerly and then I'll be as good a medicine man as anybody. I thinks it over but I steals out a little of his medicine and gives it to the doctor to have it assayed on the quiet, and the dock he tells me a couple days later that it ain't nothin' much and costs about two bits a gallon to make and won't cure nothin' and that the tagger fat ain't nothin' but some doped up taller that ain't no good 'cept to grease harness with same as Eph and Zeb done. Well seein' he ain't honest I aims to learn him a lesson and I beats him down till he sez that seein' I and him has been quarrentine partners he'll take fifteen dollars. I writes up a bill of sale and he reads it, but I won't let him sign it fer a while and on the quiet I writes myself a bill of sale fer that big diamond he wears in his shirt front which he sez was the eye of a heathen idol in India. I reckon it was worth a couple thousand any way. So jest before we are ready to go I gits a chance to steal this diamond and pin it inside my pants laig. He asks me about the formerly agin and I hands him the bill of sale fer the diamond soter folded up so he will think it is the bill of sale fer the formerly and lays fifteen dollars on the old board table in the quarrentine place. Well sir I hope to drop dead if he didn't reach into his vest pocket and take out a leather case with five more diamonds as big as the one I stoled and put one in his shirt and shake hands good bye. I goes down to the joolry store and asts Abe Minsk what this here idol eye is worth and he l[a]ffs and sez that suckers has been knowed to pay as high as a dollar fer a hunk of glass that size. Tricky folks is tricky folks and you caint make nothin' else out of 'em," sez Bill. On the way back to the ranch I tries to figger how Bill aims to win out agin family fights and buckin' hosses, not to mention fake formerlys and diamonds. Bill shore leads a busy life.

Bill Has Trouble [20]

Bill finished his job breakin' hosses and the next thing I hear he is tendin' bar fer old man Kennedy. The oldest Briggs kid tells me a few days later that a bunch of boys from down the river has come to town with a race hoss and has matched a race with Kennedy's sorrel. He sez that Bill is goin' to lose his shirt fer he's doin' most of the bettin' and that the boys from down the river has stoled Kennedy's hoss out one night and run him against their hoss and that the hoss from down the river beat Kennedy's hoss two len'ths of moonlight, and they run 'em fer blood all the way. The next time I am in at the ranch I tells them about it and the boss asks if Bill is bettin' any real money. I tells them that I hear there is about two thousand dollars up and that Bill has bet the most of it and right away the boss's wife she wants to know where Bill got all that money. The boss is still fer a spell and then he sez, "Bill is shore headed wrong. He is shore goin' to have him a pair of striped pants or a wooden overcoat if he keeps on." His wife wants to know what he means, fer she likes Bill same as all the women folks does. He don't answer her but he looks at me straight and sez, "Shorty, you keep out that hoss race and all the bettin' and all the trouble that comes up afterwards." "Why?" sez his wife. "Bill aint never done nothin' wrong, and he aint never started anything he couldn't finish neither." And she shakes her head like a sassy colt. "I know," sez he[,] "[b]ut he'll start once too often and he'll start sumpthin' he'll have to finish." When the boss looks and talks like that I know he savvys what he's talkin' about and aint tellin' all he knows either. When the Sunday comes fer the race he tells me before I start to mind what he told me. He sez Kennedy's hoss will win but fer me to keep out of it and I promises him I will.

There had been a heap of excitement about that race and the odds was ag'in Kennedy's sorrel and the big black hoss from down the river was a big favorite. I shore did want to git my little bit of money down on the sorrel at the odds they offered fer I knowed that Bill and Kennedy wasn't as easy as some folks might think. But I had give my word to the boss and so I kep out of it.

They was to run a mile and that made it twice around the old half mile track jest outside of town. I'll never furgit how they brought the big black and the sorrel to the post and they was to start at the pop of a gun. The black had a jocky up all dressed in colors. Jose, a little Mexican that had been wranglin' hosses in that country since anybody could remember, was on the sorrel. The black drawed first place and when the gun popped he lep right out in front and Jose took the sorrel right in behind him. As soon as they was on the back track the sorrel went around the black. The black come alongside ag'in but he couldn't pass and was carried wide on the turn. As they come down on the half the black come along side once more but he couldn't pass and was left outside on the turn. The outfit that owned the black was all tryin' to holler sumpthin' to their rider but in the noise and rush nobody could hear a thing. Both hosses was doin' a lot faster time than folks reckoned they could and when they pulled out into the stretch both riders was whippin' and the sorrel came onder the wire a good len'th in front.

A lot of small bets was paid off then and there and then everybody went back to town where the big money had been hung up. There was not as many at Kennedy's bar as I had figgered there would be, and one feller comes in and sez loud enough fer every body to hear; "All you boys that aint paid off your bets yit jest let the stake holders hold 'em fer a spell. That race wasn't fair. Our hoss was fouled. He was carried wide on all the turns and bumped and crowded." All at once I sees what's up. Bill's sorrel saddle hoss is a dead ringer fer Kennedy's race hoss, and in the night—Shore! The trick is as old as the hills. They had baited 'em with Bill's saddle hoss. It was crooked work on both sides and now them boys didn't aim to pay the big bets off. I went over to the billiard hall where a lot of the money had been hung up and Bill and Kennedy was there. Baldy that run the place had several of the envelopes in his private desk. The man that had spoke his piece in Kennedy's place come in and Bill sez to him, "Baldy sez you told him not to pay off." "I shore did," [t]he feller sez. "That race was crooked all the way through." "The race was run fair today," sez Bill, ["]And I'll give you two to one and run it over two weeks frum today. [A]nd speakin' of crooked work I reckon you fellers thought because you run our hoss one night before he was in condition that you had the race cinched." "You're a liar if you say anythin' like that," sez the feller. Before you could see what he done Bill has laid his six shooter over that jasper's head and he is out cold and he sez to Baldy[,] "Git them envelopes out here 'less you want to meet yore great grandad right now." The feller on the floor is hit purty hard and I steps outside to see how things look. It looks bad. Three fellers is hangin' around but jest then Bill and Kennedy steps out. Two of 'em don't say nothin' but one jumps behind a big post and cuts down on Bill knockin' some dust out of the slack in his shirt. His head and shoulder is purtected by the post but his rear end he has furgot about and it is stickin' out plenty. Bill breaks him down the first shot and then gives him two more. Kennedy has drawed but the other two fellers hold plum still and the fight is over. The Town Marshall comes along and me and Kennedy walks up to the jail house with him and

Bill. I tells Bill I aim to stay right there and see that the other crowd don't start noth-in' but Kennedy he takes me to one side and sez, "Never mind Shorty. You go down to my place and have a drink and then drag it fer home. There's enough of us here to han-dle this here ruckus." I goes over and sez so long to Bill and we talk a little while and then all at once I see what the boss has been seein' fer quite a spell. Bill aint jest a reck-less happygolucky cow waddy. There's a streak of desperader in Bill.

The Boss knows there's been trouble as soon as he sees me and when I tells him he don't say nothin' but he hitches a team to his buck board and starts fer town with his hat low over his eyes and that old pipe he smokes is showin' like a coal of fire in the dark.

Bill Says Goodbye [21]

[T]he boss comes back from town and sez that I have to go up and tell what I know about Bill's ruckus. I aint none too keen about doin' it but I know it will go a long ways toward clearin' Bill.

He sez that old Baldy wants to have Bill arrested fer holdin' up his place with a gun before they try him fer the shootin' but they have done beat him to it and swore out the warrent fer the shootin' and then they got a lawyer to go and throw the big scare into Baldy. They tells him that if he starts any thing they will close him down. Because he don't dast aid nor abet no gamblin' in his place and that he might be tried fer tryin' to hold money that was put in his keepin' onlawful.

They takes me out to the hospital to see the feller that Bill shot and asks me if I know him but I don't. The feller hisself don't seem none too glad to see me. I has to tell them what I seen and a little feller is there to write it down and he writes so fast that he is settin' waitin' fer me to talk most of the time. I looks at the paper and he is writin' sumpthin' in a furrin language fer I caint read a word of it.[22] I asks a office feller that is there what soter language he is writin' in and he sez it is Egypshun. I can see right then why that there woman Cleopatry had so many husbands. Them folks didn't waste a lot of time a talkin'. They could write or say a heap in a mighty short time.

When I gets back to the ranch the boss tells me that the feller Bill shot up is one of Rildy's cousins and the feller that got his hair parted with Bill's six gun is a soter rela-tion of hers too. Which, I sez, accounts fer them Briggs kids a knowin' so much about that hoss race. I tells the boss that I wish there hadn't been no hoss race but he sez that it didn't really make no difference fer Bill was headed fer trouble and if it hadn't been the hoss race sumpthin' else would have touched things off.

None of us like to think of Bill bein' up there in jail waitin' fer the trial but we caint help it. There was another dance over on the river and me and Eph and Zeb we goes. Rildy was there and she has the feller that Bill hit along with her. She tries to talk to me but I don't git alone with her none because she might tell sumpthin' which I never said. It aint long till she is up to her old tricks fer she caint keep her nose out of trouble any time. She sez loud enough fer every body to hear that it seems nice to have a dance without Bill bein' there to start trouble. And Zeb he speaks right up and sez that he reckons she ort to be plum suited on account that her and Bill been runnin' opposition on seein' who could stir up the most trouble fer some time and now she's got the road all to herself. That sort of makes her turn red but the feller with her sez that he reckons that Bill won't be doin' no dancin' nor makin' no trouble fer quite some time.

I speaks up and sez that frum what I seen there was some of them that quieted down before Bill did. Jest then Eph he puts in and sez, "Well folks Bill aims to change his occapation as soon as his trial is over. He aims to take up barberin'. He mightn't shave as gentle as some people but he can shore part a man's hair the purtiest of anybody in these parts." That shore gits a grin frum the crowd. Rildy she gits plum nasty then and talks about hay shakers and pumpkin shuckers, but all the women folks shore does give Eph and Zeb a chance to ask them fer a dance. Jest as Rildy is makin' a wise crack she chokes on her chewin' gum and most dies off and when they git the wind back into her she and her feller leaks out fer home.

Well as soon as the feller Bill shot was able to be carried into court the trial come off. It was a nasty affair and the hoss race trick was brought up and it was proved to be so crooked on both sides that the evidence didn't mean much either way. But the real thing was the shootin' and me and Mac was both there to swear that the feller cut down on Bill as soon as he come out at the door. When the prosecutin' attorney made his talk he sez, "To think that this cow boy, gambler, and bar tender, should go free when he came out and fired his pistol at the heart of this fine young man who had got behind a post to save his own precious life!" But when Bill's lawyer gits up to make argyment, [h]e tells the jury that this feller's heart must be in a funny spot judgin' frum where he was hit. The judge raps fer order and the trial goes on. The jury is out half a hour and they comes in and turns Bill loose.

The boss soter weakens and he tells Bill he had better come down to the ranch fer a spell but Bill is jest as good as the boss and sez he aims to look around a little. I know it is all off with Bill on that neck of the range fer he has made more enemies with the crooked hoss race than he did with the shootin'.

A few days later a feller frum the Star Livery comes to the ranch. He is leadin' Bill's big Sunday hoss and has Bill's saddle and bed in the buck board. We was all lookin' fer bad news but he tells us that the United States has gone to war with Spain and that Bill has gone and [j]ined the war. The boss is plum tickled fer he allus did try to trade Bill out of that hoss, and my old outfit is so near wore out that Bill's outfit shore does come in handy and I gives mine to Eph and Zeb. That night at supper we talks a heap about Bill and the war and the boss sez, "Well I never reckoned there'd be much of a war with Spain but now that Bill's mixed up in it I reckon there'll shore be a rumpus of some kind.["]

Eph and Zeb was soter broke up about it and when us boys went out to the bunk house I stopped and looked over at the mountains that showed up so plain in the bright star light and Zeb sez: "Bill will shore miss them mountains. He liked them and most likely there won't be none like that where the war is at."

Eph was quiet fer a minute and then he sez, "Bill is born fer trouble all his life but I shore do wish I was like him." It struck me funny that this quiet boy Eph wanted to be like Bill but I have since thought it over and I reckon that was about the biggest compliment Bill ever got.

Katherine Field –36

RIDIN' SCHOOL

I've heard 'em say, in ridin' schools,
They've got a reg-lar book of rules.
The man that wrote the book explains
The way to set and hold your reins.

And other lessons facts reveals,
About your elbows and your heels.
You read and practice, then decide
If you have really learnt to ride.

A cow man doesn't give a care
'Bout how you ride, jest so you're there
Nor how you hold your hands and feet.
The main thing is to hold your seat.

You learn more from a buckin' hoss
Than any school you come across.
Fer you and him can soon decide
What's onderneath each other's hide.

6

Shorty and the Professors

Introducing the Professor [1]

Things changes a heap around the old ranch, Bill bein' gone, and then the boss and his wife gits them a house up in town and Zeb is the foreman down at the farm ranch now. The place seems soter lonesome fer we don't git to see the boss's wife only when she comes down fer a visit sometimes. The boss reckons I am to look after the outside work and he is goin' in fer politics seein' he got elected to the state senate now.

Then all of a sudden it looks like more trouble. The boss shows me a letter frum a perfesser that sez he is comin' out to study what he calls nat'ral conditions. I tells the boss that I reckons almost any of us could write and tell them what soter condition we was in without them sendin' a man way out here on the train to look us over. But he allows this here feller is what you call a analyser that is goin' to tell all the schools and the government what this neck of the range is good fer.

Well, I sez I suppose old Ann Elizer will be a heap of bother 'fore we are done with him. That gits Eph and Zeb a goin' and we calls him Ann Elizer from then on out. Well when the time come fer me to go and git him I learns that he is gettin' off at a station that is about ten miles farther away than if he had got off up in town. That don't surprize me none though fer I know that the boss has been soter slippin' mental like since he went into the state senate and so a feller ort to know that by the time a feller got down to where he was tangled up with the main government he would be purty bad.

I takes a team of mules and a wagon and goes to git Ann Elizer. It is a purty long drive there and back in a day, so I goes as far as Brigg's ranch and stays over night, which is about the closest I can git without campin' out. Next mornin' I leaks out fer the station and when I git there the station agent and me we augers a heap about this here stranger that is comin' among our midst. It is jest train time when up rides [Rildy] Briggs on a plum good hoss and turns him out in the little corral back of the station house. She aint there to show off that's a cinch fer she has on her old dirty ridin' skirt and her dads old wore out hat and coat and her hoss is shore warmed up. She has jest took a notion to foller up and have a look and she has done it on the sudden like. The train slacks up long enough to dump a couple of trunks on the platform and out frum one of the cars steps a man with specs on and [r]ight away I know [i]t is Ann Elizer. He is walkin' fast and has a big satchel in one hand and a little flat satchel in the other. Before he gits to the platform the train is fannin' up the line. He is young fer a perfesser and he shore talks a heap and I see right now that he is a goin' to be a lot fussy.

He tells us who he is as if we don't already know. Then he looks over at Rildy's hoss and he sezs to me "Is that your Hoss?" I shakes my head and p'ints to Rildy. "That hoss is very warm," he tells her. "I reckon I know it, seein' I warmed him up myself," she sez. "Why don't you take off the saddle and let him roll?" he wants to know. "Don't you know it is good fer a animal to roll.["] "I don't see you rollin' none," she comes back at him and he gits red in the face and then he laffs and if Rildy didn't slap him on the back and jine in laffin too and I never see her look as purty before fer all her dimples shows and you kin jest see the Devil a dancin' in them eyes of hern. "If you stay in this country you'll know why I left that there saddle on," she sez, "And if you don't you mebby won't need to know. But one thing Mister. Don't you take too much stock in what these one brained hay shakers and banty legged cow punchers tells you," and she walks to the end of the [platform] and takes a look out at the mountains and flats while I loads on his trunks. We got most nigh home before he gits any ways out of hand and then he wants me to stop the team so's he can git out and poke around at a cactus which he gives a crazy name.

He pokes about fer a spell and then he looks at old Spike the off mule. Spike is standin' all hipped over like he allus does. "Why does that animal favor his leg?" he wants to know. Mebby he aint favorin' it I sez. Mebby he's savin' it fer sumpthin'. Look out! I hollers but it is too late fer he has grabbed Spike's hint laig and Spike has kicked his pins from onder him right now. His laig aint broke but I can see it is goin' to be sore fer a spell. He manages to git back in the wagon where he belongs and he asks, "What do you use that animal fer?" Well, I sez, [s]o fur we been a usin' him fer a mule and have got tollable results. "He's vicious and dangerous," he sez. No I augers. He had on a closed bridle and when you took him by the laig he jest didn't savvy and he kicked fust and thought afterwards. Ann Elizer he looks at me and durn if he didn't grin ag'in. "You have no way of provin' wheather he thought aytall either before or after he kicked," he sez. "And regardless of what the animal's intentions were the result was disasterous to myself." We was still fer a mile or so and then he busts out ag'in, "When you mentioned that that mule was savin' his laig fer sumpthin' were you tryin' to tell me that perhaps he meditated violence?" Well, I wouldn't say that, I sez. When we was havin' supper that night he seems to think sudden like and then he sez that he has lost his little portfoley case that had all his papers and formerlys in. He reckons he lent it up ag'in his trunk on the depot platform and that he aint saw it since. We was tryin' to figger it out fer I minded seein' that there little flat satchel and caint figger what's went with it. Zeb speaks up fer the fust time that night and he sez, "Rildy will fetch it over here day after tomorrer." We looks at him plum amazed and I asks what he means. "You said you aimed to stop at Briggses," he sez. Well what about it? I wants to know. That aint got nothin' to do with it. "No?" he sez. "It's got this much to do with it. Rildy saddled up and follered to be there jest out of curosity and impydence. She sees that little satchel and ditches it till you go and nobody caint say it aint left accidental. She tells the agent she'll lope up and ketch you and give it to you but 'stid of that she takes it home and her and her folks will make out all they can a readin' it tomorrow, and then the next day she will put on her glad togs and come a weavin' in here and larn all she kin by talkin' and listnin'." The perfesser looks at all of us and asks, "Did any one tell him about that girl?" We all shuck our heads no, and the perfesser wipes his specs and remarks, "Mister Zeb, [i]f that young lady appears at the time you mentioned with that case you are a wonder."

"I wouldn't say that," sez Zeb, "I don't know much and I don't even know Rildy Briggs, nobody does, but I know that much about her." The cook and Eph agrees with Zeb and reckons the portfoley case is good as settled. We had a room fer the perfesser but he gits a sleepin' bag out of one of his trunks and it is plum practical. None of us has ever seen nothin so light and so warm and he allows he is bunkin' in the bunk house with the hands. You know we caint help but like him and we puts hoss linnyment on his kicked laig and we tells him about Bill and the medicine man and he laffs plenty. He allows that the world and the folks is about the same wherever you go and we finds he has been plum to France and Chiny. But he is tired and he jest smokes a ready made cigarette and he goes to sleep and snores in a way that lets all know he is a purty good man if he is a perfessor.

Rildy Brings the Portfolio [2]

Well sir, the second day after the perfessor comes up drives Rildy Briggs in a buck-board. She has the portfoly satchel with her all right. I am shoein' a couple hosses and helpin' Eph around the corral, so happen to be among them present. We don't none of us say a word about Zeb's purdictions 'cause he don't want us to and neither does the perfessor. She shore lands talkin'. We puts her team up and lets her ramble right along.

After dinner[3] she goes right at the perfessor and before we know it she is through and has pumped more outen him than we figgered he'd tell inside the comin' year. He has a pair of high powered glasses, so she is a showin' him all the country in range of them lookers and tellin' him all about it fer her uncle is a prospector and she knows the names of all the rocks and strattys in sight and out of sight to hear her tell it. He gits his papers out and sez she checks up right in the rack with the dealers at Washington and all the he school marms back east.[4] He caint ride nor walk on account of bein' kicked by that mule, so he hires her and her team to haul him around next day. Which is a good bargain fer Rildy, seein' we board her and the team.

The perfessor kicks about his face and lips chafein' and gittin' sore. "Well," sez Rildy, "If you mind, you ast me why I left the saddle on a sweaty hoss. Now I'm tellin' you. If you pull the saddle ofen a hoss in this country when his back is hot and tender and the hair wet and mashed down, his back will chafe a plenty and then you got a sore backed hoss.["]5 That evenin' we caint help but notice Eph. He is about half mad at Rildy and about half stuck on her. He sasses her a little and he don't look none too pleasant at the perfessor. She moves right into the boss's wife's room and leaves us right early after supper.

Next mornin' she tends to her own team and has things ready fer a soon start. Eph he starts to shovel out a lateral ditch but it aint no time till he is back at the shop jest a cussin' flashes. Somebody has greased his shovel handle with cookin' grease, and he swears he seen Rildy stoppin' her team at the top of the hog back, and he knows that she has the perfessor's glasses a watchin' him tryin' to hang onto that there greasy shovel handle. Then we all recollect that when she drove off she hollered back, "Say Eph! If you don't know what to do, git a piece of broke glass!"6 And that is jest what he has to do. Git a piece of glass and scrape that there shovel handle down.

It is late when I git in that night so I don't hear much more about things fer Rildy is up with the crew next mornin' and as soon as she gits breakfast she leaks right out fer home. She has been gone mebby half a hour when the perfessor allows that his high power glasses is gone. Zeb is tickled and he bites off a chaw and sez, "Most likely Rildy took 'em. She'll soter keep in tech with ye fer a spell." I sez mebby she wanted Eph fer to come down and git' em and that shore makes old Eph bow up like a wheel mule on a muddy road. Zeb and the perfessor has been talkin' about [gophers] and how bad they are about makin' holes in ditches and causin' the whole ditch to wash out endurin' the night. The perfessor has a little writin' machine7 which he plays like a pianny or a organ and he has set down and wrote a letter to the science man back east to git the fambly hist'ry and habits of all gophers. Zeb allows he don't care where they come frum nor where they go to as long as they keep outen his ditches.

The perfessor sez he aims to ride to town and mail the letter right now, so we saddles up old Barney with Eph's saddle and gits the stirrups geared up to fit him. Most new hands tries to lope fust off but the perfessor starts out on a walk which is plum sensible. Then mebby the perfessor's kicked laig was still a little short of the lopin' stage.

I was there when the perfessor gits back. He has took the whole day fer the ride but he has done it all right. Eph hollers and tells him he will turn the hoss out but the perfessor looks like he thinks Eph is stringin' him and starts to do it hisself. "Look out!" Eph yells but it is too late. The perfessor has pulled the bridle off before he does the saddle and to make it worse Old Barny's head is turned away frum the corral gate instead or toward it and the gate is open. The perfessor charges at him but there aint nothin' to hold on to and he gits knocked down and run over. We all runs up to see if he is hurt which seems to surprise him and to do him credit I will say he wasn't mad nor skairt neither. We tells him not to take them sort of chances fer Old Barney aint above kickin' a man once he gits the upper hand like that.[8]

"Where will he go?" he asts. Well, I sez he waters over on the Sandy Arroyo and Eph and me will corral them tomorrow and git the saddle. Jest so you aint hurt. That's the main thing. We tells him that even a old hand sometimes gits keerless and spills his hoss and it aint no joke if he gets left on foot away off frum anywheres. After supper he gits a pencil and paper and starts to figger and purty soon he calls me and Eph over and shows us. He has a whole plan of the corral drawed and cross marks to show where him and the hoss was at. "I made three mistakes," he sez. ["]I should a closed the gate, I should a took the saddle off first. And if you must contend with open gates or doors you should release the animal with his head toward them." Me and Eph shore thought a heap more of that boy right then and I got a sneaky feelin' he might even outfigger the gophers, which aint been done so far, but that old boy shore does think hard once he makes a mistake.

When we goes out to the bunk house he stops and looks at the moon a shinin' on the mountains jest like Bill used to do and then he walks inside. Zeb is settin' there a smokin' his pipe and what do you think? The perfessor's glasses is a layin' on his bunk. He looks funny at Zeb and Zeb grins and sez, "Oh, she took 'em all right. I see her put 'em in one of the nose bags she had to feed her team. So I jest took 'em out and put in a old boot and a [couple] hoss shoes to make up the weight and she snuck around and slipped it into the buckboard and drove off smilin' and hollers back that she'll be seein' me a long ways off. I tells her shore take a good look. I jest let them rest fer today so's you'd know how it felt to have her around much." The perfessor he reckons it looks like Rildy has the whole crew to buck but Zeb tells him he will shore wish fer a bigger crew before he gits finished with that gal.

The Second Perfessor Arrives [9]

A couple days later Rildy Briggs' kid brother brings back the case fer the perfessor's glasses and leaves it on the bunk for him, and after he has a good big bait he leaks out fer home ag'in. Frum what he sez he is actin' on his own and Rildy is plum mad at Zeb.

We was all in a good humor when in drives the boss with a plum new perfessor to help out the fust one. Next day the boss goes back to town and leaves us with it and we ain't none too well pleased neither. The cook he sez to me, "Shorty," he sez, "Do you reckon that all these here perfessors is comin' here because the boss is gone or do you reckon he left because he knowed they was a comin'?" Well I sez I reckon I'll say what the fust perfessor said when the mule kicked him, "Whatever the animal's intentions was the result was disastrous." The second perfessor was a heap different frum the fust one. Always wanted to ast questions and argy. The fust perfessor is a heap different too fer he gits mighty high chinned and throws in with this one. I see right off they had been in cahoots fer he fetched two little flat saddles[10] along and how would he savvy to do that if they hadn't been writin' letters. They didn't ride around none fer a day or two but jest set around and augered, and both moves into the boss's part of the ranch house. The fust mornin' we ketched the second perfessor shavin' with a little affair that was like a hoc.[11] We made him show us how it worked and Zeb allows it will be a good rig fer a married man fer then when the old woman cuts her corns or rips up old clothes with it all she can do is spile one blade and not the whole razor. "You don't like women?" asts the second perfessor. "I been married twict," sez Zeb as if that was enough. "I never was," sez the perfessor. "You're a smart man," Zeb sez and walks out. But that was the start of it fer right off they got to talkin' at the table about women votin' and how smart women was.[12] That riles Zeb and finally he ups and sez, "Women will vote and in time they will run the government fer they have the real government idee. Give a woman enough cloth to build a quilt and she cuts it all up in little patches and sews it together again to make a lot of work and expense, and when she has got that done she gets all the other old women in and the whole passel of them works it full of cotton and makes a whale of a fuss jest to make work fer the whole mess of them that she could a done in a couple of hours with a sewin' machine if she'd a left things as they was. And if a kid gits sick they git advice frum the old maid that leads the village choir 'stead of frum a old woman that smokes a cob pipe and has raised ten head of her own besides a crop of grand children." Well, Zeb soter has 'em there so they lays off till the next day and then they starts on a other lead. They start to talk about dry farmin' and about plowin' deep and then shaller and how it will keep the m'isture in the ground. Zeb he gits the beef and biscuit swallered out of his mouth and sez, "That is pervidin' that dirt lays there. Why man if you plowed the grass offen this here country the spring winds would plum change the map and the whole surface would jest drift around between the Powder River and the Cimmaron plum continuous."[13]

Well that holds 'em fer a spell but the next day we gits in Eph's little chore hoss, "Chunky." Now [C]hunky has got away and has been runnin' out fer a matter of three months and when Eph lets the hammer down on him he suns Eph's moccaisons and skins up his hands and nose some.[14] The perfessors wants to know how he got skun up like that and Eph tells 'em that old Chunky broke in two with him. "Impossible," sez the second perfessor. "Oh yeh?" sez Eph. "Well if you want to know it he plum swallered his head and fell to staves." They goes out to the corral and looks at Chunky and the second perfessor sez, "The animal seems to have become reunited." And then they laffs.

They gits out them little saddles and I see they aim to do some ridin'. The second perfessor tells Eph to saddle a hoss fer him and Eph allows that if he aint able to saddle up he aint able to ride very fur. The only hoss we had kep up was old "Gander." Now Gander was a big long gaited hoss that was a good coon tailer but he had been run after hosses till he was a hoss fool.[15]

Before I knows it the fust perfessor has that postage stamp on him and a bridle with more reins than there is strings in a Navaho rug weaver's machine. Let me wrangle the past'r I sez.[16] Gander is a hoss fool and he might cold jaw on you. There's a few old mares and some young stock in there and you might git him runnin'. "I'll thaw his jaw out if it gits too cold," [h]e sez. Well, I warns him he's an old coon tailer so look out. "A colored gentleman that makes clothes," sez the second perfessor[.] "Have him make you some of these western riding clothes." [A]nd they laffs some more.

Zeb comes along about then and he sez, "He'll likely bust you outen the clothes you got on," and me and Eph laffs. Well, Gander is lazy when he aint woke up and I see the perfessor a whippin' with a little stick he packs and kickin' with his little spurs while the other one sez sumpthin' about Gander bein' "[v]ery spirited."

It looks like every thing is goin' to be all right fer we see the hosses a comin' along down off the mesa in the paster, but about three hundred yards frum the corral the old mares and the broncs cuts back on him and he whirls old Gander and takes after them.[17] They makes fer some little arroyos and cactus ground and Gander he throws his head into the crown piece and then roots fer the bridle. The slam most takes the perfessor out of the saddle and before he can git his balance they are jumpin' ditches and dodgin' cactus and down he comes.

We goes out and gits him and he is shore a wreck. One shoulder busted and mebby more damage so Eph gits the spring wagon and the other perfessor and they all go to town. What surprises us is that the stirrup is still on his big slab [footed] boot when we gather him up and the strap is on the stirrup. When they was gone I rounds up the paster and we gits the saddle offen old Gander and we finds that the stirrup straps is set on little pieces of spring steel so that if a feller is drug they will come off and let him loose.

Zeb looks at the saddle and at me and then he sez, "Shorty, I always knowed them little saddles was built to fall off from but I never dreamt they was so complete."

Zeb Loses a Trick [18]

When Eph gits back frum town he tells us that the fust perfessor is busted up so he will be shut in from now till a lot later. In a few days he takes the second perfessor and goes in to see him and they come back with the report that the fust perfessor aims to go back home as soon as he is able to travel. But the second perfessor gits a gentle old hoss and his little dinky saddle and keeps right on a nosin' around the country.

About that time I have to go out and join a work and by the time I git back I have most forgot all about things. Well, one day that pest of a Rildy Briggs rides in fer noon and she is dressed up in a new divided skirt and all her outfit sets mighty good on her and bein' tall and slim she did look good on her hoss.

I knowed there was sumpthin' in the wind fer her and Zeb hated one another like p'izen and while we was eatin' it cropped out. If she didn't up and ask Zeb right out before all of us to take her to the dance over on the crick next week. Zeb he reckons it's soter fur to go to her house and back but she heads him off by tellin' him that she will meet him at Wilson's ranch which is right on his way to the dance. He caint say no and as soon as she has made the date and swallered her grub she steps up on her hoss and makes fer home.

The perfessor he reckons she's a fine lookin' young woman and I agree with him but I also tell him how her and Zeb agrees and that I aim to keep out of the whole thing. Well, come the night fer the dance and the perfessor he saddles up and goes along with us and Zeb saddles his old hoss Tobe and takes his big pack hoss Red to put Rildy's saddle on. We wanted him to take the buckboard but he won't. He calls his dog Shag and they start. Now when Zeb is ridin' Tobe and packin' Red he takes the dog Shag always, and when Red gits too fur behind he hollers "Bring up the pack Shag!" and the old dog fetches the pack hoss up behind him right now.

The dance was a good one and they had good fiddlers. Rildy come in her ridin' skirt but went into the bed room and put on another one she had fetched tied behind her saddle. The perfessor had a good time and so did we all, exceptin' Zeb. A young feller that had jest come to that neck of the country got to follerin' Rildy around and you bet she didn't do nothin' to make him quit it neither. I looked fer a fight but Zeb kep his head till it was time to go home. Then she come to Zeb and sez that this new feller is goin' right apast Wilson's and Zeb can save hisself the trouble of takin' her home.

He is shore b'ilin' mad but he sez all right. He tells her he will git her hoss for her seein' old Shag won't let a stranger take him. He rides up on Tobe leadin' Red and old Shag follerin'. The new feller helps Rildy onto Red and then starts to git his hoss. Zeb pops spurs to old Tobe and hollers "Bring up the pack Shag!" and away they go. Red is as fast a hoss as Tobe and before she knows it Rildy is goin' too fast to quit her hoss. She can set a hoss up[19] and slide him and she is a whole lot better rider than Zeb is but I knowed that he had onbuckled her curb strap when he went to git the hoss and she hadn't no chance to hold him. It was mean and the perfessor yelled some mighty strong words after them as they cut away accross the flat.

But the next thing we heard that gal let a yell out of her that carried plum to the foot hills and then some and the sound told us between yells that both hosses wasn't jest runnin' along but was doin' their best and along with the noise we could hear somebody whippin' till they got too fur away. Then there was some soter jumble in the noise and one hoss was still a goin' and the other seemed to have slowed down or stopped. We follered till we found Zeb a settin' longside the road plum helpless and Rildy was plum out of sight and hearin'. Zeb hadn't nothin' to say and old Shag was still fussin' at Tobe fer Tobe always did fight Shag. Some folks in a buggy fetched Zeb along and I led Tobe. When we got to Wilson's ranch Rildy was there and onsaddled. She shore laffed and told what happened and this is what she sez. "You know when that fool dog took to my hoss I knowed what was up and somebody had onbuckled my curb strap. It made me so mad that I took my quirt and went to whippin' and as I come alongside Zeb I shore whaled him a few but Red went right on apast and that Shag dog took to Tobe and Zeb got throwed in the scuffle. I managed to bend old Red at the cross road and here we are."

When we got home the folks with the buggy was jest bringin' Zeb in and we struck a light in the bunk house and peeled his shirt and looked him over. They was no bones broke but he was skun up and there was three welts that proved Rildy wasn't lyin' when she said she quirted him but what made us laff there was two dog bites on one of his elbows.

He swears he will kill old Shag but I tells him that the dog don't know no better than to take to the hoss that's behind. "That may be," he sez, "But he don't have to start chawin' on me when I'm floppin' around on the ground half dead, and then try to run my hoss out of the country." Eph he grins and sez, "Rildy wasn't usin' the jaw strap on her bridle. Pears to me like you orta put it on Shag."

But he caint git a rise from Zeb. He's plum licked, and he shore does cripple around fer a day or two. The perfessor remarks, "I was introduced to Miss Briggs but in view of what took place I don't think I shall press her acquaintance."

Rildy and Zeb Have a Date [20]

The following story repeats the incidents of "Zeb Loses a Trick," although it was probably written first. Possibly the pressure of a deadline led Kiskaddon to submit a rejected earlier version. It is included here mainly for its revelation of Rildy Briggs' motive for snubbing Zeb at the dance, and for its closing paragraph revealing Shorty's feelings about Rildy.

Well, seem like after the fust perfessor fell off that hoss he lost his likin' fer these parts and the Boss tells me to haul his outfit up to town because he aims to ship hisself frum there as soon as he is in shape to go. The second perfessor is up to see him a couple of times and then he leaks out fer home and that jest leaves us with the second perfessor.

It don't look like there is goin' to be a lot a doin' fer a spell and I think if we could even git a letter frum Bill it might soter wake things up. Then, things starts right where they mostly are in the habit of startin'.

Rildy Briggs rides in fer dinner one day and she cottons right onto Zeb and he don't want no part of her but still he can't shut up and let her be. When we set down to eat she gits right acrost the table frum him and he aint got no chance to dodge. When we git done eatin' she braces Zeb to take her to the dance that is goin' to be over on the creek that week. Zeb he tries to back out, sayin' it is so fur he caint git to her place and back to the dance after he has got through with his day's work.

That don't do no good fer she sez she is a goin' to be at Wilson's place fer a few days and that aint fur off his way to the dance and he can stop and git her. Zeb is beat hands down and he has to say yes. But he tells me he don't trust her none and he allows there's deviltry afoot only he caint figger what she's up to.

That evenin' when he starts to the dance he don't take the buckboard. He takes his saddle hoss and his pack hoss fer her to ride and Old Shag his dog. Now that pack hoss is faster than the saddle hoss and the dog is learnt to haze him up if he gits to[o] fur behind. All Zeb has to do is to holler, "Bring up the pack Shag!" and Old Shag takes to the hoss's heels and fetches him up right now.

The perfessor goes to the dance too. He don't know nothin' about quadrilles but he can waltz and that like and him and Rildy dances togather considerable. But the feller that she cottons onto is a feller that has jest come into the country and is workin' fer the old man Dobbs. That feller is a young hay shaker and you can see that he has been a big hit with the farmer gals where he comes frum. He is so stuck on hisself that he is plum disgustin' but she keeps follerin' him about like a friendly pup and all the dance Zeb gits with her is the fust one.

When the dance broke up we all soter kep together because we reckoned there would be some fun before it was all over. We was right. She comes out with this here new hay shaker and tells Zeb that seein' he is goin' the same way they are that he aims to ride along with her and Zeb. Zeb sez allright and goes and gits his hoss and hers. The new feller helps Rildy onto the pack hoss, as if she couldn't bounce onto a hoss easier than airy one of them. Zeb is already on his hoss and when she lights a straddle he lifts his hoss and takes out on a dead run and hollers, "Bring up the pack Shag!" and Shag shore charges that hoss and away they go. The new feller is quick and he makes a jump fer the bridle but the dog takes to him and the hoss is runnin' and kickin' and he knocks him loose and as he goes a rollin' Old Shag quits the hoss long enough to grab a mouthful of his pants and then takes right in after the percession. We run to our hosses and take out after 'em too. We know what he has done. He has onbuckled her curb strap and she caint hold her hoss, and they are goin' out accross the flat like the Devil beatin' tan bark. Eph yells, "She'll kill him on hoss back, bit or no bit!" She ain't got no rope I hollers. "She's got a quirt!" he yells back. We aint got over a half a mile when we comes to Zeb's hoss millin' around with the reins flying and the pore old gentle feller is skairt plum to death. We pull up and there away in the distance we hear the other hoss a goin'. The old dog is tryin' to hold up the saddle hoss. We look aroun and then we see a dim shadder of a man tryin' to git onto his feet. It is Zeb.

We make the dog quit and take Zeb's hoss over to him and he is so weak and shook up he is plum helpless. He is sick to his stummick. And I tells them to git him on home and I'll git on and see what has happened to Rildy. When I gits to Wilson's paster gate I don't see her and I am shore skairt but I rides on up to the house and there she is pullin' the saddle offen Zeb's pack hoss. The hoss is purty excited yet but I snub him up to the saddle horn and git ready to take him along. He done you a dirty rotten trick I sez and he aint no man aytall. "He onstrapped my bit," she sez and than she bust out laffin'. "Aint he shore dumb?" she asks. "Why I tuck him over there to give that there good lookin' smart Alec a reg'lar good old Missouri frailin', and then the thick headed cuss he turns on me. Bill would have done it," she sez. Much as I liked Bill it made me soter mad when she sez that and I takes fer home.

When I git to the bunk house Eph and the perfessor has took Zeb by force and set him on his bunk. He has got some of his stren'th back and wants to kill Old Shag. He was only a doin' what he was learnt to do I sez. "Oh, Yeh ?" sez Zeb. "That there she devil took to me and my hoss with her quirt and like to cut the face and neck off me and she kep sickin' the dog till he tuck to both hosses and then she got ahead and Shag tuck to my hoss till he got him to kickin' and buckin' and when I was throwed he lit in and chawed me up after I was down." We all had to laff as mad as we was. We stripped him and doctored him up. He had three awful welts acrost his face and neck, and his clothes was all tore and he had four of the wust dog bites I ever seen on a man.

Jest as we are gittin' in bed he busts out agin. "She aint a goin' to git away with this," he sez. That makes the perfessor sore and he sez, "She has already accomplished it. And my prediction is that you will fare rather badly in any contest with Miss Briggs." That mighty nigh starts a fight but Eph joshes 'em and I blow out the light and we go to sleep.

That is they go to sleep. I lay awake and try to figger why she wants Zeb to lick the new feller. It's the fust time I been mad at Rildy but all the same I caint help thinkin' what if she had been throwed and dog bit. But all the same I wish I wasn't no runt and then mebby her or some other woman would pick me to do sumpthin'. 'Stead of that she jest keeps on usin' my stuff and givin' me a shove or a slap on the ear and bossin' me around like I was a kid, when she knows it don't set none too good, but she keeps right on a doin' it and seems to think it's a heap of fun.

Shorty Rescues the Second Perfessor [21]

After Zeb gits spilled offen his hoss he is pokin' around fer a few days on account he is so sore and stove up he caint hardly travel. He gits some of the linnyment that Bill has got offen the medicine man and is rubbin' it all over hisself. He sez that he found it onder the eves of the bunk house in a space between the rafters. He allows it is mighty good stuff but the perfessor he gits a lot of fixin's out of his trunk and he takes a bottle of the linnyment to the kitchen and works fer quite a spell and when he gits done he tells us that this here linnyment is a fake and aint up to much. Zeb he allows it is good stuff and is a helpin' him whatever it is and so they have a argyment, which aint no help seein' Zeb and the perfessor aint none too friendly no way.

The day follerin' I goes up to the mountain paster to git some saddle and work hosses and I takes the perfessor along, hopin' it will keep him and Zeb soter seperated till things blows over. There has been a big rain up above and when we git to Brushy Creek it is up bad. I tells him we had better wait till the creek runs down which won't be over a couple of hours at most. He laffs at me and wants to know what I'm skeerd of. He sez that there little creek aint over fifty feet wide right now and that a feller can jump acrost it most times. I allows him that p'int but I tells him that a man is crazy to ride sech water.

Then he told me that he has swum as much as three mile at a time in the ocean and that I am tryin' to pick a load into him. It wasn't no use to argy with him so I jest gits off and loosens my cinch to let my hoss rest till the water run down; likewise the perfessor. I hears him start and looks and he is ridin' right in. I yells at him but it aint no use. Boy! Howdy! Old Chunky rolled plum over but he got his front feet on the bank and scrambled out. A rope aint no use in that brush water so I runs to where the current swirls in ag'in the bank and grabs a stout brush to keep me from bein' pulled in. The perfessor is rollin' like a tumble weed only he is out of sight most of the time but luck is with us, and jest as he washes in ag'in the bank he happens to come up wrong end to. But them puffy ridin' pants is what saves him. I grabs him by the seat of the britches. All the pants that he wasn't occupyin' was full of water and they shore did go squersh when I takes a holt. But they was made of good stuff and stands the drag till I gits him swung around to where I land him.

He is a game old cuss fer all through that rollin' around he aint strangled on account he knows enough to hold his breath while his head's onder water and to grab a breath whenever his head comes up, but he shore has been rolled and pounded around and lost his specs. He rests and the sun and wind dries his clothes and when the crick runs down he helps me git the hosses and take them back to the ranch. He offers me a good days pay to ride to town and send a tellygram to his home town fer a new pair of specs. He claims that his specs was made to measure same as you would send off and git a pair of boots and this here place where he is sendin' has his eye measure, and takin' it all through it does sound mighty sensible, so I does what he wants.

Now it is still early in the evenin' when I git back from town next day but Eph he is hangin' around the corrals, he is oneasy and sez the cook wanted him to keep clost by fer

Zeb and the perfessor has been jawin' at one another consid'able. Now Zeb is a nasty fighter. He is big and stout and he can rassle and he kicks and butts. Besides he aint above chawin' on a feller if the goin' gits too tough. Things was all right till we was at the wash bench a washin' up fer supper and the perfessor was a talkin' to me about the crick and what happened up there. Zeb he horns in. "You school people is all alike," he sez. "All you do is go around and git into trouble and depend on somebody to help you out. All you got to do is shut your mouth and keep outen them kind of places. You all talk about science. When a feller sez he is scientific it jest means he's crazy."

"Who called on you to preach a sermon?" the perfessor asks. "Who's goin' to stop me?" Zeb asks. The perfessor grins right nasty. "Oh, mebby a woman, mebby a horse, mebby a dog," he sez. Zeb makes a dive fer onder holts but he misses and rolls on the ground fer the perfessor can shore side step. He makes another dive but he misses and gits a kick as he went by that shore did knock the dust outen his pants. He sees that his man aint so easy so he straightens up and comes in a swingin' fer the perfessor right and left, but somehow the perfessor keeps away from them licks and all the time he is shootin' in quick straight punches that is shore puttin' a face on Zeb. Zeb sees that he is licked if he don't go to the ground with him and he makes another dive fer the onder holts and lays hisself open fer a right to the jaw. He goes down but gits up and goes at it. It aint no use fer he is jarred and dizzy and the old perfessor walks around him like he is tied and pours it to him. Then he gits a chance and lets pore Zeb have it fer a knock out. What surprised me the most was that when Zeb got his bearin's and knowed where he was at he ups and shakes hands with the perfessor. "That was what you might call a little science," sez the perfessor. "I reckon as how it was," sez Zeb.

The Perfessor Buys a Horse . . . and a Dog [22]

In a week or two Zeb and the perfessor has got over their ruckus and is both pirootin'[23] around lookin' fer more trouble of some kind only they don't know they are runnin' their snouts into trouble but jest run into it soter dumb like. I shore wisht that Bill was back fer when Bill started sumpthin' the whole world and Bill hisself knowed what was a goin' on. But these here jaspers was plum apast me.

One mornin' the perfessor sez that he is goin' over to Lem Sikes place. When he is about to start Eph hollers to him and sez, "Say Prof! Don't leave nothin' at Lem's place and don't bring nothin' back frum there fer if you do airy one you'll shore be sorry!"

You see Lem is one of them fellers that has a team and wagon and a lot of tradin' stuff. The more he trades the more stuff he gits. The more of that kind of stuff he gits the poorer he is. He has a few scrubby cows and hosses and some bean ground and a little patch of alfalfy. He likewise has a wife and a lot of kids not to speak of a whole passel of dogs. But the principal thing he has is time.

The next day old Chunky, the hoss he rode comes into the corral without no saddle nor bridle on and we know that he has been turned loose or else he has got away frum the perfessor. We was worried some but long about sundown here comes the perfessor a ridin' a old pacin' mare that is a most as old as him.[24] He has a snaffle bit on her and he is leanin' back and plow linin' her around and his head is raired back like a coffee pot lid. But wust of all he is a leadin' a old pot houn' alongside jest as solem as you please. "Oh Lord," sez Zeb, "where is onkel Tom and Little Eva at?" Don't rib him none, I sez, and let me find out what Lem Sikes has done to this here man of eddication.

After supper I gits a talk with him and asks him about the old mare and he ruffles right up and sez, "You see, Shorty, these western horses are all treacherous and vicious. They are abrupt in their movements and tender mouthed. This animal I purchased is of the best blood and easy gaited and gentle. I got a different bit too so she will not become used to this miserable style of loose reined riding like the horses in this country." Man, I sez, That old mare is a star gazer that don't look where she's a goin' and she turns about as quick as a team and wagon.[25] "Well," he sez nasty nice like, "If a man knows where he is going he should at least be able to direct his horse and as far as turning quick, that is a minor affair. The average cow puncher works for thirty five or forty dollars a month and is on call twenty-four hours a day, so if you figure it down fine his time is so valuable that if he is real quick he might save about two cents worth of time on 500 turns."

That shore made me wish he hadn't licked Zeb but I helt onto my temper and sez, And thet there houn' dawg? "That dog," he sez, "is a trailer. I got him to hunt coyotes with. He will follow the track of one till he tires him out and I have a small pistol with which to shoot him when I overtake him." That houn' you mean? I asks. "The coyote!" he yells and I knows I got him on that one.[26] What has Lem done with all the coyotes this here dawg has ketched? I wants to know. But he bows up and quits me.

We had to keep the houn' in the chicken corral or else Shep and Shag would a took him apart and seen what made him go. One mornin' right soon we heard the old houn' bellerin' and looked out and there he was a goin' at a trot out accrost the flat and the Perfessor was side wheelin' along behind on the old mare and she seemed to be lookin' fer the mornin' star. I slaps a saddle onto the fust hoss I can grab and takes out after him. I don't git there soon enough fer when I am about fifty yards away the old mare steps right into a dog hole and down she goes. She cain't even fall down quick but upsots soter like a load of hay and the perfessor is slower yit and lets her lay down on his laig. I was goin' to jump onto her head and oncinch the saddle but that aint needed. She laid right still and after we had loosened the saddle we had a job to make her git up. She seemed to think it was right comfortable where she was at.

The perfessor is on a cane fer a few days and when the houn' comes back we puts him back in the chicken corral. The perfessor takes and lets him out fer a spell every evenin' fer exercise he sez. One evenin' we was jest a goin' in fer supper when we hears the old houn' start bellerin' and he shore can beller. He is makin' fer a shed a little ways from the house and we all wandered what he was after but we didn't have to wait long. He was a trailing Old Topsy, the black cat, and she has a nest of kittens in that shed. He don't have no trouble ketchin' up to Topsy. She is right out to meet him and jumps right up on the middle of his back and starts to work with her teeth and all four feet. The houn' lets out some awful yells and takes out. Topsy has got a good holt and she is ridin' him out accross the paster and makin' the fur fly every jump. She stays fer about two hundred yards and then jumps off. All that worries her is the fact she has to walk back. When the houn' gits his bearin's he makes out fer Lem Sikes' place in a long lope. "Well," sez Zeb, "Lem's going to be one dog poorer ag'in." "Yes," sez Eph, "He'll feel a heap more contented there where there aint no body nor nothin' got ambition enough to bother him none." We all set still fer a spell after supper that night fer it was soter purty outside with the stars beginnin' to show. Then a bad thing happens. A old toad hops out in front of the porch. Eph jumps up and ketches him and sez to the perfessor, "Here, perfessor, you take this here varmint and train him a little and you might git him to ketch that old eagle fer ye that lights up on the butte sometimes."

The perfessor gives him a nasty look and sez, "I see I will have to give another yokel a lesson about minding his own business." "That is if you can," sez Eph right pleasant. The perfessor limps into the house and we goes to the bunk house. Eph, I sez, I am bettin' you a dollar to a doughnut you'll have that there perfessor to lick as soon as his laig gits well. "And I am bettin' you a new pair of boots agin a Stetson hat that I do it too," Eph sez. I holds out my hand and we shakes. "That's a bet," sez Eph.

Eph and the Perfessor Says Good Bye [27]

When I gits back from the next work I sees Rildy Briggs' saddle layin' in the corral and I knows that trouble is right close bye. Eph and Zeb gives me a big hello like them two boys always did and helps me onsaddle and onpack and drag my bed into the bunk house. The cook gits me to one side and tells me that there is some soter deal on only he don't know what it is and that the Perfessor is actin' plum loco. He has seen him fightin' the air like a boxer when there wasn't nobody near him and he has a jumpin' rope hid out and when he thinks nobody's lookin' he skips the rope jest like some school gal.

Well, I tells the cook that this is the way that perfessional fighters trains and the perfessor is likely gittin' ready to give Eph a lickin' fer the talk he made about the toad. "He'll never do it," sez the cook. He licked Zeb, I sez and Zeb is a heap bigger and stouter than Eph, besides he is trained. "I didn't see old Topsy skippin' any ropes nor pawin' the air before she cleaned up on that houn' dawg. She was jest nacherly a rough scrapper. So is Eph. There won't be no time fer boxin' and trompin' around if he ever goes in. He's a plum cross between a wild cat and a bull dog. I've seen his kind before."

When we gits to the table the Perfessor don't talk to nobody but sets up straight and prowd like. Rildy she talks a plenty. She sez that about three weeks ago some folks come apast their place in a covered wagon and Lem Sikes's old pot houn' was a follerin'. They told her that he come into camp the night before all clawed up and they kep him. They named him Scratch on account he had cat tracks all over him. They said he looked like a good possum dog so they aimed to take him back to Missoury along. We all gits a big laff and Zeb allows he might be all right fer possums but he shore aint no good fer cats. The Perfessor has been lookin' mighty frosty but now he looks so red and hot that he could thaw out a tollable good sized ice berg.

After supper Rildy saddles up and starts home. She sez her brother will meet her on the way. I saddles up and goes along till she meets the brother. As soon as we are on the way she tells me that Her and Eph and Zeb and her uncle has got up a irrigation company. Seems like she had watched the perfessors a little and they was plannin' a scheme. They had found out that sugar beets would grow on this ground so they was lookin' things over. But Her and Zeb and Eph and her uncle has took up dry claims all over the ground they was lookin' at and they have even staked one out fer me to file on. Her uncle bein' a minin' man knowed how to form a company and so they did and took out their water rights in Brushy Creek and Sand Creek. It don't take but short ditches and small dams to turn them two creeks out onto the flats and their places is right below Clay Flat and they aim to make a big reservoy there because that ground holds water like a bottle. Old McDougal the attorny is handlin' the law part of it fer them and the boss is all bowed up seein' him and the perfessors aimed to make a real estate affair out of it but the boss was careless and slow about gittin' started so they beat him to it. That was as far as she got because we met her brother and she went on home and I went back to the ranch.

Next day the perfessor talks to me and I am plum surprised. He tells me that him and the boss was a aimin' to git holt of a big piece of land and put water on it and that he has depended on the boss to git folks to file on the land and take out the water rights whilst he is interestin' some capital in the scheme and they allowed to make a good piece of money out of it but the boss has fooled around and before he knowed it them hay shakers has beat him to it.

The Perfessor is as mad at the boss as he is at the others and sez he is all fed up and goin' in a day or two. He seemed soter friendly to me and allowed we had allus got along.

That night Rildy's uncle comes in with a lot of papers and things and he does a lot of talkin' and the perfessor is so mad that he walks out and don't care to listen. He is white and dangerous. Old uncle hollers after him. "Hey you! come back here you might learn sumpthin'." Well in the next few minutes we all learns sumpthin'. The perfessor walks back and punches Uncle three times in the face and clouts his jaw so sudden that the old feller has two black eyes and is knocked out before he knows it. Eph gits white and begins to shake all over and starts toward the Perfessor. The Perfessor comes at him jest like he done fer Zeb but it aint no use. Eph flies at him like a wild cat and grabs him so he caint box. He can rassle but that [aint] no use neither. Eph is like a wild man. He can take a lick that would stop a common man and he is fightin' with his feet and knees and elbows and buttin' too when he gits a chance. The old house shakes till the wall lamp dances up and down on it's nail and they send table and chairs and every thing a flyin' fer they are rollin' around like a pair of tom cats and you caint tell which is which fer a minute and then Eph plants hisself on top and gives him the cyclone finish.

The business talk is over. Uncle leaks out fer home and the rest of us turn in fer the night. Next day I helps the perfessor pack and takes a team and wagon and hauls him to town. As we are startin' Zeb comes over to the wagon and sez, "Eph sez tell you he wears a number seven hat." The perfessor asks what he means by that and I tells him about the bet. When we git to town he gits his ticket and checks his baggage and then he takes me and gits me the best pair of boots that we can find ready made. I shore have to thank him and he don't seem to care that he has a black eye and one ear sticks out from his swelled up jaw like he had the mumps.

We don't see the boss and I don't want to. But jest as the train is ready to pull out here he comes. He has been drinkin' and is all bowed up. He starts right in to give the Perfessor a cussin' out and the perfessor tells him that he ain't nothin' but a big dumb moss back. The Boss turns purple and his big mustache bristles like a bob cat's whiskers and he tells the perfessor that he aint nothin' but a he school marm and aint fit fer to be noticed by a man. The boss's big stummick is stickin' out temptin' like and the Perfessor socks a punch into the pit of that stummick that knocks the wind plum out of the old man, and then he starts workin' on his face and jaw so fast it is surprisin'. [T]he boss tries to fight and flails and stumbles around but he caint land nary lick and purty soon the Perfessor gits him one in the jaw and he sets down on the platform so hard that his pants splits and some of the buttons pops offen his vest, which ain't surprisin' seein' he is so big and fat that he is a considable strain on his clothes anyhow.

The perfessor gits on the train and they are jest pullin' out. He hollers "So Long Shorty!" and waves to me. I waves back. Then I look at the Boss. He shore looks like a wreck settin' there with his nose a bleedin' and one eye shet and his watch chain busted. I don't wait fer nothin' but I git to the stable and hitch up that there team and pound 'em on the tail with the line.

Shorty Turns Diplomat [28]

Well me and the cook goes out to look at them claims and then he gits a hoss and pokes around fer a day or two more. When I goes in to file, so does he. I have a good claim but what do you reckon? He takes a claim right in the middle of Clay Flat where they aim to have the reservoy. Nobody hadn't thought of that till plum now. "It might make a difference in how they handle the ditch stock."[29] He sez.

I was jest gittin' fixed to make a trip into the lower country when one evenin' just about sun down in drives the boss with his little team and buckboard. He has an old travellin' bag in the back and is wearin' his high heeled boots. He climbs out of the buckboard slow and careful like and holds to the wheel. He gits his bearin's and takes the travellin' bag out but then he loses his balance and sets on the ground. He looks all around but I know he caint see very fur so I just watch the show. He gits to the yard gate with the old travellin' bag bumpin' agin his laigs. I put the team away and then I go in to see him.

He was a settin' there tryin' to light a seegar. Fust he got the match away out in front of it and then he was tryin' to git a fire started in the middle of it. Finally he gits it goin' and then he sez, "Shorty things is come to a turrible pass. Them fellers wasn't no more perfessors than I am and that there little irrigation scheme was all a blind. 'Cause they tried to git some of us ranchers to sink some money into it but what they was a layin' fer was to put over a big minin' swindle and they was all fixed up to do it fer they have got away with it a couple of times before. How they keep out of the pen beats me. They aint nothing but a bunch of high class swindlers. All they got me fer was a little time and grub but they got a few friends of mine fer some before I got wise to 'em and that makes hard feelin's between them and me." I tells him what the cook has done and mebby so we can rig it up for a good place to raise feed and winter stock on them claims and it might turn out good after all. "But that ain't the wust part of it." He sez. "It's the town and the wife. I shore been livin' a awful life. All she does is to go to a lot of little doin's that aint fitten fer a seven year old kid if the kid is got any sense. She goes to some other woman's house or has a lot of women come to her house and they set and play a half cocked game. When they git through they have some weak tea or chocolate in little bitty cups that don't hold a good swaller, and eat some sand-witches that it would take three of 'em to make a bite.["]

"I cain't fit in around no sech doin's as that but what makes it wuss yit if I go down to Johnnie's place and play poker she howls on account I smell of likker and tobacco smoke. If I go to the livery barn and talk fer a spell with the boys she sez I smell like a hoss. All that women up in town does is to go around with their nose stuck in the air a tryin' to smell sumpthin they don't like. Why she's lost ten pounds and she has got so fur along in sassity that she is beginnin' to want a surgical operation." I looks at the old man fer a spell and I sez, Don't you reckon there might be some soter idee that would work? "I aint got no more idees" he sez. "I've come back to the old ranch to stay." Do you reckon[,] I sez[,] that she might come back here and be like she usta? "That's too much to hope fer," he sez. Next day I made excuse I needed a few things before I started for the lower country and the boss let me take the buckboard and go to town. When I gits there I don't go to the livery stable but I goes and puts the team in the stable at the house where the boss lived. The Missus is there and she comes out right now and begins to talk and I can see that the boss is right. She has lost a lot of weight and she aint spry and sassy like she usta be. Well, I sez, we shore miss you a heap but it is goin' to be good to have the old boss around once more. That's why I come up. To git his slippers. It will look a heap more home like with him there. 'Course there won't be no women folks, but it will be better than it was. And then I soter stops and studys a minute till I can see she is all ears thinkin' I got sumpthin' wuth while to say. And then I sez I reckon though if Zeb and Rildy gits married they might manage to move in and that would be a heap better. She would make the place more womanish and home like. Then I goes down town fer a couple of hours.

When I comes to the door fer the boss's slippers she is shore up and a comin', she has packed two suit cases and is already to drag it fer the ranch. The boss is surprised all right but he caint figger it out. There is a dance at the school house the follerin' night and she goes and she is as tickled and lively as a school gal. How she does watch Zeb and Rildy. Next mornin' I am packed and saddled to start to the lower country. She gits a chance and she sez to me. "Shorty, who told you Zeb and Rildy was goin' to git married?" Well nobody in particklar as I recollect. I sez. "But what give you the idee they might?" she sez. "I don't see that they take much notice of one another." I reckon you're right, I sez. "Well then why did you talk about them gittin' married and her movin' into my house?" she wants to know.

Well, I sez, I didn't reckon they would, but if they did that there plan was possible. Any thing can happen. And if you was here like you usta be why they'd never think of it. Now I gotta be a goin' I sez. She blushes like a kid and looks at me and asks. "Did you miss me that much?" We shore did every one of us even to Shep and Shag I sez. "Shorty," she sez, "You're a diplomat." I reckon I am I sez. I don't blame you fer callin' me any thing aytall. It was a mean sneaky way to do but if it only worked I'll be even lower down than a diplomat what ever that is and I'll not care a cuss neither. She laffs and sez "It worked all right Shorty and when I called you a diplomat I didn't mean to take it back." So I leaks out for the lower country but I knowed one thing. I am goin' right close to Wilson's place and old Mis Wilson used to be a school marm and I aim to stop there and find out jest what they mean when they call a feller a diplomat.

Shorty's Boss Buys a Mule Team [30]

Well things got soter settled down and the boss and all the folks that has took up claims has gone in pardners and is goin' to make a real feed and past'er place out of the deal. That is all except Rildy and her uncle. We don't look for no more trouble till Bill comes back frum the war. Then all to once the boss rides in leadin' a span of mules.

We all goes to look at 'em and the Missus wants to know where he got 'em. "I got 'em off Lem Sikes," he sez. "Lem got 'em frum some folks in a covered wagon and he had a bill of sale and give one so I reckon it is all right. They are young and when they git fat I reckon they will make a good team. We need 'em, for the old team is gittin' a lot of age on 'em and these is good for a long time." The wife she looks at the mules and sez, "Good fer a long time? Them mules won't never be good no time. Git 'em fat and they'll pay you back by keepin' some body crippled up and a lot of stuff broke as long as you got 'em. You said your self that nothin' any good ever come frum Lem's place and now you gone and done it. What did you go near there fur any how? Did you pay him cash yet?" The boss looks down his nose and sez, "I give him a check." "Send Shorty to town right now with a letter and stop that check and let Zeb take the mules back," she sez. "No Dear, I don't do business thataway," he sez. "Put the mules in the back shed Shorty." "Turn 'em out on the range and set Shep and Shag on 'em," she sez. "Yes, I know what you think. You wish a lot of times I had stayed up in town and minded my own business. Well I didn't and I ain't a goin' to." "Now now Dear, every thing is a goin' to be all right and don't go and git so fussed up," he sez.

Next day the boss allows Eph can hitch up the new mules and fetch some wood down frum the hills, so Eph he harnesses them up and puts 'em to the wagon. Him bein' a Missourian, is fond of mules and he is right pleased. I am all saddled up to go, so I opens the gate fer him and he gits up on the seat and starts. When he does them mules looks back and then away they goes. Eph he is a pullin' for all he cost but all he can do is to clear the gate posts and away he goes out through the paster jest a foggin. They take up the road along the fence and I bounce my hoss and takes after the mules a buildin' a loop in my rope, but before I can git to 'em they hubs a post and throws Eph and the wagon box into the bob wire fence. They busts the reach out of the wagon and circles back and fetches up agin the corral fence, where Zeb and the boss gits 'em. I git Eph ontangled right soon and he is cut up soter bad in the wire. The boss keeps a lookin' toward the house oneasy like, and shore as the good Lord made little apples here she comes. She helps us git Eph into the bunk house and doctor him up with some of the medicine Bill still had left frum the show. Then she looks up at the boss right happy and sez. "Don't you go and worry Dear, every thing is a goin' to be all right." Them mules was used to workin' with blinkers on, I sez and it was them open bridles made the trouble. She jest keeps a laffin' and sez, "Oh yes you must work mules with closed bridles." "Yes and they'd orta work women folks with closed mouths." sez the boss.

The follerin' afternoon the boss and Zeb hitches up the new mules to the spring wagon and puts on some posts and wire and goes to the upper paster. It comes dark and they ain't in so I starts out to meet 'em. About half a mile frum the ranch I meets 'em. They are ridin' the mules and ain't got much to say. We gits to the ranch and the missus and the cook comes out when they hears the dogs, and Eph is hobblin' along behind. The boss seems to have trouble gittin' down and Zeb goes to help him and, pop! sumthin hits and Zeb sets down and grabs his laig. The boss don't have no more trouble gittin' off fer the mule bucks him off right now. We gits Zeb into the bunk house and starts to take off his boots. The boss seems to be soter awkward. "Take both hands," sez the Missus. "I cain't," he sez. "I musta sprained my wrist when that mule bucked me off." We finds Zeb's laig ain't broke but it is shore bruised up a plenty. We all manages to git to supper. And the boss tells us how it happened. He sez, "We found a bad place in the fence and it kep' us later than we figgered. We was cuttin' across to the road and the mules kep spookin' at shadders on the ground. Well, they come to a place and stopped and I give 'em a lick with the whip. It wasn't no shadder aytall, it was a little arroyer. The mules jumped it but nacherly the spring wagon didn't. It throwed us out over the dash board and the double trees busted. There wasn't no stay straps on and they took out and left us. They took out the way we come and shore nough we found 'em at the gate and rid 'em home. I felt a leetle lame in the shoulder from divin' over the dash board, and am tryin' to git down slow like when Zeb comes to help. That's when the durn mule kicks Zeb in the laig and bucks me off." The Missus she pats him on the head but she sez right wicked like. "Don't you go and worry dear, Everything is a goin' to be all right."

We had company fer dinner next day. Lem Sikes and the sherriff. They was in a two seated buckboard and had two fellers with 'em with handcuffs on. They was the fellers that had traded Lem the mules. Follerin' in a wagon was two big Missourians that the mules had been stolled from and they was there to prove their property, which they shore done. "Did you cash that check?" the boss's wife asts Lem. "Yes," he sez, "And I used the money to pay off some debts in town that had been pressin' me fer quite a spell." 'Stead of gittin' mad she got tickleder than ever. After dinner the sheriff and Lem goes to git the mules. The Sherriff goes in fust and gits crowded agin the stall. Lem yells and jobs the mule with a pitch fork and the mule kicks and hits the fork and hits Lem in the mouth with the handle and cuts his lip plum through and knocks two front teeth out. When we looks things over the sheriff has some ribs broke. The Missourians gits the mules tied to the back of their wagon. One of them is to drive the sherriff's team and Lem rides in the wagon. The sheriff looks at me and sez, "Shorty, seein' yore the only able bodied male citizen here abouts I debatize you to buckle on yore hog laig and ride herd on this bunch as fur as town." I saddles up and strops on my old six shooter. As we was startin' the boss he growls and cusses about havin' to lose more time appearin' in court ag'in them mule thieves, but his wife she puts her arm around him and sez. "Now don't you go and worry dear, Everything is a goin' to be all right.["]

—*Sketched from life by Katherine Field*

THINKIN'

It's an easy job herdin' "Parada." Yore old hoss is standin' close bye.
You are watchin' the drift of the shadders that's made by the clowds in the sky.
There's a breeze blowin' over the mesa. It pulls at the brim of yore hat.
You feel soter careless and lazy, but it sets you to thinkin' at that.

Of the towns where the folks herd together with sidewalks and plenty of light.
They are sheltered and out of the weather, they sleep in a house every night.
There's plenty of good drinkin' water and places to eat night and day.
They live like a man really oughter, you wish you was livin' that way.

You know lots of outfits and bosses but that's jest a cow puncher's chance.
You begin when you're young wranglin' hosses, and wind up a cook at some ranch.
You figger it's really a pity. You've been on the range since a kid.
You would shore like to go to the City, but what could you do if you did?

Your idees git twisted and broken. You reach fer your papers and sack.
You reckon you'll do some more smokin', you turn with the wind to your back.
How things will work out there's no knowin' but the cattle are startin' to stray,
So you'd better git up and be goin' fer thinkin' don't help anyway

7
SHORTY GOES HOME

In November of 1936, after Roosevelt's defeat of Landon in the Presidential election, Kiskaddon probably visited his old home area around Trinidad, Colorado, with the following two thinly veiled autobiographical accounts being the results.

Shorty Goes Home for Armistice Day [1]

Not long after the boss bought the mules, I gets a chance to go up North and I goes. Then along comes that Boer war[2] and we was all tryin' to break and sell all the willer tail hosses in the Western states to the British government. After that I got a chance to go to Australia. I didn't like it so good as the old U. S. A. so I comes back. I drifts into Arizona fer a spell, and then by a fluke I got back East.

By that time the war is on and I lies five years about my age and enlists. When I gets back home I lands a job in town and so I ain't never seen the old ranch or the boss nor Bill since thirty-seven years ago. On the way back to my apartment I sees a gasoline ad with the pitcher of a cowboy on it, and when I turns I looks in at a show window that has a mirror in it. It makes me jump. Would anybody ever think that the little gray headed man with specs on had ever been a cow hand? Hardly. The next mornin' I goes to work and there is pitchers of Roosevelt and Landon everywhere jest like Bryan and McKinly used to be.[3] That settles it. I went to the manager and told him that I wanted six weeks off startin' election day. He looks at me and sez. "You been with us about twelve years and it's tellin' on you. Yes, but be sure and be back when the time is up. Where will you go?"

I tells him. "That's right, you go out there and git some of that western air," he sez. Well, I votes and then I starts out. I meets a lot of friendly folks along the way and it is a nice trip for I take my time and visit as I go because I got a lot of time to make it out home by Armistice day[4] and that is when I aim to git there. When I git out to the old short grass country I remember what the boys said about plowin' it up, and they was about right.[5] It shore made me feel bad. One thing I could see and that was that the old days was over and no mistake. I stops at an auto camp jest outside the old town the night before Armistice day fer I aim to go in next day. In the mornin' I drives in. There is a garage where the old livery stable used to be so I parks in there and goes out and takes a look around the old county seat. Things has changed a lot. No kids ridin' bur-ros on the street. No hosses tied around, jest cars. There is a sort of department store built where the old saloon used to stand. There is a movin' pitcher show in the opry house where Bill fought the Mask Marble, and there is a new depot too. The old jail and courthouse is like they always was. Nobody gives me a second look fer strangers is plenty. Lots of highway travel.

I goes into a bar room and takes a beer to soter clear my throat, then I asks him if he knows a feller by the name of Bill Bascomb. "Shore, him and Eph Lathrop is up at the jail now," he sez. That was enough. I goes right up to the sheriff's office. There is a right purty young lady there at the desk. Is Eph Lathrop and Bill Bascomb here? I asks. She sez they are. What's the charges and what's the chance of gettin' 'em out? I wants to know.

She smiles and a sassy dimple comes in her cheek and she sez. "Well, there ain't much chance. Mr. Bascomb has just been elected sheriff fer his third term and as long as he is in office Mr. Lathrop will be his chief deputy."

That shore knocks the props out from under me. She presses a button and in comes a big fat feller that could jest about ride in a wagon box let alone top a bronk. I looks at him careful and then I know it is Bill. He looks friendly but careful like at me and then he asks, "What can I do fer you?" right dignified. Well, I sez, I'd be right pleased if you would put on that there dance like you done in the paster with the willer breshes, accompanied by the two dogs. It would shore show off that girlish figger of yourn. He looks at me a minute and then he sez, "Well, there ain't no more tobacker Injuns fer you to tie crazy colts to, and if you rode a half broke hoss into town I'll throw you in right now.[6] But frum the looks of things you would do about as well on a bronc as I would on a dance."

Then he hollers, "Oh Eph!" Eph knows me right now and he wants to know where I been and how come I got back after all these years. So I tell him that I allowed to come back and spend Armistice day with him and Bill or whoever I could find of the old gang. I told Bill I knowed he would be in it seein' he was in the old Spanish war. "Yes," sez Bill, "I was in it but this time I got in with a engineer outfit and we was away down in south France. We was loggin' out turpentine pine to use fer timber and cor-duroy roads. We had a onery little drunken cuss along that shore put me in mind of you. He had been a cow puncher in civil life. That is if he ever was civil. Well the sta-ble sargent is from Montana and he gits this little varmint to day herd all the convales-cent stock out on the forest reserve while the grass is high. He did so well that he makes a night hawk out of him and puts work stock and all out at nights."

"Well, one night this here little devil is confined to quarters for some cussedness or nother and they sends a couple of other men out with the stock. That night come a storm and scattered the herd and we ain't got the half of them by noon the next day.

The top cutter knows I've been a cow hand so he gets the little cuss out of quarters and tells us to saddle up and git them hosses. This wrangler goes to the boys and finds where they had a bunch when the storm hits. He saddles up a big awkward lookin' bay and we starts off. I had heard he knowed hosses but it looked like he shore had picked a pore mount. We got to where the herd had been and he looks around at the ground and grass and ferns."

"He grinned and sez. 'The luck is shore with us.' We hadn't gone far when that crazy hoss of hisn begun to snuff and nicker and go toward a bunch of timber. [Shorenough], there was some of the strays. He started me along the track of the storm and he trotted back and forth like a bird dog. Purty soon I hears that hoss ag'in, and we gits another bunch. As soon as he throws 'em to me he starts off in a long trot. Settin' loose and easy over his long stirrups. We eats supper on time and has all the work stock besides some Frog stock that we had to cut back.

"'That little drunken cuss is a wonder,' sez the captain. Well, I sez, he knows hosses. He knows they don't drift ag'in a storm. That big puddin footed hoss he rode was a hoss fool and will run squallin and nickerin' to any hosses he can find. The wind had turned and was blowin' right back frum where it blowed durin' the storm. It was made fer him and the hoss he was a ridin'."

"The captain looks at me and sez real polite like, 'I suppose the wind and weather was different for the other man, anyway he got the stock.'[7] That made me mad but what can you do in the army?"

That's right I sez. "What do you know about it ?" Bill asks.

Well I sez I was there. I lied five years about my age and I got in with no previous service. Besides they wasn't so partickler about the weight and height as they was in the Spanish war. Yessir but the funniest thing happened to me was the time I got the shoes.

"What shoes?" Eph asks. Well, I sez you see it was like this. We had got outfitted with a bunch of salvage stuff and there wasn't a pair of shoes in the whole issue that was smaller than a seven and you know I wear a five. I put in a extra pair of salvage socks to sort of fill them out and got by the best I could.

Well, one day I gits a pass and hikes down to the little village near camp and starts to take on a little of the old Vin Blink.[8] At the same table is settin' a awful neat lookin' soldier and I knows on sight he is a dog robber.[9] He is drunk enough to talk and the little feller tells me that he is the Colonel's orderly. We git up for a couple more bottles when the old demmy leiter[10] is run dry and I see that he has on a new pair of russet leather shoes and they are number fives. Right then I gits a idea. He has a good start and I figger that few fellers my size can give me a start and drink me down. Besides he is about fifteen years less experienced in the ways of the wicked world. I am still goin' good when he begins to fade out. I gits him out the back door and sets him up ag'in the wheel of a old cart in the shed and takes his shoes off. I tries 'em on and they fit perfect.

Well, I swaps with him and puts mine on him and sticks the extra socks in his belt so he can do as he likes about usin' 'em.

That is about the most terrible deed I done in France.

Bill and Eph gits tickled, and worse tickled than what I expected. We gits out the bottle and has a drink and then Bill leaves Eph in the office and takes me out to scare up some old friends. The first place we stop is a shoe store.

"Do you know this here runt?" Bill asks of the feller that runs the store.

The little cuss looks me over right careful, and I do him, and then I know who he is. "If he wasn't so gray and wore specs," sez the store keeper, "I'd swear that he was the durn mule skinner I told you about that stoled my shoes in France."

Well, son, I sez, I am him and I have went gray headed jest a worryin' over that there crime. But seein' you got a whole house full of shoes now I reckon you ain't a sufferin' none.

He laffs and reckons I must have got his mind started on the shoe business. He calls to his clerk that he is goin' to be out fer a little bit and to watch the store.

"We will take him over to your aunt's and show her this here villyun that stoled your shoes on a cold and stormy day in a furrin land," sez Bill.

Shorty Finishes His Visit [11]

We knocked around that day and I did get track of a few old-timers. But every time I asked about somebody, Bill or Eph would say, "Let me see! He died jest after we got the ditch changed or after we got the road built." It got under my hide so bad that after awhile I was scared to ask any more.

But there was one old lady I shore run foul of, and that was the old man Wilson's granddaughter. Bill took me out to where she was a-runnin' a hot dog stand at the edge of town on the highway. "Do you recollect this here feller?" Bill asks. She looks at me a minute and then she sez, "Shore I know the scamp. It wasn't enough that he throwed walnuts on the dance hall steps and made my uncle bust his tail bone so it bothered him all the rest of his life, but he has to go and steal the shoes right offen my nephew's feet when he's in a furrin land a-fightin' fur his country." "Oh, yes," I sez, "I can mind when you let two fellers fight over a dance with you till they wrecked the place and broke up the dance. And I mind when the other gals was so jealous that they wouldn't speak to you, that you went and halfway promised to marry three single fellers at one party jest to make 'em bust up with their gals. You wasn't no dove of peace yourself." She made out like I made her mad, but she was tickled pink, and made us stay and have a hot dog and a cup of coffee. She got a big kick out of tellin' us all about the different fellers she had kept company with. She had been a purty gal with a dimple in her chin, but now she had three chins and the dimples seemed to have got sotar discouraged and quit altogether.

The next day Bill allowed I and him was a goin' to the high country. "It won't take long," sez Bill. "It used to take a couple of days to ride it, and now it only takes a couple of hours to drive it." We took Bill's big car and throwed in some skid chains for fear it might snow. Things was changed along the road and it made me feel bad, but Bill didn't mind fer he had got used to it gradual. But when we rounded the turn into the little old mountain town I was so tickled I wanted to bawl. It had changed less than any thing. There was quite a few of the old boys still livin' there, but we only saw three or four of them. Old Mac was still runnin' the pool room. He took me back into a store room and turned on the light. They had electricity even up there now, and took some tarp and an old blanket off from sumthin'. We looked and then Bill busts out laffin'. It was the cigar Injun I had tied my bronc to forty years ago. It had been fixed and pieced back together again. He had kept it up in front till about ten years back. "It brought me more trade than it did before it was busted up," sez Mac. "Everybody wanted to know how it got busted up and I would tell them. Finally there got to be so many stories about it that I give up and put it away. But I would shore like to see you two fellers try to make the run you did down the street now."

We both felt homesick when we left the old place and we talked a heap about folks and places on the way back to town. Bill had some work to ketch up on and I went to the little pitcher show where the old opray house used to be.

The next day I told the boys that I aimed to take my field glasses and drive down to the old ranch and have a look at the valley frum the top of lone tree butte if I can git there fer the fences. "You can make it all right," sez Bill. "You will be up there with Lem Sikes." "What's he a doin' up there?" I wants to know. "He's a restin'," sez Bill. "Did he ever do anything else?" I asks. "Well," sez Bill, "there's them that thinks so. You see, when the war was on and everybody was dyin' off with the flu like flies,[12] Lem hung up quite a record. Lots of the folks was sick at the same time and a lot of the young fellers was away in the army. Folks got to where they couldn't take care of their selves or their stock or their neighbors. Like usual, Lem didn't have no work of his own partickler, so he lit in to help Old Doc Preston and all neighbors. He was everywhere in that old flivver of hisn with the brassbound radiator. Nobody knowed when he et or slept, fer he jest kep a goin' all the time, and he was shore a life saver to a lot of folks. Well, jest about the time the rest got well Lem took down, and when old Doc Preston come to see him Lem sez, "Well, Doc, jest like always, I'm away behind the whole settlement even with the flu. The rest is all either dead or well, and here I am only startin' in. I always was slow and careless like that, but it don't make no difference now, fer I ain't a goin' to pull through no how." Old Doc tries to cheer him up, but he caint fool old Lem. He knows he's due to cross the big divide. "Doc," sez Lem, "I'm soter glad I'm a goin'. I've rested a heap in my life but no ways near as much as I would like to a done. I hope Judgment Day don't come too soon or I'll still be tired when the horn blows. This last six weeks has plum wore me out. Now, Doc, I wisht we could talk folks into buryin' me up on lone tree butte. There won't be no alfalfy nor irrigatin' up there, and it will be fur enough away that I won't hear them mowin' machines a goin'. That hay harvestin' is plum tiresome even to listen to. And then, besides, Doc, if I git sent to Heaven I'll be that much further up the road. And if I git sent to hell I'll have a down hill start, which is quite a savin' on a man at that."

"Pore old Lem. He never took nothin' serious; not even hisself. But Doc and all the valley didn't call him no joke at the finish. They all went [together] and made him a grave up there like he sed and made a big marble monument with readin' about him on it. So you see you and Lem can have the butte all to yourselves and you can rest assured that fer the fust time in yore life, Lem will be there but won't try to trade hosses with you." When I went to the old ranch I went alone. I went up onto the butte and copied the stuff they had wrote on the monument about Lem, and looked out over the country with my glasses. How everything had changed. I drove around for a few hours. It didn't take long to get about the country in a car. Then I went to the old ranch itself. They had put up new buildin's and the old ones was a wreck. So I prowled around in the old bunk house. They was usin' it fer a calf stable. I looked and felt in the places in onder the eaves between the rafters where we used to put small stuff that we wanted to keep. All I found was a salve box. By bein' careful I got the dust and dirt off from it without spoilin' the label. I was soter dim but you could read it all right. It was the last box of that Tiger Fat that Bill had bought from the medicine man. Guaranteed to restore youth. Cure baldness, stiff joints, and otherwise recondition any man in need of repairs.

Well, I stays till I see the sun go down behind the mountain and then I goes up to town and packs up and goes to Bill's office. It was a little late but he was still there with Eph. I sez [goodbye] to them and then I hands him the box of Tiger Fat. "Here is sumpthin' I found under the eaves of the old bunk house," I sez. "I reckon you need it a heap more now than you did when you bought it off the Medicine Man." They look at that box and then they shore do laff. I shakes hands and starts. Eph calls after me, "You got the same Idee you allus had. Allus leave 'em laffin' when you say goodbye." I stopped fer a lunch with Old Wilson's granddaughter at the edge of town and then I heads the old car East and sets her at fifty an hour because I don't like to say goodbye myself.

All Dressed Up

Things is pickin' up as most folks knows,
So I sent to town fer to git new clo'es.
Some onderwear and a big hat box,
A couple of shirts and a passel of socks.

Some overalls and other truck,
Three red bamdannys throwed in fer luck.
My boots ain't new but they'll do right well.
I reckon I'll make them last a spell.

I'll be the pride of the whole derned spread
With a fust class Stetson on my head.
A bran new slicker tied on behind –
It's strange how your clo'es improves yore mind.

Nice new clo'es purtects the hide
And soter contents a man inside.
Clo'es does a heap toward makin' the man.
Try goin' without and you'll onderstand.

8
Introducing Ike

Shorty Meets Some Missourians [1]

Jest when the Boer war was on Folks got to shippin' hosses a plenty. I had left the old man's place and I went to work fer a feller that had a bunch of broom tails and they was a snaky lot. Some of 'em was old mares that hadn't looked through a rope since the day they was branded. Along comes a big old Missourian and we rounds up a bunch fer him to look over. He takes two car loads of raw hosses and mares. The Boss sends me along to help him ship 'em and git 'em located on his farm down in Missouri. We made it all right but it was hard on the hosses seein' they didn't know nothin' about eatin' grain and it was a job to git a hay ration that was any good fer 'em all through the trip.

When we got there I was surprised. There was more barns and sheds and corrals. And when it come to kids he had the world cheated. Some of them boys and gals was his and some of 'em was kin folks and some jest visitors that had drifted in. Sort of dismounted grub line riders.[2] He had a good corral and chute built but the first day we used the chute a kid got his foot kicked while he was standin' on the side and another got his arm broke when he was stickin' it through a crack, so he made the boys tear the chute out and it didn't take long, seein' there was so many of 'em.

He sez we will let the boys ride the broncs with the harness on and git 'em used to being rode and led and to the harness all at the same time. I gits a laff out of that fer I figgers it will be a heap of fun to see them boys bucked over the corral fence. But I was to learn sumpthin'. He had a lot of big gentle teams and he gits out all the harness on the place and harnesses up six big stout work mares and hosses and tells me to rope a bronc. I front foots one and them fellers was on him by the time he hit the ground. They puts a big tug leather halter on him and blindfolds him. Then they grabs his nose and makes him git up. Then they leads a work hoss up and ties the bronc to the hame of the work hoss's harness short. Jest room enough to handle him. They wallered him around and got a set of harness on him and it didn't take long either. Then they pulled the blind off. Them broncs could try anything they wanted to because the old harness was on tight and tied down and them big old work hosses jest walked around with 'em like nothin' aytall. The next thing one kid got on the work hoss and another on the bronc, and started out. We had a lot of 'em goin' sooner than a feller might think. Say, after they had been harnessed and wooled and drug and rode about twice they was ready to hitch up to a wagon tied to big old work hosses and was broke and workin' before they knowed it. The kids was havin' the time of their life and the farm hands joined in, and the fun of it was that the old farmer was gettin' the bulk of that work done without payin' wages.

Then, one day when he was gettin' near through with it along comes a lightnin' rod man and stops fer dinner. He is goin' to sell the farmer lightnin' rods enough to purtect his whole spread from lightnin'. The old man listens all the time and don't say nothin'. All the crowd keeps still too and listens, and they got their eye on the old man. The oldest gal and one of the hands tells me to keep my eye on the old man fer there is goin' to be some fun. They caint tell just what, but they aint never seen the old man stumped yet.

After our dinner has settled the old man gits a old pocket revolver off a kitchen shelf and loads it up and asks the lightnin' rod man to help him try the gun. He leans a old end gate rod up agin a solid board gate and they both tries several shots at it. Then the old man sez, "We never hit the rod wunst, but we hit the gate ever time." "That's right," sez the lightnin' rod man. "Well,["] sez the old farmer, "Figger it out fer yourself. The buildin's covers ten thousand times as much ground as the lightnin' rods and what a fool I'd be to think the lightnin' would miss ever thing else and hit a few steel rods because I had stuck 'em up there fer that purpose." The boys laffs fit to split, but the lightnin' rod man aint stumped yit. "Well, Mister," he sez, "you see the rod draws lightnin' and that's what makes it hit the rod instead of the buildin'." "That's figger'n by the margin of a inch," sez the farmer, "and that is a mighty close shot at so long a range, seein' the lightnin' has to come frum the sky plum to here. Tell you a better plan. You go to Job Higgins's place, that's the next place down the road, and sell 'em to Job. Seein' they draw lightnin' it will hit on his place 'stead of mine. All right, boys, hitch up the gentleman's team fer him and then we will git to work and finish up this here wild west show so Shorty can git back home. His Boss is likely waitin' fer him way out there where there is a heap more wild hosses to break and where the roosters lives on rattle snakes and the little baby chickens is raised up on tirantalars."

Well we finishes up the job in a couple more days, but what little I had learnt about breakin' hosses their way was nothin' to what I think of Missourians. I tells him this. They are a heap different in their ways frum what we are. They go in droves. They shore consume a heap of grub and likker and tobacker per head. But they are the friendliest most liberal folks you can meet. And when it comes to doin' things they shore go into action and git results a plenty.

Shorty Meets a Fool for Luck [3]

Oncet I got down into Arizona fer a spell and was a lookin' about fer a job, when a feller comes a ridin' into town, and I has a hunch that he means sumpthin' to me only

I don't jest know how. He is on a good hoss, but his outfit makes me look twice. He had everything on and along that a cow puncher don't need. Of all the fixin's and flummygoes he was a wearin' what took my eye most was a pair of leather cuffs that reached a most to his elbows and was all fixed with studs and rivets till it looked like they weighed a couple of pounds apiece.

He was a friendly cuss and we had a couple of drinks together then he tells me that his boss has sent him to town fer another hand. The bar keep and a few other folks tells me that this here feller is on the level and that his boss is a good feller to work fer, so I strings along with him.

When I git there I find a funny spread. The owner is a man that has come from the East with a heap of money and he works different to what I am used to but all the same he is a makin' money. He uses a heap more fence and feed than I was used to but I can see a heap of sense in his ways. The feller that had fetched me out from town was Ike Fenner and he would have had trouble workin' fer most old timers, but he suited this man. This boss seemed to have a lot of learnin' and he talked plum funny. He called Ike Isaac, and he kep him around because he was lucky. And I will say this. Ike was a fool fer luck. One day the boss tells me that Ike had gone out in clowdy weather and got lost. It was three days before he got back in and he was about all in. He had trapped a fresh hoss at a water hole corral and while he was a doin' that he got his bearin's but what meant more, while he was lost he had found some pretty good ore. He took the Boss along and back tracked till they found the ore and he cut the boss in on half of it. The boss in his turn sold it and put Ike's share in bonds where it would be safe, and Ike was in purty good shape as far as money went. It seems that some lady went in to git acquainted with Ike right after he found his mine but the boss got a feller to show her some fake papers on the sly and made her believe that Ike only got a hundred and fifty dollars fer his share. Ike was a fool fer luck. God had his arm around him all the time.

Well one day there was a little circus come to the town and the boss allows me and Ike can go to the show and then bring some stuff to the ranch the next day. We takes the wagon and goes to town and that evenin' in rides the boss horseback. When we gits ready to go home Ike is purty drunk and he is all stirred up about a snake charmer he has seen in one of the side shows. The boss aint much of a saddle man so he tells Ike to ride his hoss and he will go in the wagon with me. Ike is shore drunk and he musta had a small bottle on him fer it looked like mebby he'd ride all the way, and then ag'in it looked like mebby he mightn't. We was about half way when Ike slides off his hoss and gits down on his haunches and waddles around like a walkin' toad. He is makin' his arms wave. We was loaded heavy and the team couldn't run up hill. Take the lines quick! I hollers to the boss and grabs the whip and starts a runnin' fer Ike fer I knowed he was a doin' the snake charmer act and I knowed by the way the hoss was a actin' that he was a foolin' with a shore 'nough rattle snake. Ike was so drunk that when he balanced to make the forrud bow he lost his balance and set down backwards. That give me some time but before I could make it he was up ag'in on his knees and he raises his hands and fetches 'em down in the magic slam. That there snake strikes and I hear him hit. I runs up and kills the snake with the whip and Ike has started to squeal high and mournful like the snake charmer music. "Don't hurt my snake. I'm a charmin' him." he sez. By that time the boss has jumped out of the wagon and has run to help. "Is he bit?" he asks. The snake hit him, I sez. I heered it thump. Look at his hands and arms. He was a tryin' to do the snake charm act. We looks and there on his leather cuffs was the mark. The fangs had hit one on a bright rivet and one on the leather. It was most up to the elbow and with any common leather cuff he would have been bit, but them big fool cuffs saved his life.

The boss laughs and sez, "Those things are foolish and exaggerated but they saved his life. When he found that ore he put samples in his saddle pockets and I guess he is the only cow boy that has carried saddle pockets for the last thirty years. Yes, Isaac is an extremely fortunate person." He's a fool fer luck if that's what you mean, I sez.

Shorty Hears Ike Analyse Words [4]

There was four fellers a workin' at the place besides me and Ike. We had gathered the beef and shipped it. The feeders was in and to the rack and things had settled down fer the winter. We had a lot of fun about Ike a tryin' to charm the rattle snake, but the joke got stale and we hadn't no amusement in particklar.

The boss didn't have no man cook, but had a family at the place. The woman was a doin' the cookin' and the man was a makin' a hand on the ranch. The kids was a doin' jest what kids always does. Makin' you laff at 'em one day and makin' you want to kill 'em the next.

Then the school marm come to board at the place. The Boss didn't like it a bit. Fust off she had to have a gentle hoss to ride to school and the Boss didn't care to have a old pet hoss tied up to a post at the school house all day. Then too you couldn't git nothin' done till she got started to school in the mornin'. All the fellers includin' the boardin' boss would hang around and hep her saddle up and open and shet the gate and talk and giggle till it was a costin' the Boss a heap in time and he allowed to me and Bill wunst that he reckoned if things kep on he would have to put on a extra hand to keep things a goin' till school let loose on the follerin' spring. Then there was so many fellers that found excuse to stop at the ranch fer supper and stay fer breakfast that the board-in' missus didn't make nothin' out of it neither. The boardin' missus had gone ag'in the Boss's talk when she took the school marm in, so the Boss in a sly way he jest kep a steerin' all the strays in to the place to soter have a look at the gal and there went the profit fer the boardin' missus.

She was young and not hard to look at and I liked to see her around seein' it ain't botherin' me none and it keeps things stirred up and interestin'. She shore hates the Boss and Ike, and is free to tell every body how things ort to be done and sed. The oldest little gal in the boardin' family was Mollie, and she was purty and smart. Her teacher might tell her about doin' her lessons but she couldn't tell her where to pick her friends, and Little Mollie jest worshipped Ike and he shore petted her and give her presents till she was the wust spoilt ten year old kid ever was and even the Boss wasn't above talkin' some with her.

One night at supper she busts out. "Say Ike, what is a sub normal?" The school marm sez, "Mollie you're excused frum the table." But the Boss sez friendly like, "You stay right here Mollie and finish your supper, and what was it you wanted Isaac to tell you?" The school marm froze to her chair and turned forty colors if there is that many. "About what a sub normal is," sez Mollie. The Boss has the face he wears in a poker game and I see Ike is wakin' up like he knows he is in a corner. "Jest how was that word used, Mollie?" Ike asks. Little Mollie blushes and chokes but she is game. "Well Ike, the teacher told us today that some of us was associatin' too much with cow boys and that it was bad fer us because cow boys was a onder paid sub normal lot of men."

"Well we can soon clear that up," sez Ike. "Cow boys is onder paid because they are so val'able that nobody could pay them what they are really wuth. It couldn't be done and make a profit. Now this here sub normal affair is like this. Normal folks is folks that is all right in the head jest like folks ort to be. Well now you know there is a normal school kep by the state. It is kep fer folks that aint normal. They have to go there till they git normal ag'in. Take school teachers, fer instance. Most of 'em has to go there fer a spell every year till they gits their mental balance so to speak. Now cow hands doesn't haf to do that. All they haf to do is what you might call a sub normal. That means, generally speakin', they don't haf to go to school no more but jest git set right on a idee now and then by lookin' in the catalogue or readin' a news paper."

Well, that was sure a hard one to beat, and the school marm she don't even try to come back but runs out and leaves Ike with it. The Boss he don't say nothin' but them English cut whiskers of hisen is sure curled a little and his eyes is jest a poppin'. And he lent over and give Mollie a second helpin' of desert.

Next mornin' the school marm she leaks out frum there on foot with no breakfast before any body can stop her. The kids comes home and sez that she has turned school loose and told them to come back next day. We was jest a finishin' dinner when in rides old Miss Gaynor and her two big boys and she sez they come fer the teacher's things, and bein' a sassy old hen she starts in to tell the Boss sumpthin' but he won't pay no attention. The boardin' missus butts right in and sez, "All right Miss Gaynor, jest come in and take her stuff and that's all that yore asked fer. She took her funny idees with her and you keep yourn to yerself. Her and you will git to know one another 'fore school's out. It'll shore be a eddication fer ye both."

While this is a goin' on I looks out and sees the biggest boy foolin' around Ike's saddle. Ike had saddled a little brown hoss called Toby, jest before he come in fer dinner. The boy snuck away and back to the wagon when he see me a lookin'. Well, the Gaynors was loaded up and gone mighty soon and we went out to work ag'in. Tommy, one of the boys that is feedin' wants to open a paster gate and he asks Ike fer his hoss. Tommy shore does like to git up on that big fancy saddle of Ike's. Ike tells him to watch Toby. He is skittish but don't buck, only he might jump frum onder a feller that ain't watchin'. Tommy steps on him and he squats and jumps a couple of times and then he shore does buck and he throws Tommy hard into a pile of posts and breaks his collar bone. The Boss is shore mad. He walks over and gits Toby quiet and then he on-saddles. There shore 'nough is a big cuckle burr onder the saddle blanket. I tells him about that big Gaynor boy bein' around that hoss. "That's where the burr come frum," sez the Boss. "He was after Isaac and he got Tommy by mistake. Well, as I have always said, Isaac is an extremely fortunate person."

The Boss Buys a Mare [5]

The boss has a great big mare that he works around the ranch but he ain't got nothin' to mate up with that big animal and make a real team, so he allows he will go up to town and see if he cain't match her up because old man Marker that runs the Dobe Feed and Sale Corrals has sent him word that he has got in a lot of big stock and to come up and see what he can do.

Now the Old Man Marker is a pizen old reptile that is as crooked as a barrel of snakes and he is a brother-in-law to Old Squire Bane. Him and Bane does a lot of funny stuff and anytime there is a law suit Marker tries to git it tried before Bane and then he has it all his own way. The Boss takes the wagon and the big mare hitched up with an old work hoss and he sez me and Ike had as well go along. He sees to it that Ike ain't got a gun on him since the trouble he had[6] but he don't watch me and I feel a heap better when I slip my old single action Colt in onder my shirt.

Shore enough Old Marker has a big mare that is young and most as big as the one we got. But there is a freighter has pulled in and he has a big mare that he will sell. She is as good or better than Marker's only she is pore and worked down purty bad, while Marker's mare is in top condition. The freighter hitches up his mare and of course she works perfect, bein' right out of the team. But Marker is a little skittish about hitchin' his mare up and tryin' her out. Me and Ike is fer buyin' the freighter's mare but the Boss is like a lot of folks, he likes a hoss that is fat and high headed. So he sez to Marker, "If you guarantee that mare to pull I'll give you yore price." By that time Old Squire Bane and a couple more fellers has joined up with the crowd and him and Marker has a talk. Then Marker sez, "Tell you what I'll do. Here is Squire Bane hisself. You put the price of the mare in his hands and I'll put ten dollars with it. If the mare don't pull every time I tell her to, I'll give you yore money back and the ten dollars along with it." Me and Ike tried to git a word with the Boss and stop him but it ain't no use and before we knows it old Bane has the money. We got the mare hitched up but when the Boss goes to start her she throws her head across the other mare and does a purty stroke of balkin' as you ever seen. "I guess the deal's off," the Boss sez. "That mare's balky." "The deal stands," sez Marker. "How come?" asks the Boss plum white and mad. "I sed she'd pull every time I told her to," sez Marker. And I ain't told her to. Not yit." "Here, give me that money," the Boss sez to the Squire. "Listen," sez the Squire real high chinned like. "At least a dozen men here heard the terms of the agreement and as long as Mr. Marker does not tell the mare to pull, the deal will stand in any court." Old Marker grins and so does the Squire and the two fellers with him. "Got yore gun, Shorty?" Ike asks. "Shore," I sez. Ike grabs a heavy quirt off a saddle that is layin' handy, and he grabs Old Marker with the other hand. "You tell that mare to pull," sez Ike. Marker starts to argue but Ike don't. Them fellers might know all about hoss tradin' but they didn't know a lot about cowboys. Ike jerks old Marker onto all fours and jumps straddle of his neck and grips with his legs, then he grabs him by the belt and turns him up and starts to whale the pants offen him with that raw-hide quirt. "Tell her to pull. Tell her to pull," he keeps a sayin'. "Stop in the name of the law!" yells the Squire, and him and the other two fellers makes a move but I throw down on 'em with the old forty-five. "Keep out of it," I sez. "We'll take care of our own outfit, law or no law.["] By that time Ike has most whipped all the lower end offen old Marker and he yells, "Stop! Fer Gawd's sake stop! I'll tell her to pull! I'll tell her to pull!"

Ike lets up on him but he still holds him by the collar. "Go ahead and tell her," sez Ike. "Giddap Lucy. Giddap Lucy," wails old Marker, but the mare still balks. Old Squire starts to walk away but I pokes him in the ribs with the old hog laig. "If you was thinkin' of takin' a walk fer yore health,["] I sez, "it might be a heap healthier to stand still and give Ike that there cash money, seein' the Boss has his hands full with that there team.["] Old Marker starts fer his office but knowin' he has a Winchester there, I throw down on him and make him come back and the Squire has to shell out the money.

About that time the town marshall lands on the scene and wants to know what the ruckus is about. The Squire tells him but we have to check up on him and make him stick to the truth several times. "Well," sez the old marshall, "the idee seems to be that the mare was supposed to pull and her and Marker here both balked. You fellers got yore money, now give him back his mare and Shorty you give that shootin' iron of yourn to yore Boss. You might git too previous with it." "Jest a minute. Not so fast," sez the Squire. "I know the law and what the terms of a contract means and this affair is not legal in no way." "You got some cute idees," sez the marshall. "If you don't take in yore horns around this here town some feller is liable to turn you wrong end up and set yore pants afire, and mebbyso change yore opinion of a lot of things, includin' yoreself. Now you fellers git yore outfit out frum this corral and consider this here affair plum settled." Well, we onhitched Lucy and got out frum there and then the boss bought the freighter's mare. The next day I was watchin' one of the ranch hands workin' the team and I sez, "That is shore a fine mare and when she rests and fattens she'll be as big as the other one.["] "Yes," sez the Boss absent minded like, "Isaac is a wonderful person to have around."

He Was After a Road Runner [7]

The road runner discussion in Mr. King's column[8] made me think of a little affair that happened long ago. A road runner played a part. I have been told that the road runner was a misunderstood bird. In this case it was the road runner that made the people misunderstand each other.

So, if you will let me get away from Ike and Shorty for one issue, I would like to tell the story. I have changed all the names of people and I won't name the little town. No need to, you can all remember a dozen towns like that. A depot, a pump house, two stores, a couple of saloons, a pool room, a blacksmith shop, a livery stable, an upstairs opray house, and a shingle roof 'dobe church.

I had gone to town one Sunday, and about three o'clock I had started for home. I was too young to be allowed in on the Sunday amusements of a town that size so I was tired of it. Four blocks one way and you were out into the pinons. Four blocks the other way and you were out into the sage brush flats along the creek. When I got near the edge of town, I saw a couple of old folks I knew settin' in the shade of their house on the door step. They were great friends of my Father and Mother and of course the old man called me to "Git down and look at my saddle." I slid off old Snip and wrapped one rein around the hitchin' post and went in and joined them. They wanted to know if I had seen Bob down town and I told them no. Bob was their son. He was about twenty-five years old and made his home with the old folks. We got through with what little gossip we knew and the old folks had settled down to the usual subject of tooth ache and rheumetiz, which I know more about now than I did then, when a man came along the street. You could tell he was from the East. He wore a straw hat and one of them little summer weight coats, and had on tan low cut shoes. The Old Lady remarks. "Why Mr. Thompson is gettin' home early fer a Sunday. He mostly stays out late of a Sunday. Him and her don't git along no way and it's shore a pity fer he has such a purty wife. He's here fer his health and I don't see how he holds his job at the store. Him a goin' on like he does." The Old Man tried to change the subject, and by that time Mr. Thompson was goin' into his house. About a minute later Bob come in the back door and joined us settin' just inside the door.

"Where was you son?" his mother asks. "Oh, I was down at Joe's playin' draw pitch with the boys." Bob sez. She remarked right off that I said I hadn't seen him down town. The Old Man tried to change the subject again and I said that I hadn't looked in at Joes very close on account he didn't like to have kids in the bar room. The Old Man give Bob a hard look and said real mean like, "Well son if it makes you pant like that to play draw pitch, you better not take up foot ball. That's all I gotta say." Right then I saw a road runner come dippin' along the little dusty street. Out at the door comes Thompson with a double barreled shot gun. I was the only one that had seen the road runner. "What's that man fixin' to shoot at?" she asks. The house shook as Bob went out at the back door. The Old Man started to git up. That road runner, I sez pointin' to the bird. The Old Man sets down and lets out a long breath. "My Lord where did Bob go?" The Old Lady asks. Well, I sez, unless it's a long ways from here he'd orta be there by now. Then I remarked that I had forgot to git Dad's tobacker and had to go back down town. Thompson chased the road runner but couldn't git within gun shot of him and the bird got out of sight on the flats. I go out and git on old Snip and start down the street on a slow walk. I figgered Bob wouldn't try to leave town till after dark and if I could find him and sort of explain things it would save him a heap of trouble.

I mopes along past the depot, but the fellers settin' on the platform looked like they hadn't moved in two hours. I looks in at the livery stable door as I goes by, but them fellers had been there a long time fer their sticks was purty well whittled down and one of them was reachin' fer a big shavin' to cut on. No body had changed places much at Joe's. There was four Mexicans playin' at the pool room and the rest of the gang was loafin' like they had been so I could see he wasn't in there. Then, I happened to think. Him and the hotel man was great friends. I goes to the hotel and shore enough the hotel man was out at the desk in place of the card game in the side room. I asks fer Bob and he sez he ain't seen him. Well, I sez, if you do happen to see him tell him I got a right important word for him. The hotel man tells me to wait a minute and he might see somebody that could wise me up as to where Bob was. He goes out the back way and purty soon comes down the front stairs. "You might go up to room thirty-five," he tells me. "Likely you can git track of him there." I goes up and knocks. Bob comes to the door. I goes in and I sez. There ain't nothin' to be scairt of Bob. That feller with the shot gun was a tryin' to shoot a road runner. I seen the bird all the time and if you had waited a couple of seconds you would a seen him too. "You shore of that?" he asks. Shore I sez. He flopped into a chair and let out about the biggest sigh of relief that ever come from a human stummick.

As I said on the beginnin', this ain't no part of the road runner discussion, but it proves that at times the road runner can be a mighty misunderstood bird.

Shorty and Ike Meet the Boss's Nephews [9]

One day the boss gits a telegram and he looks awful worried. We try and figger it out but no chance. Things git to lookin' funny. Petersons, the family that is boardin' the hands, they moves down to the lower place and the boss takes the crew down there and starts to buildin' a reservoir. He leaves two hands to irrigate and me and Ike at the home place. Old Anton is doin' our cookin'. Then the boss has a talk with me and Ike. He tells us that his sister and her husband is a comin' to be at the ranch. He don't know how long. He braces himself and then lets out the news. They got a pair of twin boys twelve years old. He sez he will have to be away fer a spell and fer me and Ike and the two irrigaters to do the best we can till he gits back.

He goes down to the lower place with Petersons and starts some place frum there. Me and Ike flip to see which one of us has to go to town for the visitors. Of course Ike wins, bein' lucky always. So I git the mule team and a wagon and start fer town the next day. I camp at the wagon yard over night and the next mornin' I am ready when the train pulls in. A few local passengers gits off and then I sees my party. No wonder the boss run. The sister lights first, then the twins, and then the husband. The husband is a skinny lookin' worried man; the twins is all feet and ears except they have mouths as big as the average bull dog. But the woman—she has her nose glasses set on tight and is raired back plum hostile. I have an extra spring seat and I get them loaded in. I put their two big trunks in the back and I figger the kids can ride there but that won't do. The old man gits in with me and the old lady and the two kids gets in the other seat. "Where is Brother Charles?" she wants to know. He had to be away, I sez. "Wait till I see him," she sez real cuttin' like, "he will hear from me. He could at least have sent the carriage for us and let one of the hired help bring our trunks in this old wagon." I don't say nothin' fer I know it will be some distance before she gits a chance to tell the boss anything. The boys each got a twenty-two rifle and they keep wantin' me to stop so they can shoot at a prairie dog or a picket pin weasel. They always run out to where the varmints was and declare they killed him but he got down a hole. That takes up a lot of time till one of them gits a foot full of cactus and they keeps the whole passel of 'em busy so I can keep a drivin'. When we get to the ranch it is dark. Anton has supper ready, and they are all about ready to go to bed. But supper is jest over when some coyotes starts to holler. The boys want to go out and kill them and won't listen to us when we tell 'em they aint got a chance. Their dad he reckons he ort to go along. That devil Anton loans him his six shooter and the kids git their guns and out at the door they go. They are gone about three minutes and then there is a snarl and a bark and a lot of yellin' and the two twenty-twos go off and so does Anton's gun. Anton he grins and sez, "Old Shep she's make a pretty good coyote, ha?" They comes in all russed up. They had been attacked by wolves. The old man has been dog bit and so has one of the kids and one of the kids has shot the old man in the laig only it jest barked him. Old Shep must have took out when the shootin' begun. The next mornin' they sleep late but was all up and prowlin' around by ten o'clock. I slip in to the house and learn that the kids are named Rodrick and Rodney. Me and Ike calls 'em Kid and Kidney. Their mother tells that she named 'em so much alike because they look alike. Which was true. It was fortunate seein' there was nothin' else that looked like either one of 'em and if they had-n't been twins they would have been lonesome. The old man had about give up the coyote idee and had begun to ask where was the best place to prospect fer gold seein' he might jest open up a gold mine to pay expenses while he was out there or sumpthin' like that. But the old lady she said she had promised the boys some wild animal skins fer their den and aimed that they should have 'em. Ike suggested Jack rabbit hides but that don't seem to please 'em. They soon got over the ruckus they had with Old Shep and was ready to try fer coyotes ag'in. The old lady sez we ort to trap some fer she knows there is at least a hundred around the place every night. Ike tells her that he has a bait in the top of a soap weed out in the little calf paster which is empty and that there is three traps around it and he might git one. She looks at Ike and turns up her nose. "If you knew enough to conceal the traps perhaps you might get some of them." Not long after that we see her goin' out to where he told her the traps was. Ike was goin' to holler at her to keep away but I made him be still. Purty soon we hears a yell that is awful and some more hollerin'. She had got loose when we got there but she had got her toe pinched plenty in a wolf trap. It wasn't broke but it was enough to lame her up fer a day or two. "Of all the dumb ways to set a trap," she sez. "Anyway," sez Ike real polite, "It was properly concealed." At the dinner table we see that they are all right friendly with Anton. And about an hour later we see the old man and the two boys start out with Anton's old six shooter and the twenty-twos. They goes out onto the flat and lays down behind some ant hills. It wasn't long before they was a dancin' around with their pants in their hands, and they made fer the house. Anton came out to where we was and he told us. He sez, "Them fella he's want coyote. I tell him my cousin gat 'em all the time. He hide behind the ant hill, because there is so many ant hill the coyote don't look there. Mebbyso batter stay here leetle while 'cause that fella goin' to be plenty mad till the ant bites quit hurtin'."

He was right and they was mad fer keeps, the whole bunch of 'em. The two old folks set around fer a day or two and Kid and Kidney they was busy ridin' Jack, Little Mollie's old pet burro, around the corral. Then I happens to look up and some body has built a fire right close to the corner of the barn. I reckon them kids are about to burn the place. I runs to the corral but I am too late. Kid has the bridle on old Jack and Kidney is comin' up to him with a hot iron. They aimed to brand the burro. Before I can holler Kidney has socked the hot iron to him and old Jack has kicked Kidney into the middle of next week. This time it ain't a joke. Kidney's arm is broken and a wonder he wasn't killed.

That settles it. Ike lights out fer town in the buckboard with Kidney and his mother. She leaves orders fer the old man to pack and have me bring him and Kid on to town right that night, which we did. A couple days later they boarded the train fer home. Of course the Boss was right back and he allowed it hadn't lasted as long as he thought it would. But he was mad and he went right into the house and took a look around. "What did they bring with 'em?" he wants to know. Well, I sez they had two trunks. "Yes, and what did they take?" he asks. I told him they had two trunks and a bundle but I figgered they had packed in a hurry and couldn't git their stuff fixed into the trunks. "O yeh?" he snorts and hands me a letter his sister had mailed to him up in town. It read like this: Brother Charles: We are on our way home. We are through with you forever. When you go back to your miserable hovel of a house you will see that we took a few things for the boys' den. If they had been properly treated they could have gotten these hides themselves. So in view of the way we were received at your ranch I considered it no more than right that they have at least a few shoddy cheap things to take along. Please do not take any of your valuable time to answer. Emmaline.

I went into the house and looked. They had got away with the Boss's bear skin rug, a deer hide, a wolf skin, and the wild cat and coyote hides that he had hung around the walls of the big front room.

THE OTHER FELLER'S BEEF

When some fellers start out lookin' fer meat,
They get mighty careless at that.
They ain't so partick'lar whose cattle they eat,
So long as the critter is fat.

They go away up in the brush and the stone,
The same as they would huntin' deer.
And when they git up there somewheres alone,
They shoot a nice fat little steer.

They pile some rocks over the hide and the head,
And they pack the meat out on a hoss.
They reckon as long as there ain't nothin' said,
The owner won't know of his loss.

They figger there's nothin' much to it.
And it cuts down expenses a lot.
It's a good one all right if they do it,
But think what it means if they're caught.

9
RUSTLERS AND ROMANCE

Shorty Corrects a Mistake [1]

One night the boss calls Ike into the house, and when he comes out he looks like he's got sumpthin' heavy on his mind. Next day he tells me what it is. He sez he has been wantin' the boss to change his brand and ear mark. What fur? I asks.

"Well," he sez, "this here outfit on the south of us moved in here about a year ago. They bought out the brand the old man Prouty had run ever since he had settled here in the early days. They ain't a usin' that brand but by some hook or crook they have took out a brand that they are runnin' now. You know that there brand of theirs. It don't take a heap of changin' to work our brand and ear marks over into theirs. I been at him to change it because if he does the worst they can do is to eat a beef on us now and then, and it will cut our chances fer losin' down a heap. I shore wisht they was out of here." Well, I sez, I reckon the Boss will string along with you on that, because I have heard him say a heap of times that he reckons you are a lucky feller. "Well mebbyso," sez Ike, "but I wasn't till I got to workin' fer him. I and him seems to have brought one another luck right along. He is a goin' to change the brand all right, but that there chore man he hired this fall found it out and went and told it to Spud."

Now Spud was the foreman fer that spread on our south and it soter surprised me that our chore man knowed him. How come he's got anything to do with that spread? I asks. "That's just it," sez Ike. "Him and Spud growed up together, come to find out. Why does he come over here and work as a chore man when he is a good hand? Besides Spud has put on two other men since he come here. If he is on the up and up why don't he go over and git a real job workin' fer his old pardner? Reason's good enough. He's here fer a snake in the grass and the best thing is not to tell him nothin'. But the cuss is smart and he's got a long nose fer news and he finds out considable. The Boss called me in to let me know he has heard some talk. They are sore at us and he reckons me and you better not pack no guns, and he is right because that might give 'em a chance to pot one of us and fix up their own story. There is a sort of a company owns that spread and frum what I can see Spud and his bunch is a stealin' 'em blind. If they could git me and you out of here and git some of their own gang in on the quiet or else git a couple of green hands here it would make that much more fer them before the git away comes. They know the Boss ain't a range man and that he depends a heap on us two."

The boss set about gittin' a new brand recorded and Ike he sets out to be gone a few days. Jest to soter visit around the country and see how everbody was a stackin' up and he allows to stop and see our neighbors on the south his last night out and come home frum there. I tells him to make shore and let me know the time he is a goin' to land in there and not make it any other time on account I don't trust them fellers. Not any.

It was a freezin' winter and I was kep busy choppin' ice and what not, and it was time fer Ike to be back before I hardly knowed it. I figgered to go and meet him so I took a soon start that mornin'. I had crossed Cedar Mesa, and was goin' to take a little trail that led off the rim down into the valley. But I looked out across the valley and there was four fellers a comin' my way. When they got closer I could see that one of them looked like Ike and the other two I couldn't make out but kinda laggin' behind was Spud.

I figgered they would come up onto the mesa, or at least Ike would. So there was no use takin' that much extra work out of my hoss. I took him a little ways back into the cedars where the grass was good, loosens the cinch, pickets him to a cedar and pulls the bridle off. Then I goes back to the rim and watches. There was a spring on my side of the valley jest below me and there was a corral and a water lot and a little night paster and it made a mighty handy place fer a feller to camp particklarly if he was alone. When they got there they looked at a bunch of gentle cows and calves that was a hangin' around and drove some of them into the corral. They branded a big calf and then went out to their hosses. I could see right now that there was some soter argyment. Next thing, by the way one of them is standin' I can see he has throwed down on Ike with his gun. The other two goes into the corral and cuts the cow and calf and puts them in a little night paster.

When they come out Ike gits on his hoss and they puts a rope over the hoss's head and snubs him up to a saddle and they start off one man leadin' Ike, and Spud and the other waddy a follerin'. I waits till they are back across the valley and then I goes down and has a look at the cow and calf. Jest as I figgered. The calf has our brand on and the cow belongs to them. I could hear the whole story. They had beefed one of our heifers and was goin' to brand one fer us while Ike was there fer witness. There was Ike. Blood on his rope and three to one ag'in him in court. Well, it didn't take long. I put the calf back in the pen and fixed the marks and brands so's it was same like the mother's.[2]

It was gettin' late and it was after night when I rode in. I got a snack to eat and turned in. Early in the mornin' about two o'clock I reckon here come one of old Hopkin's kids to tell us that Ike is in jail fer rustlin'. The boss wakes me up and I tell him what I done seen. We hitches up to the buckboard right now because we know they got to town after the offices is closed and we can make it before any of the offices opens up if we hurry. "Git yore gun," sez the boss, "and saddle a top hoss." Then he routs the chore man out and tells him to git into the buckboard with him. The chore man was fer givin' him a talk but the boss winks at me and I throws down on him and he dresses and crawls into the buckboard with the boss and I lopes along behind.

When things opens up in town we finds Spud and the sheriff and the prosecutin' attorney, all a havin' a medicine dance. The Sheriff allows he will take a debbity and go out to the paster where Spud and the two waddys has the cow shut up. The boss and me allows we'll go along and don't nobody object. Even the chore man is fer goin', so we makes it unanimous. I had managed to git a word with Ike and tell him what I had done. A feller could git to that corral with a team so the whole purcession starts out like a parade for where the old cow is at. When we gits there Spud points her out. "There she is!" he hollers. "We bobbed the end of her tail so's we could find her easy if she got out." Yeh, that's her sez the other two waddys.

I jogs out into the little paster and drives her in and the sheriff and debbitty goes in and we has a look. They shore looks funny. "Got anything else to show us?" the sheriff asks Spud. "No." sez Spud. "But I cain't make out jest what has happened." The sheriff grins and then he says right sharp like. "Next time you'd better look a little sharper before you stir the whole settlemint up when some feller does a neighborly turn and brands a calf fer you. Now I reckon we all better go on about our business." The chore man busts out a laffin' fit to kill and Spud makes a dive fer him but he side steps and trips Spud and he lands agin the fence and like to busts his head. The boss and the sheriff had a talk and we go back to the ranch. The boss tells me that the sheriff sez Ike has got the chore man all wrong. Him and Spud did work togather when they was younger but they split up on the quiet a long time ago. The chore man is workin' really fer the company that owns the spread to our south. They want to either sell out or buy us out.

Anyhow I sez to him, I'm glad old Ike come out all right. The boss looks at me and grins. Then he sez: "Isaac is an extremely fortunate person."

The Fortune Teller Sends Ike Fishing [3]

A couple of weeks after Ike had got through with his rustlin' scrape him and me went to town. The Boss tells us the very last thing, not to git drunk, and not to git separated. We took a couple of drinks and started to look around. We sees a sign in the winder of a store buildin' which had been vacant fer some time. It says: "Madame Egypta! Tells You All!" There was pitchers on a big piece of cloth, of some Egypt ladies doin' a dance, and a boat with a lady in it. Ike said it was Cleopatra. I tells him I don't care none about seein' her do the boat ride but I shore would like to see her do her dance. "You little fool," Ike sez, "she ain't a doin' none of that. She is a fortune teller frum Egypt. Them pitchers and things is to show where she comes frum which is called the Oriental, if you git what I mean."

I tells Ike that I reckon he might be right. That there, I sez, is where they have the snake charmers, and you might could put on a snake charmin' act fer her if you could borry a snake somewheres. That shore got Ike, but he didn't say nothin', he jest went right in to where the woman was at, and I follers along. Before I could say a word Ike speaks up and sez, "Lady, my friend here wants to have his fortune told." I was so surprised that before I could talk she had set me in a chair and had got out a big glass ball. First off she asks me what year and month and day I was born. "I see mountains raisin' around your birth place," sez the lady. They was already raised when I got there I sez, but you are right. I was born at Trinidad, Colorado, and the mountains is sort of on the rise around about three sides of that town. "I see animals all around you when you was a child," the lady tells me. Hosses and cows, I reckon, I sez. "Burros," sez Ike. What, I asks? "Yes, Burros, we lived there wunst a long time ago and all them kids done was to steal burros and ride 'em around. The whole town was jest oozin' burros. The kids stoled 'em so fast that the town marshall couldn't find none to put in the pound yard. The kids' dads worked fer the rail road and the kids learnt to ride burros at the age of five. A kid frum that town had two chances and I reckon they turned out as many railroaders and cowpunchers as any town that size ever did." The lady was good natured and let Ike talk. Then she sez to me, "You are a person that loves ease and luxury." I don't know, I sez. I never had none. "You will be married three times," she tells me. "Women ain't that easy fooled," sez Ike. "You will never be rich but you will never come to want. You will live most of your life in big cities and crowded places. The time is not far off when you will make the change."[4]

The[n] she motions to Ike and he goes over and sets at the table. She dusts off the globe and shuts her eyes and don't say nothin'. Lady, I sez, if you're ashamed to tell Ike's past, present and future, don't do it. Mebby it's better if we all snuck off and sed nothin' about it. She laffs and tells me that Ike is a peculiar case. Then she gazes into the globe. "I see a large stream of water where you was born. Where was you born and when?" And why? I asks. Then I learns that Ike was born at Marrietta, Ohio, on a Sunday of the week. I tells the lady it was a good thing it was Sunday and nobody had to lose any time over sech a trifin' affair. Then she sez, "You will always do well where there is water." Which is the reason he came to Arizony, I remarks, but they don't take any notice of me. "You will soon be offered a small proposition," the lady tells him. "Take it if it is reasonable at all. It may lead to something bigger. You have been trying to study out something for a long time and the time is near when you should if you follow out your horoscope, as you should." Then she charges us five bucks apiece. Ike kicks like a bay steer and when we comes out he allows we was fools to go in there. But I asks him who it was that went in there and started it and besides I told him that anybody could tell to look at him that this five bucks was about the most money that had ever been spent on his eddication.

Not long after this the Boss hires a boy to work on the ranch. He is a new feller right frum Missouri. One night in the bunk house he is goin' through his stuff and he drags out a throw line about forty feet long, with fifteen hooks on it. I don't know how they use it, but Ike and this boy tells me that it is to throw into a crick or river and leave there all night to ketch cat fish. The boy wants to sell it to Ike for a dollar, and Ike he pays over the cart wheel right now. I asks Ike next day what's eatin' on him, seein' there ain't no place to fish around here. "Well," sez Ike, "the fortune teller told me that a feller would make me an offer and that I'd ort to take him up. So I aim to go right ahead and foller her advice all the way through and mebby my horoscope will learn me what ort to be done with this here outfit over on the South." I gits a big laff out of it but Ike he aims to foller up the talk he got from Missus Egypt. It was only a couple of days when the news come that the camp super from the minin' camp over West of us had been killed and robbed. He was comin' out frum town with the payroll in his buggy. He always done that but he figgered nobody knowed jest when he had the money along. The team tore loose from the buggy and went back to camp and when they went lookin' for him they found he had been shot and robbed. He had put up a fight for there was three empty shells in his six shooter. The sheriff made what he could out of the tracks. Our chore man was missin'.

Not long after me and Ike starts out to meet the wagon for a work over on the other side of Flat Mountain. We could make it in two days easy and we camped overnight at the corrals on Turkey Creek. Ike shoots a rabbit on the way and takes him along, though he don't say what he wants with him. We grazes our hosses as long as it is light and then we corrals 'em. And then, what do you think? [Ike][5] gits out his big fish line and starts to bait it up with rabbit meat. I tells him he ort to have worms on it too and mebby so some bugs, so I goes prowlin' around to help him git bait although I knows there ain't no cat fish in that there crick. I starts turnin' over some rocks and I see the ground has been disturbed and I calls Ike. We gits some sticks and starts diggin'.

We are about to give it up when Ike's stick hits some tin and we dig up a big sized lard pail. Inside it in a cloth poke is a lot of cash. We counts it and it is the amount that was took in the holdup. I had a sneaky idee in the back of my head to cut the money and keep it but Ike was so straight that he leaned backwards and so square that his corners all stuck out like a store box, and I knowed it was no use to speak of it. Ike sets and smokes fer a spell and then he sez, "Our chore man is missin'. I was wrong. He was in with Spud and that outfit on the south of us."[6]

Well, we circles around when we got near the wagon and tells them we had come in by another way to that we took and as soon as we can we tells the boss. It is jest noon and he has an excuse to send old man Cline in to town with a buckboard fer some stuff, but Cline had a letter to the sherriff too. Spud was there with two hands but he looked purty peaked and worried so at noon next day he allowed he would ride in home and the other two hands could bring his hosses. He was lame and said a hoss had fell on his laig. A little after midnight a debbitty sherriff comes into camp. He wants to borry the buckboard. We had covered up our work at Turkey Crick as well as we could, and it was dusk when Spud got there. He found the money had been dug up and was lookin' fer tracks and signs when he was told to "Stick 'em up," but he didn't do it and took to his gun, and so got killed.[7] They already had the chore man. He had been shot bad in the holdup and had come into town fer a doctor but died before they could learn anything from him or help him any. Well, we were rid of that gang on the south and the Boss is tickled. So is the sherriff and all peaceful citizens. Some laid it to the fortune teller, some laid it to good detective work, but the Boss and me jest reckoned that Ike was a fool fer luck.

Ike Has Trouble With His Hat [8]

Spud and his crooked outfit was gone and the company had put a foreman in charge of the outfit over on the south temporary till they got things arranged fer permanent. We was all breathin' easier.

So I remarks to Ike that it was shore fine to have things goin' smooth and peaceful once more. "Oh yeh?" sez Ike. "Well let me tell you there's as bad or wuss stirrin' right now." Meanin' what? I asks. "The Widder Morton," Ike sez. "Her and the boss is sashayin' around each other a heap right now." The boss ain't no hand with women, I sez. "He don't have to be," Ike allows. "She's a widder and widders makes their own chances. No sir. It won't be no time till they are spliced and here she will come with that ten year old brat of hern and her dad, and what a place this will be. I allus said it was hard luck when Tom Morton got killed but I never allowed it would hit me."

What's eatin' on you Ike, any way? I asks. She's a nice woman and that kid is all right, so is the old man Dix. Besides it ain't been but a few weeks since you took her to a dance yourself. You bought a new hat special and you must a give it to her fer I ain't seen it since. "You been talkin' to Johnny Burke," Ike sez. I tells him I ain't but he won't believe me so he busts and tells me about it. "Yes you have, but I'll tell you jest how it was. I went to town fer to git a new hat and borried the boss's buggy to take Mis' Morton to the dance. Me and Johnny was a havin' a few drinks. We was at Louie's place most of the time. He has my new hat out of the box a showin' it to Louie. He talks me into puttin' it back in the box and wearin' my old one till I git to Mis' Morton's. Well, I done that durn fool trick of lettin' somebody tell me what to do. I ties up the team and puts my new hat on and goes in and gits her. I been drinkin' some and don't notice nothin' except that she acts sorter funny. There seems to be a bad smell around but I cain't figger it out. She don't stay long at the dance and on the way home I notice the smell is wuss. She don't hardly say good night and goes into the house right now.

I goes on home and when I lights the bunk house lamp I find out what it is. Somebody has slipped some thin slices of Limberger Cheese onder the sweat band of my new hat. It was a hot night and it had melted and stunk things up soumpthin' horrible. There was Limberger Cheese in the bar lunch at Louie's and Johnny was the only feller had a holt of that hat except me. There's a goin' to be a dance at the Sand Creek school house Saturday night. And I aim to take him to a cleanin' right there. When folks ask what I pitch onto the little runt for I aim to tell 'em cold turkey. That will explain things as well as gittin' even with him."

Now this Johnny Burke is about one size bigger'n a jockey. He generally works fer some outfit durin' round up time and the rest of the time he is around the smaller hoss outfits. He is well liked and is a good little hand. But he is as tricky as a box of monkeys and a devil from the hide to the core. I reckons mebby Ike is makin' a mistake, but then I remember Ike's luck.

We git to the dance a little late. The Boss is there with the widder, and festivities is at full swing. Ike joins in fer a dance or two and then Johnny Burke goes out fer a smoke between dances. Ike follers and I follers Ike. Johnny is standin' by the house with some other fellers and Ike goes right up to him. "You dirty little cuss," sez Ike, "you know you got a lickin' a comin', don't you?" "I hope you know what you're bawlin' about," sez Johnny. "Nobody else does." Ike makes a dive fer him but Johnny sidesteps and trips Ike and he butts into the rock foundation of the house fit to bust his head. It's a good thing he hits the rocks or he would a ruint the side of the school house. He is nigh telescoped. Johnny helps to git some water and fetch him around and he fusses around like he was skeered he had killed Ike. Ike is sick and dizzy enough that he is willing to set around and let his stummick settle and his head clear up. Then some of the older women git to dancin' with him but that makes it wuss, fer down from onder his coat is a big red hair tail a wavin' and floppin' around while he is dancin'. He sees folks a laffin' at him and he comes to me and we gits it loose. It is one of them hair tossels that some people put on work bridles. Some feller has fixed it up with a fine wire and a little teeny fishin' hook jest purpose to fix onto the other feller. He must a had it in his pocket with a little cork over the hook. Ike starts lookin' fer Johnny, and I knowed he was right fer Johnny was too anxious to help with Ike when he was knocked out not to be up to sumpthin'. But Johnny had gone so Ike allowed he had been fool enough fer one night and he leaks out fer home. I feels sorry fer him and goes along.

When we gits home Ike is madder than he was on the start. He gits peeled down to his onder clothes and he is jest a walkin' the floor and a cussin' he allows if he knowed where Johnny was at he would foller him up and shoot him on sight. He would too fer Ike was jest that mad. I stalls around hopin' he would cool off. I goes and fills the big wooden bucket with water fer the mornin' and sets it on the bench outside and puts the dipper in it. Ike is still a walkin' the floor by the time I am ready to go to bed. Then as he gits near the door a big splash of water hits him in the face and the dipper comes a whizzin' in and takes him right in the forrud. Ike lets out one yell and runs out at the door. There is a crash and a splash. I grabs my six gun and runs out. Ike is pickin' hisself up. He has fell over the water bucket. Then we hears a hoss a runnin' out across the paster and somebody a yippin' and yellin' fit to bust. That's him now, I sez. He snuck back here ahead of us and listened and looked then he put that bucket in front of the door and throwed the water and the dipper. I looked fer Ike to do almost anything. He did look funny a settin' there in his onder clothes with his shin cut and all over dirt and a lump on his head as big as a aig. Ike, I sez, I bet he is a batchin' with old Happy Jack over at the cedar corrals. Let's saddle up and go over there right now. I was a gettin' plenty mad myself. But Ike acted funny. He set down on the edge of his bunk and looked at the floor. He wasn't like Bill. I starts puttin' on my clothes, but all Ike done was to say real sad like, "Aw, what's the use?" Then he lays down and turns his face to the wall. Ike had quit cold.

Ike Meets a Romance [9]

A few days after Ike had been to the Sand Creek dance he saddles up one mornin' and he had a wicked grin on his face. I wasn't long learnin' why. The Boss comes out and sez, "Boys, I was comin' over by Cedar Corrals yestidday and Johnny Burke and Happy Jack is breakin' hosses there. They had broke out some for the Old Man Dix. I bought 'em off him. Good young hosses they are too. I figger you boys had better go over and git 'em today. Make it back tomorrow sometime."

When we git started I sez to Ike, the Old Man Dix must be a honest hoss trader to start in a dealin' with his future son-in-law. Ike is still fer a spell and then he remarks, "If he knows I'm a comin' he might hide out. If he don't I'll git a chance at him." Meanin' the Boss or the Old Man Dix? I asks. "Johnny Burke!" Ike snorts. Well Ike, I advises, you done had a couple chances at him and frum what I could see you didn't do so good. Ike turns in his saddle. "Git this through your head, you half growed runt. Mebby he did git away with a little but this time it's goin' to be different. There's goin' to be one cyclone finish." In which case, I sez, I reckon I'm supposed to stand with my hat in my hand while they sing Rock of Ages, and then appear in court fer a witness ag'in Johnny. Ike don't say a word to that.

By that time we had come out of the canyon and was headin' out across the flat to Cedar Corrals. Right ahead of us is another rider. First I thought it was a slim boy but when we git closer I see it is a woman in a divided skirt. She is ridin' a big rangy bay that is a good run walker and drivin' a couple of pack mules. Out ahead a little jennette is trottin' along with a bell on. She slows up and lets us ketch her. She shore is some purty woman. Her big hat is tied down on a mop of dark curly hair and her eyes are green as jade. She grins when she speaks and her teeth are so white they flash. But you could see the very lurkin' devil in her sassy face, but yet you had to like her anyhow. Her stock was good fer fifty mile any time and her ridin' outfit was no plaything. Her little shop-made boots was brush scarred, so was her stirrups. The brass bindin' on 'em was all jagged.

"From up in the hill country?" Ike asks. "Yes," she sez, "I'm Jessie Burke. I'm goin' over to Cedar Corrals to see Johnny. I stayed at Mr. and Mrs. Dorman's last night and come on from there." Ike looks worried. So you are Johnny's sister, I sez. She looked at me soter funny and then a dimple comes in her cheek and she sez she is. I see Ike is lookin' at her with his mouth an eyes wide open. Don't bite the lady, Ike, I sez. "Whaddaya mean?" Ike growls. Well, I sez, I see you ridin' up close to her with yore mouth wide open and that there's what you might call a bad sign.

"You're like all little fellers. You need somebody to ear you down once in a while," she tells me. I bet you was like that before you growed so big, I sez. We all three laffs and when she laffed I tell you it seemed to make even the mules happy. I know you'll like Ike here, I tells her. Him and yore brother is great friends. In fact they are what you might call playmates. But I see right now I ain't gettin' nowhere. It's a purty view out across the flat to where it breaks off into the lower canyon but they don't see it. They don't see me. They just see each other. I knew. I had a spell like that wunst when I was younger and I shut up because I knew they was in another world altogether. When we drops down into the canyon we are just around the bend frum the corrals, she stops. She looked at us straight a minute and then she sez. "I got to apologize to you boys. I told you a lie back there. I am Johnny Burke's wife. Not his sister. I don't know what made me do it. But we better have things straight I guess."

When we got to the corrals the dust was a flyin' in the big square corral. Seems like a bunch of fellers had made a hoss round up and that big pen was jest a boilin' with hosses. Johnny and Jack come out and spoke and all acted like the best of friends seein' Johnny's wife was there, but I knowed when her and Johnny looked at each other they had had a heap of trouble to git along with each other and he would about as soon she wasn't there. We helped her git her packs and saddles off and by that time the Boss and the Old Man Dix drives up in a buckboard. There was a whole lot of kids had worked on the hoss round up and they was beginnin' to chouse the herd of hosses in the big square corral. "Don't razee them hosses in a square corral; you'll kill or cripple some of 'em!" old Happy Jack yells. "We ain't a hurtin' 'em!" the kids yells back. "Stop it!" yells Old Dix. "There's a couple loose posts a layin' in the fur corner and they'll crowd one another onto 'em and git crippled." "Naw they won't," bawls a big loose mouthed boy. Johnny starts into the corral to throw the posts over the fence and I go with him. I tells the kids to lay off a minute, but just as Johnny starts to pick up a post that big kid yells, "There he is!" and smears a big loop among the hosses and the other kids are lined up across the corral. The hosses crowd each other to our corner. I grab a picket and make it onto the fence but before Johnny can look they have crowded a young mare against him and she kicks twice like lightnin' and hits him fair both times. Well, that's the end of Johnny Burke. We carries him out and the kids is all still but the big mouthed one. He is doin' his share of talkin'. Jesse steps onto my hoss. She builds a loop with one flip and she don't even swing her rope but shoots it right over his head. It settles to his middle as she spurs my old hoss.

All that saved him was that I had loosened my cinch when we stopped. It throwed Jessie when the saddle turned and Ike grabbed the hoss and the Boss cut the rope. But she is on her feet before we can grab her. And she smashes that kid in the face with a piece of wood till he looks different the rest of his life. We git her cooled down and then of course she starts to cry like any other woman.

Old Man Dix puts her in the buckboard and takes her to Dorman's ranch. The Boss tells me to take her stock and her outfit back to her Dad's ranch in the hills and have them come down and git her when the funeral is over. I makes a two-day ride of it and they are shore upset when they see her hosses a comin' in but they don't seem so worried when they find out it is Johnny that is done for. The old folks go and git Jessie and I stay there with her brother and I learn that Jessie was married for four years. Her dad had give her a nice little place and a few cattle, but Johnny only stayed a few months and then he was driftin' around a lot of the time after that. She had worked hard and worried a lot.

When she got back home with her folks she didn't look as sassy as she did when I first saw her but I believe she was purtier. I was all ready to leave the next mornin' and she come out to say goodbye. After she had said goodbye to me she got red in the face fer a minute, then she looked straight at me and said, "Tell Ike to write," and I agreed with the boss that "Isaac was an extremely fortunate person."

Cap'n Beasley Goes in for Cattle [10]

One Sunday we was foolin' about the place when a wagon drives up. Old Man Dix was ridin' alongside. Out climbs a feller that is six feet high and about as wide, but he comes down over the front wheel as easy as a big bear. The other feller is big too but he is raw boned and don't have the weight of this one. Old Dix interduces 'em to us. He sez: "This folks, is Cap'n Beasley and Jed Tatum. They used to go to school with me back in the state of Maine. Cap he took to the sea and Jed he took up farmin'. They bought the outfit over on the South and aim to be neighbors to us fer a spell." We shook hands all around and they onhitched the team and come in fer dinner.

It seemed like they wanted to clean up their range before winter and was around givin' out the word that they was goin' to make a work. Old Dix was in charge in a way, but the old Cap was the real boss. We had a few head to brand up and we did that in the corral before we started. They stayed the next day. A few of the bigger ones we heeled and it shore tickled me to hear the old Cap talk to Jed. "Look, Jed," he sez, "that's why they leave hosses standin' with the reins a draggin'. They tie to the fence and the other beasts would run foul of the lines and bust 'em and hurt the hoss. If he's loose and beasts bothers him he can git away too. See! That thing they call a horn on the saddle—that's really a forrud bitt. They take turns on it with the line and they can cast off with no trouble. If they want to they can make fast and tow 'em anywheres. If they heave the line on a big 'un they heave a stern line on him too and hold him fore and aft."

The Boss asked him about his crew and he said, "Oh I paid 'em off and sent 'em ashore. They was jest eatin' up the boardin' house and tormentin' a few beasts where they wasn't needed." We got a bunch of hands together and made the work. When we cut the cattle I was surprised.

Old Jed was no buckaroo but that farmer knowed his cows. What got us was that he cut all the culls and old cows and sorry stock. By the time they was ready to ship they shore had a big shipment but it was a bad lookin' one. What do you suppose? The rest of the owners got the idee and cleaned up their herds and there was a good bunch of stock left on the range and all the culls was off the feed. It wasn't till then that we knowed what a lot of wuthless stuff had been around there. They was sellin' them fer what they could git on the market seein' they would never be wuth any more and would be out of the way. Jed and Ike and a couple more fellows was to go with 'em.

When we got to the station Old Cap goes in and sez: "I come to see about the cars fer Tatum and Beasley." The agent is a sullen cuss and he jest looked at old Cap right cold and turned around and sed nothin'. He picks up a old magazine and looks at it to rile old Cap. He is havin' some fun to hisself. "Know anythin' about them cars?" Cap asks, and I see old Dix and Tatum grin. The feller looks up at the Cap'n and then back at the magazine. Cap reaches out and slaps him offen his chair so sudden you don't see how it's been done. Then he grabs him by the neck and slaps his ears down. The agent starts to talk but old Cap shakes him till his hair flutters. His collar button busts and his eyes sticks out plum terrified. Old Cap takes him out on the platform and asks him about them cars ag'in. Well, he seems to know a heap more about 'em by then, shook up as bad as he was. Cap didn't seem to even remember about it, as soon as we got our cars he helps load and sees the cattle on the way. Next he goes up to the hotel bar where he has enough money planted to pay off the extra hands. That done he gits a couple of rooms where we can clean up. We all go to the barber shop but before he paid off the extra hands he gives me some cash and tells me there's a show in town and fer me to go and git five good tickets.

After we clean up an have supper it is about time fer the show. Well, one thing is shore. The old Cap knows how to work and he knows how to play. I asks the bartender why a feller as smart as Cap goes and buys a spread and don't git a count on the cattle. He tells me that old man Dix knows about what is there and he was the go between. And besides Cap and Jed looked over the tax reports because they figgered that people wasn't likely to pay tax on cattle they didn't have.

But when we was ready to leave town the town marshall arrests Cap fer mussin' up the agent, and he had to wait and give bail before he could leave. We knowed what that meant. We would be called fer witnesses. A few weeks later things was all set and we got notice to appear. It was to be tried before Judge Thomas. The Boss allows it may be soter tough because Cap is a Yankee and a sailor and cow man. Old Judge Thomas is a strict Texas Baptist and his dad was a Confederate soldier. It shore set me a-thinkin' and I got ready to do my best, no foolin' and after thinkin' a day and a night I allowed mebby I was ready.

When the trial come up the prosecution asked every witness what the agent was a readin' when he didn't answer Cap's questions about the cars. That was what I had counted on because they was goin' to make out like it was railroad papers and orders like. They all said it looked like a magazine or sumpthin' but they hadn't noticed patticklar. When it come my turn I sez: Well, it was a funny soter book like. It wasn't a Bible and it wasn't a magazine. It was a story or sumpthin' that is called a Koran. They looked at me soter funny and the Judge takes the witness. Yes, I tells him, the book looks funny and I goes back and picks it up. I hadn't no business to do it, but I did. I moved the marker he had in there but otherwise that's the way it was. I hands the judge the book. The old judge looks at the book and the marker and asks the agent if he belonged to any church and he sez not. He admits he uses tobacco but don't drink. The defense lawyer butts in and allows that the evidence of the agent cain't be counted on seein' the oath on a Christian Bible don't mean nothin' to a man that has a leanin' to a heathen religion. The judge hears the case through and finds Cap guilty of disturbin' the peace and fines him a dollar and cost. And the way he looks at that agent would bore a hole through him. When the thing is over Cap and the Boss gits me off to a card table in the hotel bar and asks me where I got that old Koran book with the back busted off?

Well, I sez, I'll tell you. You heard me speak of the perfessors that stopped where I worked a couple years ago? The boss allows he has. You see it was like this. One of 'em left this here Arab bible when he went away. I have kep' it fer a curiosity in my war sack and it has been packed and slung around till the back was about off anyhow, so I took the back plum off to make it look a little like a magazine. Then I got a pitcher of General Grant on a card with flags all around him that little Mollie used to keep in one of her school books when her folks run the boardin' house here and she had lost or furgot. I puts that in fer a marker. Say! When that old Southern Texas Baptist got holt of a heathen bible with General Grant's pitcher fer a book mark, he was ready to give the Cap'n a bounty on the feller that had it. He figgered the agent was a radical Yankee and to top it off had soter gone Mohamedan.

Cap and the Boss laffed till their eyes and noses was so red you would have swore they had been bawlin' fer a week. Then we took another drink and went home.

Stockings and Watches [11]

As I said, Ike took to the hill country. We all knowed the reason. Johnny Burke's widder. The Boss hates it because he reckons Ike brings good luck around the place besides bein' a good hand. He tells me to go along with Ike as far as town and do what I can. "Not that there'll likely be any chance," he sez, "but you might could turn him." I knows Ike has some money invested in our spread and I hate to have him goin' wild and foolish like that myself.

Ike don't seem to relish my company but he don't git openly hostile. We has a couple of drinks in town and he thaws out and starts tellin' what a wonderful woman the widder is. Right now I git the idee. I shakes Ike fer a spell and mopes over to see Betty Crandall that works in "The Ladies' Fashion Store." We has a talk. She is about half onwillin' on account she likes Ike purty well. I promises her two tickets fer the show the next week and that done the business. I finds Ike oiled up about right and I tells him he'd ort to take his gal a present seein' he ain't so well knowed to her yet and that would soter break the ice a little.

He goes fer the idee like a hungry burro to a alfalfa stack. We goes over to the store and starts lookin' about. Betty she shows Ike a pair of stockin's like we never seen before. They was so thin you could kinda see a lady's bare leg through 'em if she had on short onderwear. I kicks about it. A price like that, I sez, fer a pair of stockin's that won't wear no time. Besides she wears boots most of the time. Git her a big ribbon or some of them cloth flowers. Betty laffs at me and sez I don't know much about what women folks like. She puts her hand in the stockin's and shows how they are all silk and tells Ike that they ain't fer hard wear but jest dress up stockin's and the mayor's wife and Judge Thomas' wife wears 'em and they are jest the thing. Ike he sez he'll take 'em. She allows she'll make a gift package of 'em. That's the only good idee I see in the whole deal, I sez, fer if you don't Ike will pack 'em in his pocket. And if he don't furgit and wipe his nose on 'em they'll smell like tobacker and pieces of calf's ears anyhow. She shore makes a purty passel out of 'em and Ike starts out plum joyful fer the hill country.

A few days later we hears that he is over at Cap Beasley's place and a couple days later he comes weavin' in. Nobody sez a word about it but the first night we was all together at supper Ike busts out and tells the whole story. "Boys, I shore jumped myself two wild cats. I don't know which was the worst, the Widder Burke or Betty Crandall. I visits along the road some and about ten o'clock the third day I comes up to Burke's ranch. I figgered she might be there alone and she was. She give me a bid to light off and come in. She was pleasant enough and so I goes out to my pack and gits that package of stockin's fer her. She shore peels her teeth and grins when she sees that purty passel Betty had fixed, but when she onwropped it her face gits so long she could a et oats out of a churn and then she begins to git mad. I tries to calm her down but it ain't no use. She was bad enough on the start when she was polite and sneerful like but I tried to tell her that Betty Crandall had jobbed me on the deal and she didn't git me right. She threw the stockin's out the door and told me to take 'em to Betty Crandall whoever she was and to shet the paster gate as I went down the canyon if I had brains enough. No wonder pore Johnny stayed away frum home and battled bronchos. I shore furgive him fer what he done to me. He never could git even with the world nohow."

Didn't she like them thin stockin's, I asks. "Thin stockin's!" Ike snorts. "Thin stockin's nothing. They was a pair of big cheap cotton stockin's. Why a woman could a got 'em on if she had a number ten foot and a leg as big as a gate post. They was striped black and white and red and the stripes run round and round like a barber pole. Wait till I see Betty Crandall." When the Boss gits me alone he tells me I shore done fine and as usual he sez, "Isaac is a very fortunate person." Which I reckon is so.

The Cap'n and the Boss seemed to soter go in pardnership. Over at the half way creek where Ike and I found the pay roll money hid they have started a ditch and a dam because they can lead the creek out on a flat there and raise alfalfa. The ditch is to be two miles long. Besides they are makin' an awful big reservoir on the flat. I looks at Ike and at them shovels and scrapers and plows and sez. Ike, it's here. I seen it in Colorado and now it's here. He knows what it means too and allows we are in fer it. Bob wire and irrigation. It's soon goin' to be forks and shovels instead of ropes and saddles.

One thing shore, it helped the old Cap'n and the Boss git away with a lot of crooked fellers that used to be visitin' and pokin' around that neck of the range. Whenever one of them lit they would try and make him build fence or work on the dam and ditches, and them boys ain't good post hole diggers and shovel or scraper men. When two or three of 'em got camped at some old shack on the range Cap and the Boss always had reason to send a couple men there too to do some lookin' around. They sent men that it wouldn't do to fool with either.

Squint Waller was about the worst range tramp in them parts. He was a feller that was in town about half the time and was always hatchin' a scheme to beat some feller out of a few dollars. He was one of the kind that would land in with two hosses and stay a month. He would mebby help saddle a young hoss and braid the boss a quirt, that was about all. Well, when he left they was always so glad to see him go they would tell him a pleasant goodbye and hope he died before he ever come back that way. The old Cap'n shore fixed him. He tried it a couple of times but the old Cap had him on the hard labor before he knowed it and had him framed so it was a week or two before he could git away. He always got wages but he soon kep clear of Cap. He never come near our place on account of Ike pestered him to death every time he showed up and he was no match fer Ike any way you'd take it.

One day Cap and I has gone to town fer a load of stuff and the mail when Squint comes to the Cap'n with a tramp lookin' feller. He sez the feller has a wonderful watch to sell fer forty dollars. He tells Cap that seein' he always give him a job whenever he come out to the ranch he will put in ten dollars to make it a sort of a present seein' he can't buy him the watch outright. They tell Cap that Solly Schwartz at the jewelry store will give him fifty but he will have to wait ten days fer the money. The feller sez he must have the dough right now and he will take forty. Squint whispers right suspicious that the watch might have been stolen in some other town seein' it is so plum valuable. They was talkin' the deal over in The Antlers Bar. Cap looks serious and tells the feller to go down to Solly's and he will meet him there and have the watch appraised. He is no sooner out the door than Cap seems to think of sumpthin'. "Here," he sez, "give me that ten bucks quick. Solly will beat me to it and buy that watch ahead of me if he finds out he can't git it on time. Wait right here till I git back, you boys." In about half an hour the Cap comes back , and he has on a fine big Stetson hat. "Did you git the watch?" Squint asks. "No," Cap sez, ["]I got a good watch and seein' I ain't been wearin' the sort of hat a cow man ort to, I reckoned I'd git me one and I knowed you would be proud to know you was in on the first real hat I ever wore, so I took the ten and put it in on this hat. Ain't she a beauty?["] Po[o]r Squint. He sort of strangled and said yes, and then he went out of the door. He was about the saddest feller I ever see. The bar-keep buys the drinks fer me and Cap and he is still laflin' when we leave on account he heard the whole deal. I reckon the watch was a phony. I'll never know.

THE WRANGLER

Oh yes he's the wrangler, a big lanky kid,
That started to work 'bout the same as you did.
He ain't got chaps and boots like the rest of the hands.
He wears tattered old pants and a pair of brogans.

He rides an old saddle that's got a long tree,
With some gunny sack blankets in onder, maybe.
He has only one spur that he ties to his shoe,
And a limber old rope that he has to make do.

He sometimes gits lonesome while watchin' his herd,
But he keeps a tight mouth and he don't say a word.
He takes out the remuda, and brings 'em back in
When it's time fer the boys to change hosses ag'in.

Now you and me, pardner, has done had our day,
We cain't make a real hand, but I'm willin' to say,
If they give us a chance we would really enjoy,
Jest to wrangle the bunch, like we did when a boy.

10

Hell among the Yearlin's

Ricky Comes and Goes [1]

One day I rides in to the ranch and I sees a kid's saddle throwed under the shed cow puncher fashion with blankets over it. I examine it and it is shore the finest kid saddle I have seen. Ike comes out and I ask him about it. "Well," Ike sez, "that belongs to Ricky. Ricky is Old Cap's nephew. His Ma bein' Cap's sister. He is thirteen and has been fired out of school. His dad is the money man behind Cap. He seems to give the kid more money than he'd ort to but he don't want to be bothered with him. His Ma don't want to be bothered with him and she sent him to Cap. Cap sez he is shore pizen and don't want him about. He sends him out to the ditch camp. The kid is doin' sumpthin' with an open fire and cedar wood. The sparks set fire to a big tent and burn it up before the kid has a chance to do anything. Him bein' left there alone fer a little while. So the Boss fetches him here till they can find another boardin' school fer him. He ain't a bad kid and he is shore hard. He never had a home and he has been sent from one school to another all his life. Jest trained and trained, that's all. Him and Scutt, the little dog, is friends and him and the cook has throwed in together. But Carver, that new ranch hand, shore hates him and there ain't no love lost. The kid is a match fer him at that."

Ike starts out and before I git to the house I hear some shootin' back of the store house. Around the corner comes the kid with a big rat he has shot and Scutt at his heels a waggin' his tail. That kid has the cutest little double shot gun ever made. He tells me he has to load his own shells on account he cain't git shells fer that small a shot gun, and that he has a set of moulds fer a round ball that fits the gun and fer sixty or seventy yards it throws a patched ball purty true. I asks him if he has shot the rabbit that hangs around the corral and he sez, "No, he don't do no harm. You can git him any time you want to. If you let him be, mebby you'll have more rabbits later on. Besides Scutt likes to chase him and he knows Scutt cain't ketch him. They got to have sumpthin' to do." I looks at that kid, too old fer his years. He shore had never been a pet. Carver comes past and speaks to me, then he wants to borry the kid's little gun to shoot at some quails in the paster. The kid seems willin'; he tells him he ain't got but eight shells loaded but he can have them. I ask the kid why he let Carver have his gun and he tells me he won't

131

do a lot of harm with it. I go up to the back porch and the cook comes out when he hears Carver start shootin' he has a big laff and the kid winks and grins. Purty soon Carver comes back and he is shore hot. He sez the gun ain't wuth a cuss. The kid sez nothin' and cleans his little shot gun. That night at supper the cook keeps talkin' about Carver tryin' to git us some honeymoon quails. "Well," the cook remarks, "I've heered of tryin' to throw salt on their tails but when a feller starts tryin' to throw rice at 'em I reckon they must a been honey moon quails." "Who was throwin' any rice?" Carver wants to know real savage like. "Well anyhow," the cook sez right pleasant like, "that's what the kid loaded them shells with."

Me and Ike busts out laffin' and so does the cook but the kid looks straight at Carver and only grins and Carver he looks hostile at the kid and sez sumpthin' or other. Things goes along smooth fer a spell. Ricky helps the Morton kid move hosses from one camp to the other and watch fences. They git along fine togather. Then one day Carver finds out about Ricky burn[in]' up the tent. We was eatin' dinner and he tackles the Kid. "Ha Ha; you went and burnt up a tent and your uncle run ye out. Didn't you?" Carver sez pointin' his knife at Ricky. Ricky looks at him but don't answer. "Har Har!" Carver laffs. "I reckon thet will hold ye fer a spell. Cain't talk eh? Cat got yer tongue?" That is jest baby talk to Ricky and he looks at Carver and grins. "The tent was jest an excuse," Ricky sez. "He fired me because I won too many pennies off him playin' pennywinkle. He's a poor loser." "You couldn't beat old Cap playin' cards nor no other game," Carver allows. "You don't play it with cards," Ricky tells him, "you play it with pennies and a funnel. I'll show you after dinner and I'll win all the pennies you got. That is if you got any and ain't afraid to play." Carver allows he will have to be showed. So, after dinner the kid goes out with a funnel he borrows from the cook and sets down on the wash bench. He puts the funnel in the belt of his pants and then he lays back his head and puts a penny on his forehead and tries to flip it into the funnel without usin' his hands. Wunst he does and twicet he don't. He explains that each feller takes five turns and the one that ain't playin' furnishes the pennies. Carver allows he will go it a round and go first. He sets down and fixes the funnel and Ricky is gitting him a drink of water out of the bucket with the big dipper but he hands Carver a penny with his free hand. Carver lays back his head to fix the penny and when he does Ricky dumps a dipper full of water into the funnel. Carver is a slow thinkin' feller and before he knows it his pants is plum soaked and Ricky has dodged past the cook into the kitchen. It's a good thing Carver didn't take after him because we was all laffin' till we couldn't have done a thing to have stopped him.

Ricky never talked about it. He never talked about anything he did and young Morton rode in to get him to help move some cattle and he rode away for a couple of days. Things seemed pretty peaceful. The next week the boss tells me they have got an old hoss buyer who is willin' to buy up all the fuzz tail ponies on the range and ship 'em.

The boss and Cap figger it is a good riddance and are plum tickled to make the deal. The old hoss buyer comes to our place and he has his grandson along. The boy is Ricky's age and is plum mean. His granddad tells everybody the kid is so bad he has to keep him along with him. That kid shore thinks he is plum onmanagable, and he struts about like a tom turkey. He tries to start sumpthin' with the Morton kid but Young Morton is sensible and keeps out of his way. So does Ricky. The old hoss buyer goes over to the ditch camp to see Cap and the boss takes him. Carver sees his chance and he tries to rib up a fight with Ricky and that kid. Ricky ain't afraid but he tries to dodge it. He tells me and Ike that he has all the trouble he wants and hopes he don't have to fight. I asks him if he thinks he can lick that kid and he grins and sez, "He don't act like a kid that ever fought much." But it ain't no use. The kid and Carver crowded Ricky too far. The fracas started when the kid went to use Ricky's saddle. That's the only time I ever saw Ricky lose his temper. Carver has butted in. Ricky turns on him. "Aw shut up you poor feeble minded joke," he sez. Then he turns to the kid and sez, "All you need is a couple of punches in the nose to make you bawl like any other spoiled baby." The kid makes a wild swing fer Ricky's jaw and rushes. Say! Ricky shows he has learned about as much boxin' and hard hittin' as a kid his age can ever hope to know. I've seen worse work in the ring. He don't dodge back; he steps inside the swing. His left smacks twice on the kid's nose and his right shoots in a wicked punch to the kid's stomach. The kid staggers back off balance and Ricky peppers his face a dozen times before he is knocked off his legs. He comes back like a tiger but Ricky has it all. He is too quick and too strong, and besides it would take that kid five years to learn what Ricky knows about boxin' and rasslin'. Another minute and the kid is settin' on the ground again. The kid jumps back and tries to grab a rock and when he does Ricky is right on top of him and stomps his hand till it is out of the game. Then the kid runs and gits behind Carver and I see him and Ike is about to mix fer Ricky downs that kid and begins to work him over a plenty and him squealin' like a stuck pig. Ike is standin' Carver off. So to stop more trouble I pulls Ricky off. When that old hoss buyer come back the kid runs to him and tells a big story. He hunts Ricky up and starts in to tell him off. Ricky looks straight at the old man and sez, "If you're that kid's granny you better take him to a doctor. I think he's got a bad hand." Then he walks away and leaves the old feller gappin' fer sumpthin' to say. Well, the old feller was so mad he left and the hoss deal fell through. Was Old Cap mad? "That Whelp," he sez. "No good, I tell ye. A Johner frum the day he was born. Look what he went and done." Cap, I tells him, the kid wasn't to blame. "Neither am I," Cap roars. "They got to git him out of here."

It wasn't many days till Old Jed drove up in a spring wagon. He had a wire fer Ricky. They had found another boardin' school fer him. He was to start next day. He never changed face, but he rubbed Scutt's ears and begun to pack his stuff. He give the cook his little shot gun and put his ridin' gear in a sack. He asked Jed if he'd stop in so he could give it to the Morton Kid. "Why Ricky," Ike sez, "don't give that val'able stuff away. We'll keep it fer you till you come back." Ricky's hard eyes got a little dim but his voice was steady. "They won't let me come back," he sez. "They don't let me stay no place. But I'll be a man some day and then mebby—" he stopped. "I'll say you'll be a man," Ike sez and walks toward the corral. Old Jed got ready to start next mornin' and I could see he didn't like the job, but the kid told him point blank not to worry because he was only doin' what had to be done anyhow. Scutt wanted to foller and we had to tie him up. The boss had done started Carver over to the ditch camp with his bed and a team, which was sensible from the way Ike and the cook had been lookin' at him. Ricky gives Ike and me each a card. "That will always find Dad," he sez, "and he will know where I am. He's all right only he's always busy. I'll write him about you boys." We gits on our hosses and starts out and Ricky climbs into the spring wagon with old Jed. "Gawd, what a man," Ike sez. "Who?" ["]Why Ricky of course." Ike turns in his saddle and looks back. So do I. And there is the little feller settin' beside old Jed with his hat pulled down over his eyes and as straight as a ramrod. I wisht he'd look back and wave, I sez. "Not him," Ike answers short and sharp. He ain't the lookin' back kind, and shore 'nough, as the wagon topped the hog back, we watched, but the little feller never turned his head.

Cap Takes to Mules [2]

Old Cap liked to git about and see what was a goin' on but he was soter handicapped on account he had to drive and there was a heap of places where he couldn't git with a spring wagon or a buckboard. He was too heavy fer most of the hosses and besides he wasn't the build to fit right comfortable onto a shifty cow pony. He is about to give it up when he gits a notion. We had a great big wheel mule we called Jumbo and he is plum gentle and a fast walker. We had no mate for Jumbo so the Boss sells him to Cap. Cap gits a big saddle and him and Jumbo goes into pardnership. Him and the mule gits along fine. He likes to brag about Jumbo. One night in the hills Cap kinda lost his bearin's so he gives Jumbo his head and of course Jumbo goes right back to his feed box. After that Cap allows Jumbo has more sense than all the hosses in Arizona put together.

He gits so fond of Jumbo he hates to ride him hard, so he tells the Old Man Morton and Jed to keep a look out fer another big mule that is a good traveler, because bein' big and heavy he needs two mules. Which is a good idee seein' that Cap does a heap more travellin' around since he learns how handy it is to ride than to drive.

I had been sent over to Cap's place to help with some work and one day Manuel Cordova rides in on his top hoss. A big buckskin which Manuel allows is the best all around cow hoss that ever looked through a bridle. He has just finished workin' for another outfit, and he stops to ask Cap what he will pay by the head to git some wild cattle led out from up in the rough country. Cap don't like him and he don't mind lettin' Manuel see it, but he stays to dinner. There is just me and Cap and the cook. Manuel don't onsaddle but I have turned out my hoss. I have another one in the corral but I ain't saddled him yet. After we eat Manuel starts on Cap some more about them steers. Cap tells him mighty plain that he ain't interested and besides the round up has worked that country and got what is there. He sez he has been up there and ain't seen no steers, so if Manuel is so much better than anybody else why don't he own an outfit of his own and not be around breakin' hosses and fightin' wild cattle in the brush. And if there is any cattle up there he don't want 'em right now anyhow.

Manuel gits mad too. "You are a smart man, Captain," he sez. "Those steers are from three to six years old and still you don't want them. Mebby you think they raise you some calves? Mebby you like to start a dairy with them. Mebby you walk the old mule around behind the wild steer. Mebby you get him in a spring wagon, No? Perhaps you make a ditch to him and get him with a boat." Manuel like all old cowboys hated farmin'. He knowed hosses and cattle but he didn't know old Cap. Cap moves about twice as quick as most men his size and age. Before Manuel knowed it, Cap had grabbed him and throwed him out at the door about three times as far as I ever allowed a hundred and fifty pound man could be throwed by hand. He picks himself up and then picks up his hat. He walks out to the corral and takes my rope off the saddle. Then he leads his hoss out of the corral and shuts the gate and gits on. He is takin' his time. I don't like the look of it, not any. Cap goes to the door. Don't go out there I sez, he aims to start sumpthin'. "If he does," growls Cap, "I'll pull him off that yaller billy goat he's ridin' and beat him to death. I can lick a whole crew like him." Manuel builds a loop in my rope and rides over to a high post where Cap has a weathervane and ropes it off. He starts to build another loop and look around fer sumpthin' else to tie onto. Out of the house busts Cap. I yell at him to come back, but it ain't no use. Manuel lifts his hoss and drops a loop right around Cap's middle and away he goes. He don't jerk him down but he just leads him a little faster than he could run without help till he gives out and falls down. He gits a rough fall and a hard jerk. Then Manuel throws off his dallies and leaves Cap and my rope behind and lines out. Before Cap can git back to the house he is plum out of rifle shot.

Cap wasn't as mad as I figgered he would be. He was sick and shook up purty bad. It looked to me like it might have done him a heap of good to rope him and bust a fall out of him. He seemed soter puzzled. Finally, after he got his wind and took a drink, he sez, half to hisself and half to me, "That feller wasn't so bad, come to think. He could 'a broke my neck if he'd wanted to, or he could 'a drug me to death. I reckon he jest wanted to take a fall out of me, and you cain't blame him a heap neither. Shorty, a rope is a turrible weepin in a good man's hands." The cook nor me don't say nothin' to nobody about the affair and the funny thing neither does Manuel.

In a week or less in comes Old Man Morton with a big bay mule as big as Jumbo. He ain't old and is a runnin' walker. Cap is shore pleased with him. He names him "Sambo." Between his business and Jumbo and Sambo Cap is shore a busy hombre. A couple days later he takes his big spy glass and starts out on Sambo. He don't git home at dark and we was worried. "Do you reckon he depended on Sambo to fetch him home?" Jed asks. "Well if he did," sez Old Man Morton, "he is plum out of luck. That mule was raised at Joe Gray's place forty mile from here." In the mornin' we starts out. Morton and Jed starts leadin' Jumbo and trackin' Cap. I takes the spring wagon and heads fer Gray's ranch. When we parted Morton sez. "And to fix it all Manuel Cordova is breakin' some colts over at Gray's ranch. Looks like almost anything might happen."

It is late in the afternoon when I sight Gray's ranch and what do you reckon I see from a distance? There is Cap and Manuel settin' cross legged on the ground makin' marks in the dust. When I drive up they come over to meet me. "Hello, Shorty," Cap sez. "Smart mule that Sambo. I went up into the rough country yesterday to look around and I see some right big cattle with my glass jest like Manuel here said. I didn't notice till it got dark. I got off my course and I give Sambo his head. That there mule was homesick and he come right to here and made good time too. I got in before daylight." After supper I asked him if he aimed to go back in the wagon and let me ride the mule or if he aimed to ride Sambo back. "Well," he sez, "a day's rest won't hurt me or Sambo either and seein' he come all this way he ort to be allowed a day to visit. Tell the boys I'll be back day after tomorrow."

He got back jest when he said he would, and he took up a crew from the ditch camp and built a corral and paster in the round country, at a big spring. A little before it was finished in comes Manuel and his pardner to git out them cattle. Cap was shore friendly to 'em and he sez to us. "The steers they take out will more than pay fer the corral and paster and Manuel allows if we put in that camp and work them cattle some they won't git so wild from now on."

That night the cook and me was alone and he sez, "I sailed with old Cap fer several years. If he ever heard any preachin' it never cooled him down none. But I am sayin' that there Mexican boy shore improved him a heap when he busted that fall out of him."

Squint Comes and Goes [3]

When I gets back to the home ranch after my work at Cap's place, I finds a mighty peculiar jasper there. The cook said that Ike had fetched him out from town same as he had me. I didn't take kindly to that remark because I don't like no part of this feller. Whatever we talked about he always horned in like he knowed a heap more than the rest of us, and besides when he made a wise talk he always let on like he knowed a whole lot that he wasn't tellin'. He would mostly talk with one eye shut and fix his face to look real secrety like or else grin like you didn't know what it was all about. The cook gives him the name of "Squint." It shore suits him and is adopted by the hands unanimas. The Boss not knowin' his name and not bein' over fond of him jest calls him Squint too.

I asks Ike why he fetches Squint here and he looks at me and grins. "Well," he sez, "fer one thing I lacked jest a little of bein' even with the cook. And I shore fetched him some onhappy moments when I got Squint here. Besides before I gits acquainted with him I hears him talkin' to some other fellers. He is the biggest liar I ever listened to. Shorty, he is even a bigger liar than you, and you know that is sayin' a lot." And then Ike walks off a chucklin' to hisself. That shore does git onder my skin. No feller likes to be called a liar even by his best friend. But the funny part of it is that no feller likes to be told that another jasper is a bigger liar than he is. That is right peculiar but it is a line backed truth jest the same.

He is one of the kind that you want to kill a dozen times a day if you see him that often, and he always runs true to form. If one of the ranch hands wants to start a team he has to wait till Squint gits outen the road fer he is bound to be walkin' right in front of them about that time. When we are handlin' stock in the corrals and we open a gate to put 'em through we have to wait till he gits out of the way fer jest that shore he is bound to come a walkin' through frum the other corral and makes us wait till he is out of the way. If the boys drives in with hay to fill the feed racks he is bound to be doin' sumpthin' right at the first empty place they want to drive to. You have all seen that kind of fellers, but he is the worst I have seen. He was bad enough out of doors but inside the house he shore starts the cook to studyin' murder. There was a dance at the school house and of course he goes along. The women folks don't seem to take to him much but that don't bother him not any. The new school marm was there and her and me got along fine. I got as many dances with her as anybody, and she talked to me considerable. That was when the other fellers would let her alone long enough. The next day Squint had more to talk about than anybody. Ike kids me about makin' a hit with the school marm. Right away Squint shets one eye and looks at me plenty wise. "You didn't do so good," he sez. "There was a heap a goin' on there that you didn't know about." That shore makes me mad and I remarks to him. You are plenty smart. You seem to see more with one eye shet than the rest of us does with both eyes open.

We was beginnin' to figger what the finish of this Squint person and the rest of the crew would be, fer even the Boss is beginnin' to give him a mighty hard look when he gits in the road or horns in on a talk. It looked like trouble but we was spared a lot of thinkin'. It happened like this. Ike and old man Morton has fetched in some strays and among them was a plum salty bull. They leaves him in a corral with some cows overnight and then the next day the Boss tells them to put him out into the home paster.

Well, they gits him alone in the corral and then opens the gates and turns him out. He comes out a trottin' with his neck bowed. He has to go through the corral where the wagons and other things is to git to the paster gate. And shore enough there is Squint a pesticatin' around on foot. The bull makes fer him and he lines out to git onder a wagon and he purty near makes it, but in a case like that purty near don't count. That is, not in favor of the feller that is tryin' to git away. So jest as Squint goes down onto all fours to dive onder the wagon, the bull ketches up to him and gives him a turrible jolt. It knocks him plum through and aginst the hind wheel on the fur side. The bull gits his head onder the wagon and upsets it. Time he gits the wagon off'n his horns, he looks up and sees the paster gate and he leaks out of that corral plenty sudden.

We gether Squint up and he is still livin'. He ain't hurt as bad as what you might think, but his head is cut turrible and he has got sech a wallop behind that he is stove up till he cain't hardly walk. The next day he is a sight. His head is swelled so bad his eyes is most shet and he can jest cripple around by holdin' onto things. This ca'ms him down fer a spell, but soon as he begins to git better he is right up and at it ag'in. He begins to bawl us out fer lettin' the bull in where he was. Well, Squint, I sez, there was a heap goin' on that you didn't know nothin' about. The cook he cuts in and sez, "When you go to foolin' with bulls or divin' onder wagons you ort to keep more than one eye open at a time." That shore touches him off and he is plum rim fired fer a spell. The way he cusses us all out is right interestin' to hear. When he slows up one of the ranch hands cuts in. "Squint, you been a gittin' in the road of everybody and every-thing all yore life, and when you keep on like that you can figger that sometime you will git in the road of sumpthin' that's a goin' to knock you outen there." That sets him a goin' again and he allows that we are a rotten lot to pick on him when he cain't take care of hisself, and that he knows he will be out a month's pay before it is all over. "No you won't," the Boss tells him, "yore wuth a heap more like you are than you was before. You git full pay fer two weeks and by that time you'll be able to git in everybody's road ag'in and you can go bother some other outfit." Squint gits mad fer a couple minutes but it ain't long till he has one eye shet and is tellin' 'em big as ever.

One mornin' the boys goes out to take down a beef that was killed and hung up the evenin' before. Ike is comin' fer the storehouse with a quarter that is most gittin' him down, and there in the door is Squint. He shets one eye and shakes his finger and gives Ike some orders. "You fellers ort to put that there meat in the other corner of the storeroom from where you been a puttin' it," he allows. "You see the mornin' sun don't git to that wall, and by the time the evenin' sun gits to that wall and it gits warm it is most night and time to hang it out ag'in." There is Ike a standin' with all that load of beef. He dassent knock Squint over on account of him bein' crippled. He finally eases past him and when be comes out frum there he is so hot his clothes is smokin'. Well Ike I sez, you shore did git even with the cook that time. Ike don't say a word, but he is mad till mighty nigh noon.

About three weeks after Squint gits hurt he allows he is able to travel so the boss takes him to town and pays him off. We don't see him fer a couple of months and then one day me and Ike goes into Harry's place fer a couple of drinks and we hear Squint's voice. He has his back turned and don't see us. He is tellin' about the bull affair. One feller grins at us, but Squint is so busy with his windy that he ain't noticin' nothin'.

"Yessir, fellers, that little kid walked out into the corral jest as they was a turnin' the bull out. I hollered at 'em but you know how thick headed some rannies is. They never noticed and let him out. I was a ways off but I went fer there as fast as I could. Shorty was on the fence and the boss was behind a post. Ike went onder a gate and old Morton he was up on the chute. I couldn't stand there and see that bull tear a pore little kid to pieces and I run and grabbed her and threwed her into a wagon. I tried to git onder the wagon but I had lost too much time a savin' the kid. The bull hit me and then he upsot the wagon. I was busted up purty bad. I won't never know how I done it but hurt like I was I managed to grab the kid and roll onder a gate with her. The bull trotted around the corral a couple of times and then he sees the paster gate and trots out there."

I looks at Ike. He is so mad he is plum froze. You was right Ike, I sez, he is a bigger liar than I am. You ort to be proud of him. He is shore a doin' you proud. Ike walks down along the bar and grabs him by the shoulder and spins him around. "Who is this here little kid you are tellin' about?" he asks and his voice cut like a knife. "Oh, hello, Ikey!" Squint sez holdin' out his hand. "Feelin' better by now?" There comes a smack like when the baseball hits the bat fer a home run and then the gents present waits in respectful silence till Squint becomes conscious ag'in and stands up hangin' onto the bar with one hand and rubbin' his jaw with the other. "You tell that bull story like it happened." That was all Ike said. Squint's eyes was poppin' wide open like a beetle's this time. He worked his jaw a couple of times before he could make any talk come. You bet he don't shet one eye. He lights right in and tells that bull affair as clear and plain as anybody could and fer a man that ain't used to tellin' the truth, he shore does wonderful.

That night when we are ridin' home I asks Ike if he reckons he is even with me and the cook. He allows he is and that he is even with Squint too but that he will have to listen to us about it fer the next two years. He tells the boss about it a couple days later in front of me and old man Morton, and he makes the same remark about havin' to do a lot of listinin'. "You might and then ag'in you mightn't," the boss remarks lookin' at him plum straight and hard. Ike looks some surprised. He figgers the boss and him is on good terms up to right then. "Mebby you know why we didn't git that shipment of white faced yearlin's we had as good as closed the deal fer?" the boss sez. Ike still looks surprised and sez nothin'. "Well, Ike, I'll tell you," the boss sez cold and even like. "That pest you drug out here to bother the whole outfit fer yore own amusement, went and wrote to a Californey outfit he used to work fer, jest what they could be got fer.

They sent a man and he closed the deal before we had a chance to make a second bid. We wouldn't 'a overbid 'em anyhow. It would 'a knocked too big a hole in the profits. From here on up the creek if you git half drunk and find some pest you want to play with you ride toward some other outfit with him. You'll save yourself the trouble and distance of comin' by this way." Ike don't say a word. He is plum took down, fer him and the boss has built up the outfit together, but one thing is plain. The spread has growed till Ike is only a cow puncher and not worth no more than I am. The boss bein' a business man and Ike ain't. Somehow all at once I feel sorry fer Ike and I offer to quit with him but he sez, "Shorty, me and the boss didn't start all at once and we won't quit sudden. I got a lot of my own business to settle up around here and durin' that time I can figger whether I start a little spread of my own or go back to my little home town by the Ohio river and be a nice comfortable peaceful old villager."

Cap and Morton Each Tell One [4]

It don't seem long since that night at Cap's place, but I reckon it has been. We was talkin' how modern things was gittin'. Steam boats, railroad trains, telegraphs, and even a talkin' machine had been invented. And to cap it all, folks was a goin' up in baloons at the county fairs and jumpin' out in parachutes. We reckoned the world was a goin' so fast that before long people would all kill their self with the fool contraptions that was bein' invented.

"Well," Old Cap remarks, "it is shore a lot safer at sea than it was when I was a boy on the old wind jammers. I mind one time we got in a turrible storm down in the South Seas and we was blowed off our course fer several days. Then one night all of a sudden it stopped. It wasn't long before we was a rockin' on some long slow swells. Come mornin' we looked around and there we was on a calm sea. Over off our port bow about a league away was a British schooner flyin' a distress signal. About half a league to sta'board was a Portuguese bark with a distress signal. We signalled and got no answer. The second mate took a boat and we went over to the Portuguese. Her boats was missin', and the ropes still hung from the divats where they had cast off. I was young and spry and I went up a rope. The ship was deserted. I found a rope ladder and cast over the side and the boat's crew and the second mate made the boat fast and came aboard. We couldn't find much water. The mate read the log and read it. The last entry was a month old. They had been becalmed there fer weeks and had took to the boats as near as we could make out. One of the crew could read some Spanish and he done the translatin'. That afternoon we manned a boat and went over to the British schooner. We could make out more of her log. Her crew had took to the boats about a week before. That ship had come in just after the Portuguese and knew all about her, but why would they take to the boats in an open sea with a good ship under them? We found out. They mentioned that they had seen a sail to the East but it was so far off they couldn't signal to 'em. Well, they had looked through glasses from the crow's nest and they saw signs of a steady breeze about twenty or twenty-five knots to the East. They took to the boats in hope of makin' it to the course of some ship. Purty slim in that forsaken sea. The first mate was an old feller and when him and the skipper took the bearings, they had a big talk. The mate allowed he had heard of the place. It was a dead calm only three or four times a year and then a hurricane swept it and tore everything to pieces. We rested a couple of days and figgered. The sharks was so bad that we couldn't do nothin' in the water but the sail maker and the carpenter got a big idee."

"We had some machinery aboard. So they rigged up a wind wheel like a dutch wind mill and put a big fly wheel on it. Then they set a four man windlass with a turrible big wooden wheel in the middle, and we was to work four men at a time on it. It was hard to start but it was geared so high that when we got it a goin' it shore hummed. After an hour the skipper shouted the news that the ship was movin' some. It was slow work but we kept at it all we could stand. The third day we felt a kind of a breeze. We run up some canvas and the next thing we knowed we was in the track of the air current and sailin' right along. We had to tack a little but we made it. We looked back and saw by the water that the breeze had sort of curved to meet us. You see them boys had worked so hard on the wind wheel that they had made the ship go slow and not only that but the suction of the air they blowed had bent that there breeze about five miles off its course. It was wonderful work."

Old Cap lit his pipe and looked at us cow fellers and grinned. It was shore a turrible yarn to match. I looked at Ike and the Boss. Some of the boys looked at me and then we all looked at the Old Man Morton. Old Morton lit his corn cob and took a few drags at it and set his hat back. We knowed he had took the dare and he begun like this:

Speakin' of the weather and the likes makes me think of one time we was on the trail with two thousand head comin' up from Texas. We had been goin' right good till we got up into some mesa country and it was sometimes hard to make them cattle take the trails down the hills off them mesas. One night we bedded down on a big mesa and the next morning the remuda and the wagon went down into the canyon ahead of us. The herd started all right but before they went far they stopped on us. As fast as we would rim off a lead they would double back and keg up with the rest. Things was at a standstill. We would lose a week if we went back through the pass and tried the other way. We had along a Baptist preacher's son named Abner Baines. He was the only one that wasn't cussin'. He watched and worked and then he got to the boss and asked him if he thought a hard rain would do any harm. The boss was about to jerk a few doubles of rope off'n his head but he cooled down and asked what he meant. "Well," sez Abner, "this is a 'dobe hill and if it is wet nothin' could stick on it, it would be so slick.

I aimed to pray fer rain if you thought best. I don't want to disturb the Lord unneces-
sary." The boss told him if the language that was bein' used didn't disturb the Lord, a
few prayers wouldn't. Abner wanted us all to go down to the wagon in the canyon so
as to be safe when the rain came. The boss allowed we better go down and eat and come
back anyhow, and he would stay up there and see what he could do.

When we got to the wagon, Abner wanted the cook to move a little on account he
mightn't be safe when the cattle come down but the cook was mad anyhow and mighty
nigh hung the pot hook over Abner's head. But Abner was ca'm. He took off his spurs
and chaps and hat and ast us to be quiet. "If yore strippin' fer a corn dance," sez the
cook, "I might could give you some tom tom music with a pan or pot lid." We was fit
to bust fer laffin' but we had got over our mad and was glad fer anything that would
make us furgit them pesticatin' cattle fer a few minutes. Well, Abner he kneeled down
and he shore knew how to address the Lord plum respectful. He did so good that we
all furgot everything and was listenin'. Then all of a sudden the sky got dark and before
half an hour there come a reglar cloud bust. That 'dobe hill got wet and slick and of all
the bellerin' and floppin' and slidin' you ever seen or listened to, it happened then. We
jumped on our hosses and took out. The cook clum a tree. We jest got clear of the
mess before there was cattle bunched all around the wagon and trompin' over pots and
pans and buckets. But wust of all here come the boss on his hoss slidin' right amongst
'em. And he was a yellin' at the top of his voice and cussin' Abner. "Abner! Abner!" he
yells, "git the Lord stopped 'fore we all git washed down the canyon!" We was all still
fer a spell and then Old Morton sez: "Yessir, Abner shore savvied prayin'."

"When I was a kid at Sunday school," sez Ike, "we was told about two people that
told a big lie right in a meetin' house and was both struck dead. Good thing this ain't
no meetin' house."

"Don't go fetchin' religion into this here peaceful descussion," sez Old Morton.
Which remark was too much fer even Cap and the Boss, so we all had a good laff and
hunted up our bed rolls.

Stickin' to One Idee [5]

One night over at the home ranch several of us was settin' on the front porch. We
got to talkin' about folks changin' from one plan to another and losin' a lot of time and
work. Old Man Morton he reckoned it was better fer folks to stick to one idee. "Fer
instance," he sez, ["]there was old Hard Rock Jake and Farmer Tom. Jake he had a tun-
nel on the side of a mountain and Tom he took up a claim in the bottom of a wide
canyon right below and kep' a tryin' to farm without any water. It was plum pitiful.
They would go away and work till they got a stake and then come back. Jake would
dig in his mine and Tom would farm. Sometimes in a right good year Tom would make

a few beans and now and then Jake would git the notion that he was close to the gold.["]

["]They fit Injuns and part of the time they packed in water. They made a flood ditch and a 'dobe house and corral. They had put in twenty-four years in that canyon before they knowed it. The boys allowed that the next year they might gang up and give 'em a silver anniversary or sumpthin' like that, when what do you s'pose? One day old Jake shot right into a big onder ground water supply and it come a runnin' out of the tunnel. He give Tom the water fer his ranch and was a goin' to start another mine but while they was a buildin' a ditch to take the water to Tom's ranch they had to drive a tunnel through the point of a little hill and if old Jake didn't strike a right good lead of gold. Which shows if you foller one idee fur enough it will git you some place worth while even if it don't git you where you aimed to go in the first place."

Lige Jones lit his pipe and set quiet fer a spell and then he begins. "A idee follered plum out is all right if the idee is practical. If it ain't you may go wrong. When I was a kid back in the Kaintucky hills I knowed a fambly by the name of Bascomb. Old Mis' Bascomb she was one of them one-idee women folks. Well, one day she was a washin' down by the spring and the hogs got to botherin' around where she was at. She got to kickin' 'em outen the road but her bein' barefooted she hurt her toes a heap more than she did the hogs. Finally she rech down and grabbed up a rock and throwed overhanded at one of 'em. The Old Man Bascomb had left a scythe hung up in a tree and she ketched her arm on it and cut her self sumpthin' turrible. It looked like she might bleed to death but the oldest boy he heered his mammy hollerin'. He havin' been to school knowed what to do. He took her apron and tied it around her arm and then he twisted it up with a stick till he got the blood stopped. After that the old lady was plum tickled with that idee of a rag and a twistin' stick whenever anybody got hurt.["]

["]Well a couple of years later the oldest boy got to goin' out in the evenings and settin' up with the gals. So of course he got a razor and took up shavin'. The younger kids was all told to keep their hands offen that razor but the youngest boy was foolin' with the razor one day and his mammy come in and ketched him at it. He got skeert and give a jerk and a jump and like to a cut his neck in half. The blood shore popped out. Old Mis' Bascomb she grabbed down the roller towel and the mush paddle and went to work on him. The second oldest gal tried to git her stopped but she was big and stout and she had jest one idee. She got the blood stopped but the pore kid was choked to death before she did. The Old Man Bascomb wasn't so mad about it as folks reckoned he would be. He allowed the kid would 'a bled to death anyhow and besides they had a big enough fambly that they could spare one to experiment on now and ag'in."

We had a big long laigged Texas boy with us by the name of Curley Powers. He was reckoned to be a plum good liar and the boss sez to him, "Well, Curley, what do you think of this here parminint idee business[?]" Curley he rolls up a cigarette and studies fer a minute and then he cuts into it. "Well," Curley begins, "down in Texas they don't go much on idees. Not that they would bar a feller fer havin' a idee, but there is about the same things fer everybody to do and about the same things to do with and so they jest go ahead and they all come out about the same, idee or no idee. The only critter in our settlement that had a parminint idee was a big old long horned steer. He used to water at the creek and then come up and stand in the shade of our shed. Our corral was pickets on three sides and a shed on the North side. I used to lay fer him and chunk him but all he done was to run round and round the corral. I set old Shep on him but he jest went round and round the corral. He would run over anything that got in his way but you couldn't run him away from that corral till he got good and ready to leave. He had a sot idee. Old Shep got discouraged and give it up.["]

["]One day the folks went to town and left me there alone. I see the old steer a waterin' out down on the creek and I got up on the shed roof and laid fer him. I waited till he was a standin' there chawin' his cud and I jumped off and lit on his back, aimin' to ride him round the corral till he give out. But when I lit on him he bucked me so high I could see plum over the timber down along the creek. He went around so fast that he was right onder me when I come down and I lit on his back. The jar was turrible, but he bucked me right up in the air ag'in, and he was plum around and onder me when I lit. I jest couldn't git to the ground fer he had that one idee of goin' around that there corral[.] I don't know how many times he went around[.] I lost all track of 'em. I allowed my time had come, when all of a sudden I lit on the ground[.] I rolled out of the way and fainted plum onconcious.["]

["]When I was able to git up there was the steer a layin' dead. He had gone round that corral so fast and so many times that he had tore all the dirt away frum the south east corner post and he had run into it when it leaned out, and killed hisself. Him not bein' able to see it fer the fog of dust he was a raisin'. That is why I happen to be so long laigged and onperportioned like. I was split up a heap further than was nacheral after that there awful experience. Fact is you might say I am the victim of the parminint idee." Old Man Morton was a little bit peeved about the boys buildin' stories like they thought he lied and he remarks. "Too bad you couldn't a lit on yore haid a few times and shortened yore neck a little."

Hell Among the Yearlin's [6]

Between the home ranch and the south ranch laid a big strip of country we called Middle Valley. What with their fencin' and fixin' Cap and the boss had got it shut off from everybody else and was a holdin' it fer winter paster. There was a little ranch on a creek at the head of the valley that was called Dutchman's well, on account a Dutchman had settled there and dug a well right beside the creek. The creek sunk there and that was the only water in the valley except the seeps along the wash.

A family had been leasin' the place from an agent in town fer the last several years but they only had about three hundred head and had agreed to let us water there the comin' winter. Things looked all right only that Ike was fixin' to leave the outfit. He had spent all his time in slack seasons turnin' everything he had into cash. He was sore on the spread. Old Cap wanted to beller and boss around, and the boss had rigged up a room in the house and called it an office, and he was gittin' mighty high chinned too.

Cap come over to the Home Ranch one day and that night after supper they sent fer Ike. The winder to the office room was up, so I stood out in the dark where I could hear and see what went on. Ike was shore a different Ike when he walked in. He speaks right up. "All right, what's heavy on yore minds?" That aggervated 'em both. They wanted folks to act polite and scairt around where they was. "Jest this," the boss sez, giving him a hard look. "You got so much of yore own business to tend to that we don't need you around here. We are givin' you yore time and you can tend yore own business all you want to." Ike takes a folded paper out of his shirt pocket and hands it to the boss. The boss looks it over and then pulls some figgers out from his desk and looks 'em over. Then he sez to Ike. "We was a goin' to give you two dollars and a half more, but we'll settle to yore figgers." He writes a check and hands it to Ike. "We'll allow you a team to haul what stuff you have off the ranch tomorrow if you know where you want it sent," sez the boss. "Thanks," Ike sez, "but I ain't imposin' on folks that ain't as able to take care of their self as I am. I'll git my stuff and myself out from here without any half cocked help." Old Cap has been settin' quiet up to now but that teches him off and he hits the table with his [fist] and bellers, "Looka here, you lanky lubber! Git smart with me and you'll have a lot of help a gittin' out o' here right now!" "Why hello Grampa," Ike sez right pleasant, "you here? I thought you was in a pen with the weaners sence the hands had took to leadin' you around on the end of a saddle rope." Cap jumps up but he takes a look at Ike and sets down ag'in. "That's better," sez Ike right cool. "Be a good boy and Sandy Claus won't furgit ye. I fetched a present fur ye but seein' yore sech a good child fer to mind I might keep it till further on." Then he turns to the boss and remarks. "Speakin' of folks tendin' to their own business, that's exactly what I aim to do. And, in case you ever have trouble in doin' the same I might could help you some." Then he walks out.

I goes into the kitchen to have a smoke with the cook. The cook drags a jug from onder a bunch of boxes and we have a good one. He slaps me on the belt at the left prong of my vest. Then he grins and remarks, "So you was aimin' to take a stack yoreself."[7] Well, sez I, the boss is bigger'n Ike and Cap is a reglar old grizzley, besides they might 'a had things fixed to suit 'em in the office. Ike fetched me here. "Me too," allows the cook, "which is feed fer thinkin'!" He repurduces the jug and this time we takes one that is right refreshin'. The cook gits down his fiddle and tunes her up. He cuts into a real tune and he shore makes the old fiddle hum. Purty soon the boss pokes his head in at the door and asks, "What's all this noise. We got business to tend to." Old Cap shoulders past him and stands there glarin' savage at us. "That what you been hearin'," sez the cook, "is a selection frum grand opray commonly knowed as Hell Among the Yearlin's."[8] I lines my left knee with Cap's belt and don't even bother to git up. Cap is puzzled and goes back to the office. The boss looks at the cook fer a spell and the cook looks at him. I know right then that they are both gettin' better acquainted in five minutes than they have done in five years.

Next night I got in late on a tired hoss but the cook he had a drink fer me and saved a hot supper too. "Shorty," he sez, "they'll be hell among the yearlin's all right. Old Tenley Tingle and his nephew Joe was here today and got Ike and his stuff." I knowed them two. They was two Ozark mountain Missourians thet had been workin' on the ranches and ditches that summer. They each had a mule team, a covered wagon and a dog.

Two weeks later there was a big free dance and feed at the school house. It was to celebrate the fact that Joe Tingle had married Mandy Black and was movin' into Dutchman's wells ranch. Me and the cook went. Old man Morton comes to me durin' the dance and sez, "Shorty, Ike has bought Dutchman's wells. He has bought Black's cattle and sold 'em. I ast him about waterin' our stock there this winter and he sez no. Blacks has bought a hay ranch on the river."[9] That shore makes me onhappy and I don't dance with nobody except the widder Baisinger who is my best friend. I goes to Ike and asks him. He allows I can tell the boss what I like. I tells him he brought me here and he only grins and sez, "Shorty, I never had no Colt's when I was talkin' to the boss and Cap, but I knowed you was right handy with yours."

Next mornin' I tells the boss and he is shore mad. He saddles and goes to the South Ranch to see Cap. He is gone two days. When he comes back he is plenty mad. He asks me if I have used my homestead right, and when he finds out I have, he hunts up two of the other hands. Then he tells me, "We will show Ike a thing or two. We will get these two men to homestead claims at Clay Flat. That is right in the middle of the valley. We will build a big reservoir and fence some hay land. If you remember there is a place where the bed rock crops out and makes a natural flood dam.[10] But why do you reckon he sold Black's cattle?" Well, I sez, mebby he reckoned you'd push all the stuff you could into the valley and keep him frum takin' in stock to winter. Right then the boss grins and allows I am right and tells me to hitch up to the spring wagon and take them two fellers over and show 'em the layout. In the mornin' we hitches up. Jest before noon we tops the hog back that separates Home Ranch frum Middle Valley. I can see with my neckid eye but the boss pulls out his glasses and gives it some see. Looks like we been asleep, I sez, but the boss sez nothin. "Go ahead down there," he sez. I drives down there and I can see what happened. A frame shack is bein' built and a line of plowed ground marks the line of flood ditch that leads from the outcroppin' of bed rock to the best reservoir sight in Middle Valley. Ike rides up to welcome us on his big grey. "Git down and have a snack seein' it's nigh noon," he sez. The boss gives him a dirty look and asks, "How long has this been a goin' on?"

Ike answers, "Well, genrally speakin', it's been goin' on fer a spell. The boys filed on these claims and the ditch right before the last roundup and hay cuttin', but seein' they was busy, they didn't start work till a couple weeks ago. I aim to live on this place where the reservoir is and the old man can live on his place. Nice little place and spread, come to figger it out."[11]

The boss keeps his temper and acts right cheerful, but when he gits back he is plum mad and ready to do all the damage he could. They makes a work and sells off some more cattle, then they pushes everything they can into the end of the valley to keep stuff from driftin' down toward the river.

I goes to the boss and sez, now looka here, them fellers has sunk a sump in the wash at Clay Flat and that gives 'em all the water they want fer them and their teams. But two things. Fust, we are dependin' on the seep water in the wash fer stock water. Second, what about the upper end of the valley? Who is watchin' that? The boss allows that he aims to send some hands into the wash with plows and scrapers to holler out some water holes, and if Ike don't want his little paster and alfalfa field and his hay stacks et up it is up to him to fix his fences or stay there and watch 'em. I tells him that there was a big after growth when they cut the last alfalfa and in case some of our stuff gits in there and bloats Ike mightn't bother to stick 'em. The boss laffs and allows that when Ike and them hill billies lets somebody else have that stubble paster he will put in with me.

Well, one day I gits oneasy and rides up to Dutchman's wells to see what the score really is, and there I git a look. The alfalfa fence is down and scattered all over the forty acres of stubble is a passel of critters that has bloated and died. That with the short water in the seeps has shore knocked the profit out of all the winter feed in middle valley.[12]

We finally gits everything settled on the winter range or the feed[13] and the boss surprises me by tellin' me one mornin' to go over and see what Ike and the Tingles will sell out fer. I goes to the cook and asks him about it. He tells me to come around fust thing after I have saddled up. Well, I does that same. The cook he purduces the jug. We has one, we has two, we has three. The cook fills up a half pint flask and sez, "Make two of it and talk to 'em." Well, I goes over and wants to know what they will take and sell out. All they does is to take me up to the Dutchman's Wells and show me where the creek is runnin' a wheel which taps the onderflow and allows the Dutchman's Wells Ranch to raise twice the feed they have been raisin'!

The boss ain't a whole lot pleased when he hears that and he reckons he has to go over and see Cap. I asks him what's the matter with Cap comin' over here, but he tells me he don't want Cap over here because he is on the fight and wants to go over to Middle Valley and warn them folks they better never try to run cattle in there or he'll make it plenty hot for 'em. I git the boss's angle. Ike is a good rifle shot and them two hill billies is past master with a rifle. And the whole three of 'em has nerve enough to tackle a buzz saw and give it three rounds the start.

We go over to the South Ranch in the buckboard. Cap is shore rairin' mad and I can see the boss is plum fed up on him and would be mighty glad to git out of partnership with him. Cap is goin' over to talk to Ike, he sez. Well I goes out pirootin' around and I finds four sharp tacks. I goes into the shop and gits a awl and a screw driver. I rips a little place in the britchin' of Cap's mule harness and punches a hole with the fine awl and purty soon I has four tacks in the two britchin's. The rip don't hardly show the heads is between the leather and I dabs a little dope off an axle on the points where they stick through.

When we start next mornin' old Cap has the boys hitch up his big mules to the spring wagon. He takes a new hand and has him saddle up and go along. The new hand is a hard lookin' feller and he has a carbeen onder his stirrup leather. Cap comes out and lays a Winchester back of him in the wide wagon seat. The mules is fat and frisky. The boss and me are in the buckboard and Cap starts off. He went down a little hill below the house and the britchin' comes up on the mules. Them tacks done wonderful. First the mules spooks and then they starts to run and kick. Old Cap sets back and breaks one line and then the team quits the wagon tracks and upsets the spring wagon on rough ground. Cap and his shootin' iron go a flyin'. Cap tries to git up but no use, he has a broke laig. I help git the mules and while the rest is workin' on Cap I works on the harness and gits the tacks out. Cap's laig is broke between the knee and the ankle. The spring wagon is a wreck, so the boss takes him to town in the buckboard and sends me back to the home ranch. I tells nobody about the tacks, but all I wished was it had happened at the beginnin' of spring instead of winter.

Ike Gets a New Job [14]

About a week after they had took Cap to town with a broke leg the Boss goes in to see him. He comes back all fussed up. It seems that Cap and his side kick is not the main owners of the spread on the South. But that it belongs to a big company back east that has sorta gone into the cow business for a side line. They own a big lot of shippin' and they want Cap back on his old job with the company. They figger he is worth a heap more there. And there you are. Cap leavin' soon with a busted leg. Old man Morton laid up with the rheumatiz and his grandson ridin' in to tell us that the outfit on the south has got to start feedin' right soon. How come they got to feed soon? I wants to know. The Boss tells me that Ike has bought a lot of feed and cattle in the south valley from the little outfits and while they was pesterin' him in Middle Valley he has put them all up onto the South Ranch range and kep' 'em there till they took their cattle back. And now him and Old Tenley Tingle and a couple of hands is over in the

South Valley finishin' 'em out on the feed he has bought and the South Ranch has been et out so bad that they have to feed their beef hay to stock cattle this winter.[15]

The worst of it is, they want us to go over and help git started. I asks Old Morton's grandson what is the matter with Manuel and that new tough guy doin' some feedin'. He tells me they are both gone. They didn't git along none too good. Tough guy gits to settin' on Manuel's hosses. They had some words about it. Manuel finds there is a reward out fer this jasper and so he turns him in. The kid sez that the feller will have a steady job fer a long time and Manuel ain't goin' to work none this winter on account he has to lay off and spend his summer's wages and some of that reward money.

The kid and me puts our outfits into the spring wagon and starts over fer the South Ranch. When we git there we learn the cook aims to stay if it is agreeable but Cap's old pardner is goin' to go back with him. The cook tells me that Ricky's dad is one of the directors of the company and that fer some reason he has got in touch with Ike. That shore does mix matters up.

Well, we had got a couple new hands and was startin' on the feedin', the Boss bein' there that evenin' when in comes old Tenley Tingle and Ike. They has a couple of beds along and makes down in the bunk house. Of course, they comes in fer supper. They acted like nothin' had happened. The cook seemed happy and was kiddin' Ike about how the gray hairs was beginnin' to show above his ears, and the Boss asks old Tenley Tingle how things was a goin' fer him. Tingle lights his pipe and gives a wicked grin.

"Come to think of it,' he drawls, "this here year makes me think of a year we had back home. We had been havin' bad luck fer a spell but this season we raised a spankin' big wheat crop. So all we had to bother about was the thrashin' bill and some old stale debts that we had got used to a long time ago. We had the wheat stacked and ready when the wind begun to blow. It blowed hard and steady. Then come a earthquake. It would shake turrible fer a spell and then stop but the wind kep' right on a blowin' steady. It kep' that up fer two days and nights. When it was over we went out and looked. What d'ya s'pose? We didn't have to thrash aytall. The earthquake had shook out all the wheat and the wind blowed the stray and trash away so all we had to do was to shovel it up and put it into the barn." The Boss looks at him and remarks, "I suppose all that hadn't hurt the barns any." "No not to speak of," old Tingle answers. "You see, we had a lot of hogs and as soon as the rumpus started they all run and crowded onder the barn and as you might say, sorter absorbed the shock. The house did slide around some, but it finished up [closer] to the well and the wood pile than what it was and made things handier all around. And speakin' of hogs, the wind scattered the straw over the ground we aimed to plow fer fall wheat. All we had to do was to take the rings outen the hogs' noses and turn 'em out on that ground. They tore and rooted it up a plenty. Then we sold the fat ones and put the rings back into the rest of their noses and harried the ground down and seeded it. It was the most plum agreeable season we ever had." The Boss remarks that he don't doubt such things happen sometimes and when he sees 'em he knows he will be considerable interested. We knows the old cuss means sumthin' but we can't figger him out. Next day we know. In drives Ricky's dad and another company man and they tell us that seein' Cap is leavin' and Morton not able to run the spread they have made a deal with Ike to ramrod it. The Boss don't look none too happy, but he is up against it. They all git togather in the front room of the house and talk it over and they reckon as soon as Cap can move they will go into town and sign papers and Cap can come out and git what stuff ready he aims to take with him. Meantime, Ike is to stay right there and set on the lid. When I asks Ike about it he tells me that when he left our outfit and the [trouble] started in Middle Valley Ricky's dad started in to write to him and ask him what the row was, seein' Cap had wrote sumthin' about it. He told them the truth. Then when they found how he had moved in on their range when they moved on his'n he gits more letters. He still tells things straight and lets 'em know he aims to keep right on with his own affairs and advises that they do the same. It seems Ricky's dad thinks a heap of his boy by now and that Ricky is gettin' to be a right good sized sensible young feller. The old man talks it over with him and asks him about Ike. The boy gives him his idee and the old man allows that Ike has shore played a good level headed game and wants Ike to meet him at the ranch.

I tells Ike I am glad things turned like they did and he looked tickled and sez, "Shorty, did you ever hear that old sayin' All on account of a horseshoe nail?" I tells him I have, and he remarks that hoss shoe nails ain't had much to do with this, but he reckons a few tacks or fine steeples might have done sumthin' toward it. I asks him what he means and he sez: "Well, I know Cap and his mules. I know you. It ain't like them mules to have a ruckus with Cap. I've knowed some funny things to happen when you was around. So I have looked them harness over. You would have to be lookin' fer it to see it but it looks to me like the britchin' had been doctored a little. Well, it saved a rifle fight at Middle Valley and got Cap outen here and put me and my old friend the Boss back to where we will likely be friends again."

The Boss and me goes back to the home ranch and I know the Boss reckons he has had a fall took out of him because he don't talk about business aytall only jest common things that happen every day and don't mean nothin'. I tell our cook about it, and he sez: "Shorty, you ort to a' said to the Boss like he allus said to I and you. Isaac is an extremely fortunate person."

The Old Timers

A bunch of old longhorns that's peacefully grazin',
Like forty years back you'd still see on the range.
When you come to think of it, it's really amazin',
The way that the people and cattle both change.

I used to allow it was cruel and dirty
To pen up the cattle and cut off their horns.
In a feed lot a muley may look sort of purty,
But out on the range he looks mighty forlorn.

They didn't feed cotton cake, beet pulp and silage.
There wasn't no corn chop and hay by the bale.
But how them old critters could put on the milage,
A goin' to water or hittin' the trail.

They may have looked rangy and tougher than leather,
But they had lots of beef steak wrapped up in their hide.
They could fatten on grass and stand all kinds of weather,
And it didn't hurt much if a few of 'em died.

II
Last Stories

Shorty's Boss Buys Purebred Bulls [1]

Things got to changin' around the spread and all the old hands was gone. Even Ike went. I got a letter from Ed Gray, a feller that had been with us a couple of years before and he allowed there was a job fer me up where he was at. He asked fer me to let him know right away. One of the other hands wanted my two hosses so the next day I sold 'em to him and told the Boss that I reckoned I about had it made. He seemed a little surprised but soter pleased fer I knew he was about through with the old style of cow hands. I sacked my saddle and put my bed in a box and got on the train. I had been with that spread quite a spell, but somehow I felt like it was time to drag it and I wouldn't be missed much and I wouldn't miss nothin' much.

When I got to the new job they told me the Boss had gone to a stock show. That seemed funny to me fer all I knew about a stock show you could put in a Durham sack and still have room fer a half day's smokin'. He left orders that if I come to let me work around the home ranch till he got back. It was shore an up to date spread and the boys had a closed shed to hang saddles and harness in. I felt soter ashamed when I hung my old rope and brush scarred saddle up alongside the rest. My bed had been on a hoss a lot and it didn't look or smell like it ort to in a bunk house like them hands had. But Ed was glad to see me and the boys was all friendly so it wasn't so bad.

When the boss did git back he sent word to Ed to bring me and come to town. When we got to the little town the Boss was there and in the shippin' pens he had six pure bred bulls. We took 'em part way home and corraled at a little ranch that night. Next day we got home with 'em. He rested 'em up in the feed lot fer a spell before he turned 'em out. You know how news travels in a stock country, and seem like every feller on that neck of the range knowed all about them pure bred bulls right now. Several fellers come to look at 'em and of course they all had the same line of talk about cattle hadn't ort to be bred too fine if you expected 'em to rustle their livin'. The bulls was shore good lookin'. There wasn't much daylight onder none of them. They was jest one solid hunk of beef and you could see they was a class of cattle that would fatten quick. When one of the fellers had left, after sayin' he reckoned they wasn't the right sort of cattle to turn out the Boss asks me my idee. Well, I sez, a feller can eat tripe and he can eat beef steak, but not many fellers take willin'ly to tripe fer a steady diet if they can git beef steak.

The Boss allows that is about his idee too, but, he sez, "You ain't heard nothin' yet. Inside the next two days they'll be three old jaspers over here to give me a real rawhidin'. I want you to hear it and git acquainted with 'em. You'll be ridin' all the time and you'll likely have consid'able to do with 'em. A feller lots of times can git a better idee of a man frum hearin' him talk to somebody else than he can talkin' to him hisself. Shonough, the next day in rides them three old moss backs. The one that started it was old Clem Boggs. He never fed nothin' and before he would shoe a hoss he would ride him till his feet was wore off plum up to the hair. He was right funny about it even if he had took a big loss from not havin' feed the winter before. "Al," he sez to the Boss, "them fat short legged bulls ain't fitten fer to turn out in this country. All they can do is to git jest about fur enough frum home to lay down and die." "Well," the Boss answers, "you'd ort to know, a lot of yore stuff went about that distance last winter." Old Clem he bites off a chaw and the other two fellers cain't help grinnin' a little. Then old Andy Harper he takes a turn at the Boss. "No Clem," he sez right hopeful, "I reckon they won't go that fur. They'll stay right at the water hole where you put 'em and every mornin' and evenin' one of the boys can ride over with a nose bag and feed 'em. In the winter time he can blanket him and in the summer time he can fix a big umbreller fer him to stand onder. You can leave a bull at six different waters and that way you'll always know where they are at." "The blanket and the feed bag idee might be all right," the Boss allows, "but they won't need no umbrellers till they git bald headed, and when they git like that they won't be no good nohow, so I'll jest let 'em stray around and suffer till they die off."

Old Andy is bald as a cue ball and he colors up consid'able. The other two has a laff on him but old Carney was game and he took his turn with no waitin'. Now old Carney had been busy keepin' jest a shade ahead of a foreclosure ever since anybody in them parts knowed him.

"Al," he sez, "don't you think them helpless critters is a big waste of time and money? You might have kept six extra steers on yore range and then you could 'a got beef prices fer 'em. That's what I'd 'a done. I reckon the result would be about the same." The Boss fills and lights his pipe and takes a minute to answer that one. "In yore case Carney," he remarks slow and easy like, "it mightn't make much difference. I have heard the sheriff fed the prisoners bull beef so it would likely be a question of weather he sold 'em or butchered 'em."

Old Carney was a good natured cuss and he got more fun out of that one than any of us. "That's right, Al," he laffs, "I ain't no bookkeeper and I ain't no cashier but I reckon I've worked fer the banks nigh goin' onto thirty year. But what we're a gittin' at is this. If you breed range cattle up too fine they won't rustle." They was all agreed on that and had a lot to say. The Boss he let 'em talk till they was through, then he sez: "Well, seein' these bulls ain't goin' to git over a hundred yards frum the water my neighbors ain't goin' to suffer none onless they let too many of their cattle git over onto me.["]

When we did turn the bulls out I asks the Boss: Do you think them fellers is so bowed up about havin' them bulls turned out on this range, or are they like a feller in a hoss trade? You know a feller never sez a good word about a hoss he aims to trade fer. The Boss gives me a big wink and sez, "You got the idee. Now act accordin'."

No, them bulls didn't stick right at the water holes. It wasn't long before they was plum scarce. I done some trackin' and as the Boss had said I acted accordin'. I rides into the home ranch and tells the Boss about it. One is shut up in a school section and the other five is scattered around across the hog back and the creek among the neighbors' cattle. "You know how they got there?" he asks. Well, I remarks, onless they was drove off, accordin' to the tracks they got to each of 'em leadin' a couple of shod hosses off'n the range. You know, I tells the Boss, them fellers said that when critters was bred too fine they wouldn't rustle. That bein' the case I reckon you got some neighbors that ain't exactly aristocratic.

We works till we gits our pure blood bulls back and then the Boss makes it a point partick'lar to tell them three gents that next time his bulls git over on their range he would take it as a favor if they would let him know and not let 'em stay and ruin their herd.

When we got things straightened out the Boss stayed one night at my camp and of course we got to talkin' cattle. "The only thing to be said fer scrub cattle," he allows, "is that they are hardy and can git about. Now speed and endurance in a hoss is a fine thing and makes him val'able and useful. But packin' houses ain't payin' no extra prices fer steers with track reckords. They buy by weight and speed don't weigh much. So, as long as they only pay fer beef, I aim to raise cattle with meat on 'em."

Bruce Kiskaddon Visits Old Friends in Arizona [2]

On Saturday, April 8, the Livestock Growers of Mohave County held their spring meet. They gathered at the Cane Springs ranch on the Sandy, forty miles from Kingman. I got a bid, and was I pleased? It had been fifteen years since I worked up in that country and I got to thinkin' about it more and more till I finally told the Missus that I aimed to be among those present or bust sumpthin' tryin'.

She agreed to go along and took her friend Mrs. Richards. On the seventh we got the old car out and headed her toward Kingman and we didn't bend her till we got there. That evening we went to the Beale Hotel where the Association had reserved rooms for us. Mrs. Chapman, the proprietor, was very cordial and friendly and did everything possible to make our stay a pleasant one.

Next afternoon was the doin's. The business meetin' was first, and, not bein' a member of course I didn't attend, but we rolled in in time for the barbecue, and a barbecue it was. They had everything a human would want to eat. And that beef! He was a dandy and had been fixed up plum right or even a little bit better than that. There is a slim chance there might at some time or place been beef that was as good, but it's a cinch there was never any better. And we had real cow camp coffee. The kind you dassent put milk or sugar in fer fear you'd spoil it.

To ride or drive over that country you'd say it was settled soter scant but they shore found a heap of the best kind of folks from somewheres. After the big feed we had settled down and was so comfortable and satisfied that we would have set still fer quite a spell if the music hadn't started in the big dance hall. Well, young folks will dance even if they are fed plum full. It took about three minutes for them to crowd the floor and start. There was a bunch of honest to God cowboys and gals! Well, don't think fer a minute the cities have the beauties all corralled. They averaged better lookin' than any bunch I ever saw. The Missus and me tried to figger out the purtiest gal there and finally decided it laid about equal between fifteen or twenty of 'em. It was a sight to see the purty silk stockin's and slippers flashin' around among the high heeled boots of the cow hands. It was the happiest crowd I ever saw, and all real ladies and gentlemen too. Not a word or move that was off color or out of line. Nobody drunk or tryin' to show off. Instead of the usual hand clappin' at the end of each dance the kids yelled fer more, and I mean they hollered. Them boys and gals could make a siren on a fire truck sound like a jew's harp. A lot of the old gray haired ladies got in there and stepped right along with the best of 'em and so did a lot of the old gents too.

Me not bein' a dancer, I sat and stood around with a lot of the folks outside that I had worked with and for years ago. They talked about the feed, the markets and fencin' and leases. There was a lot to be said on both sides of the business. If one part of the country gets rain and another don't the stock foller the feed. In case of winter storms they are liable to drift onto the fences, but on the other hand, when your stock is fenced in you know where to look for 'em. It's your own fault if you overstock your range and then too it keeps your stuff from gettin' held in three or four works every year and that saves 'em a lot of "Chousin'." Another thing mentioned was the fact that folks was payin' as much fer land that would run eleven head to the section as fer land then would run twenty-five. The older women joined in with the men on these talks and don't think fer a minute some women don't know the cow business too.

They had a big flood light rigged up to a tree and it lit up all the picnic grounds and the same lit up the dance hall too. One old feller was settin' quiet smokin' his pipe and a lady sez to him: "Say, I didn't know things like that growed on trees in these parts." "They shore do," the old feller answers. "Any time you git lost along the Sandy on a dark night, jest walk up to a tree and turn on one of them lights. They are mostly ripe about this time of the year."

At twelve o'clock the music let up fer a spell and there was another big feed. The music went to playin' and the dance was on once more. They danced all the old-time dances and the new ones too.

Lisle Henifin who used to own the Music Mountain ranch, is president of the association. He was also master of ceremonies. If everybody didn't have a good time it wasn't his fault. He didn't overlook a person, place or thing. He danced and cooked and interduced folks around till I began to figger he might be twins or mebbyso triplets. I reckon that old boy will have to hole up and sleep a week to git rested up from the work he done, fer he shore done a lot of it and done it right.

We drove back to Kingman through a real Arizona night. The jack rabbits jumpin' across the road and the stars so bright they blazed in the clear sky. But them that has ever been in Arizona knows and them that ain't, well, I can't tell 'em anyway. The next day we went out to the Diamond Bar ranch with Mr. and Mrs. G. T. (Tap) Duncan. I used to work for them, and we had a grand visit and stayed till the next day. They got a picture of Tap and me standin' side by each. The first trial the kodak seemed to soter balk, but the second shot they made it. Our wives said we was enough to make any kodak miss fire. We didn't know what they meant, but we took it to mean we was plenty handsome. The next thing we did was to go over to the King Tutt mine where we had a fine dinner at Byron Duncan's house. Mrs. Charlie Duncan took us to Lake Meade. Tap and I just smoked and talked. Seems like we didn't ever git all said that we wanted to, but Tap's wife was more ambitious. She rigged up a fish line and caught more cat fish than a cob smokin' Missouri farmer ever got on a rainy afternoon. We stayed that night at Charlie's and then come the tough job of startin' home. I had met a lot of old friends and looked out over the country where I had worked in the heat and cold. Where I had saved a tired hoss on a blazin' hot summer day and where I had got down and set fire to rat's nests to thaw out on a cold winter night. There were so many folks that I would like to have spent some time with, but I had only so much time to stay. It was a place that had been home to me for a long time and I hated to leave. We got a welcome such as old time range folks can give an old friend, and I only hope that I can go back when they have the big fall dance and have more time to spare.[3]

Afterword for the City Dweller ~ The Old Night Hawk

I am not a cowboy, or even a want-to-be any more—the work is too hard, and the pay is too low. I am well beyond the age for it anyway, which puts me safely in the never-was category. But like many city dwellers who love the West, I admire ranch people as a general rule. Besides feeding us, they are the stewards of our land and keepers of our connection with the natural world. They have come closest, after the Native Americans, to harmony with a landscape that is both beautiful and harsh. This harmony is a significant and difficult achievement, essentially in opposition to our romantic notions that are driven by need but not grounded in reality. It is one thing to love the land from a climate-controlled vehicle, but it is another to love it in the wind and sleet on horseback. Cattle as a backdrop for western entertainment are a world apart from cattle as living creatures that must be cared for and slaughtered. Standing with honesty and humility on such bedrock facts of life gives a person authority, however gently it may be asserted. Those of us in the cities could benefit by listening more closely to the stories and songs of authoritative voices from the ranges, and we can also hope that the ranchers in their struggles may be able to see us not as encroaching outsiders but as supplicants needing more from them than food.

Now I see, almost twenty years after first encountering his words, that it was Kiskaddon's authority, cushioned though it is by his humor and tolerance, that grabbed my attention and has held it ever since. The stories in this book are largely lighthearted and humorous, but they show signs of the deep currents that ran in this cowboy who became a city dweller, a bellhop, and a poet. Because Kiskaddon addressed his words so specifically to the ranching world, an urban reader must learn a new lingo to follow him, but he is worth the effort. Finishing up with "The Old Night Hawk" closes a long circle for me, for this is the poem that first caught me up in Bruce Kiskaddon's words and that is still my favorite. I hope you like it too.

Bill Siems
Spokane, October 2003

The Old Night Hawk

I am up tonight in the pinnacles bold
Where the rim towers high.
Where the air is clear and the wind blows cold,
And there's only the horses and I.
The valley swims like a silver sea
In the light of the big full moon,
And strong and clear there comes to me
The lilt of the first guard's tune.

The fire at camp is burning bright,
Cook's got more wood than he needs.
They'll be telling some windy tales tonight
Of races and big stampedes.
I'm gettin' too old fer that line of talk.
The desperaders they've knowed,
Their wonderful methods of handling stock,
And the fellers they've seen get throwed.

I guess I'm a dog that's had his day,
Though I still am quick and strong.
My hair and my beard have both turned gray,
And I reckon I've lived too long.
None of 'em know me but that old cook, Ed,
And never a word he'll say.
My story will stick in his old gray head
Till the break of the Judgement Day.

What's that I see a walkin' fast?
It's a hoss a slippin' through.
He was tryin' to make it out through the pass;
Come mighty near doin' it too.
Git back there! What are you tryin' to do?
You hadn't a chance to bolt.
Old boy I was wranglin' a bunch like you
Before you was even a colt.

It's later now. The guard has changed.
One voice is clear and strong.
He's singin' a tune of the old time range—
I always did like that song.
It takes me back to when I was young
And the memories come through my head,
Of the times I have heard that old song sung
By voices now long since dead.

I have traveled better than half my trail.
I am well down the further slope.
I have seen my dreams and ambitions fail,
And memory replaces hope.
It must be true, fer I've heard it said,
That only the good die young.
The tough old cusses like me and Ed
Must stay till the last dog's hung.

I used to shrink when I thought of the past
And some of the things I have known.
I took to drink, but now at last,
I'd far rather be alone.
It's strange how quick that a night goes by,
Fir I live in the days of old.
Up here where there's only the hosses and I;
Up in the pinnacles bold.

The two short years that I ceased to roam,
And I lived a contented life.
Then trouble came and I left my home,
And I never have heard of my wife.
The years that I spent in a prison cell
When I went by another name;
For life is a mixture of Heaven and Hell
To a feller that plays the game.

They'd better lay off of that wrangler kid,
They've give him about enough.
He looks like a pardner of mine once did.
He's the kind that a man can't bluff.
They'll find that they are making a big mistake
If they once get him overhet;
And they'll give him as good as an even break,
Or I'm takin' a hand, you bet.

Look, there in the East is the Mornin' Star.
It shines with a firy glow,
Till it looks like the end of a big cigar,
But it hasn't got far to go.
Just like the people that make a flash.
They don't stand much of a run.
Come bustin' in with a sweep and dash
When most of the work is done.

I can see the East is gettin' gray.
I'll gather the hosses soon;
And faint from the valley far away
Comes the drone of the last guard's tune.
Yes, life is just like the night-herd's song,
As the long years come and go.
You start with a swing that is free and strong,
And finish up tired and slow.

I reckon the hosses all are here.
I can see that T-bar blue,
And the buckskin hoss with the one split ear;
I've got 'em all. Ninety two.
Just listen to how they roll the rocks—
These sure are rough old trails.
But then, if they can't slide down on their hocks,
They can coast along on their tails.

The Wrangler Kid is out with his rope,
He seldom misses a throw.
Will he make a cow hand? Well I hope,
If they give him half a show.
They are throwin' the rope corral around,
The hosses crowd in like sheep.
I reckon I'll swaller my breakfast down
And try to furgit and sleep.

Yes, I've lived my life and I've took a chance,
Regardless of law or vow.
I've played the game and I've had my dance,
And I'm payin' the fiddler now.

NOTES

Introduction

1. Frank M. King, *Western Livestock Journal* (hereafter *WLJ*) 14, no. 1 (26 November 1935), Mavericks section, 17.
2. Bruce Kiskaddon, *Rhymes of the Ranges* (Hollywood: Earl Hayes, 1924), [51].
3. Bruce Kiskaddon, *Rhymes of the Ranges and Other Poems* ([Los Angeles]: n.p., 1947), 177.
4. *WLJ* 13, no. 5 (27 December 1934): 14.
5. Kiskaddon, *Rhymes of the Ranges and Other Poems*, 30.
6. In *WLJ* 12, no. 5 (28 December 1933): 7, Frank M. King quotes an *Albuquerque Journal* article referring to Field's pen technique.
7. In *WLJ* 12, no. 43 (20 September 1934): 6, Frank M. King describes a letter from Katherine Field enclosed with her illustration for "Wet Boots" which makes it clear she was working from the finished poem. On June 5, 2003, Dorothy Chapin, Katherine Field's daughter, told me that usually her mother would draw based on a poem from Kiskaddon, but occasionally Field would create a drawing that would be sent to Kiskaddon for production of a matching poem. Also, she told me at this time that her mother and Kiskaddon never met.
8. For information on Kiskaddon's standing in the world of cowboy poetry, and the obscurity of his history, consult David Stanley and Elaine Thatcher, eds., *Cowboy Poets & Cowboy Poetry* (Urbana and Chicago: University of Illinois Press, 2000). In particular, see David Stanley, "Cowboy Poetry Then and Now: An Overview," 9; Scott Preston, "The Rain Is the Sweat of the Sky: Cowboy Poetry as American Ethnopoetics," 48; Hal Cannon, "Cowboy Poetry: A Poetry of Exile," 67; and Buck Ramsey, "Cowboy Libraries and Lingo," 100.
9. See Crow's praise of Kiskaddon and Field in *WLJ*, 12, no. 9 (25 January 1934), This Week's Comments section, 4; see also his preface to Bruce Kiskaddon, *Western Poems*, illustrated by Katherine Field (Los Angeles: *Western Livestock Journal*, 1935), 6.
10. *WLJ* 11, no. 7 (5 January 1933): 4; *WLJ* 11, no. 13 (23 February 1933): 6.
11. *WLJ* 10, no. 40 (25 August 1932): 1; *WLJ* 11, no. 1 (24 November 1932): 26.
12. From Kiskaddon's introduction to *Rhymes of the Ranges and Other Poems*, 6.
13. John A. Lomax, *Songs of the Cattle Trail and Cow Camp* (New York: Macmillan, 1919), 97–99. Compare Kiskaddon, *Rhymes of the Ranges*, [27], and Kiskaddon, *Rhymes of the Ranges and Other Poems*, 221–22.
14. The dude ranch successor to the Diamond Bar claims on its website that Kiskaddon worked on the ranch and wrote poetry there in 1915; see www.grandcanyonwestranch.com.
15. Birth and death dates were obtained from California Death Index, 1940–1997, accessed through www.ancestry.com. Birthplace was given in an obituary in *The Cattleman*, January 1951, 128. I am also indebted to the genealogical work of Melanie Held, daughter-in-law of Lynn Held, for the names of Kiskaddon's parents, his older sister (Mary K. Bradford of Los Angeles, California), his younger sister

(Eleanor Kiskaddon of Canyon City, Colorado), and younger brother (Lowrie Daniel Kiskaddon, Los Angeles, California), and much other confirming data.

16. See the chapter "Autobiography" for information not otherwise noted.

17. "Bell-hop Succeeds as Poet," *Los Angeles Times*, 11 January 1932, section II, 1.

18. As told to me on August 3, 2003, Lynn Held is quite certain that Kiskaddon was only married once, to Margaret Amelia "Mellie" Larsen, but I remain suspicious that Kiskaddon laced his stories and poems with autobiographical hints.

19. The Lynn Held collection contains a clipping dated August 6, 1917, from the *Daily Free Press*, Ventura, California, entitled "Hotel Employee Joins Cavalry Troop."

20. Lynn Held told me on July 24, 2003, that according to family stories Kiskaddon appeared some time in the 1915–1917 period as one of the Keystone Kops and that he was a chariot driver in the 1925 silent production of *Ben Hur*. She believes her collection contains artifacts related to his work in movies, but they had not surfaced at the time of my visit on August 2–3, 2003.

21. See "News from the Waterhole (Hollywood)," *Farm and Ranch Market Journal* 4, no. 44 (30 September 1926): 2. This is the original name of *Western Livestock Journal*, the name change occurring on May 1, 1930.

22. Bruce Kiskaddon, *Just as Is* (Los Angeles: Hoffman Press, 1928).

23. Birth and death dates were obtained from California Death Index, 1940–1997, accessed through www.ancestry.com. The Held collection includes the marriage license of Bruce and Mellie, and photographs in the collection reveal her small stature.

24. *WLJ* 9, no. 26 (21 May 1931): 4.

25. *WLJ* 13, no. 50 (5 November 1935): 6.

26. Kiskaddon, *Rhymes of the Ranges and Other Poems*, 68–69.

27. Hal Cannon, ed., *Rhymes of the Ranges: A New Collection of the Poems of Bruce Kiskaddon* (Salt Lake City: Peregrine Smith, 1987), 1. Cannon says Kiskaddon worked at the Mayflower, but a *Los Angeles Times* article on January 11, 1932, gives his employer as the Hayward Hotel.

28. Phil Kovinick and Marian Yoshiki-Kovinick, *An Encyclopedia of Women Artists of the American West* (Austin: Univesity of Texas Press, 1998); see also *WLJ* 11, no. 1 (24 November 1932): 26, an article by Frank King about the Field family.

29. Dorothy Chapin, personal communication, 25 June 2003.

30. Kovinick and Yoshiki-Kovinick, *An Encyclopedia of Women Artists of the American West*.

31. John H. (Jack) Culley, *Cattle, Horses, & Men of the Western Range* (Los Angeles: Ward Ritchie Press, 1940).

32. *WLJ* 17, no. 30 (13 June 1939): 33.

33. Dorothy Chapin, personal communication, 25 June 2003.

34. *WLJ* 10, no. 48 (20 October 1932): 12.

35. *WLJ* 10, no. 51 (10 November 1932): 4.

36. *WLJ* 10, no. 48 (20 October 1932): 9.

37. *WLJ* 12, no. 26 (24 May 1934): 14; *WLJ* 14, no. 1 (26 November 1935): 17.

38. *WLJ* 11, no. 27 (1 June 1933): 6.

39. *WLJ* 13, no. 50 (5 November 1935): 6.

40. *WLJ* 9, no. 26 (21 May 1931): 4; *WLJ* 9, no. 54 (3 December 1931): 3; *WLJ* 12, no. 50 (8 November 1934): 3.

41. The Beverly Hillbillies were a singing group organized in 1930 by Glen Rice, station manager of radio station KMPC in Hollywood (see http://www.hensteeth.com/e_discog/hillbill.html). They were among the first to sing western songs in harmony at high speed, predating even Sons of the Pioneers. They have no connection to the 1960s television program of the same name.

42. These advertising jingles for Gorman & Monheim may be found in *Western Livestock Journal* 16, no.

12 (8 February 1938): 30; 16, no. 14 (22 February 1938): 46; 16, no. 16 (8 March 1938): 30; 16, no. 19 (29 April 1938): 19; 16, no. 21 (12 April 1938): 44; and 16, no. 23 (26 April 1938): 36. Although unsigned, their unforced syntax and well-crafted rhythm and rhyme would make anyone familiar with his poetry think of Kiskaddon.

43. Kiskaddon, *Rhymes of the Ranges and Other Poems*, 194.

44. Ibid, 212.

45. Frank M. King, quoted in Kiskaddon, *Rhymes of the Ranges and Other Poems*, 7.

46. Hal Cannon, ed., *Cowboy Poetry: A Gathering* (Salt Lake City: Peregrine Smith, 1985); Hal Cannon, ed., *Rhymes of the Ranges: A New Collection of the Poems of Bruce Kiskaddon*.

47. Mason and Janice Coggin, comps., *Cowboy Poetry Classic Rhymes by Bruce Kiskaddon* (Phoenix: Cowboy Miner, 1998).

48. Bruce Kiskaddon, *Calendar Poems*, 1951/2001, 1935/2002, 1941/2003 (Spring Creek, Nevada: Ruby Mountain Publishing, 2001, 2002, 2003).

49. Kiskaddon, *Rhymes of the Ranges and Other Poems*, 71.

Chapter 1

1. *WLJ* 16, no. 28 (31 May 1938): 34–37.

2. According to California death records Kiskaddon was born November 25, 1878. Thus he would have been ten when Indian territory was opened for homesteading on April 22, 1889, and would have had his first herding experience as a twelve-year-old boy in the summer of 1891. His story "Bill and the Medicine Man Get Quarantined" mentions Barry County in southwest Missouri, so the family may have lived in that area.

3. The phrase "a couple of years later" suggests that the family's move to Colorado occurred sometime between 1891 and 1893, in Kiskaddon's early teen years. Trinidad is in southeastern Colorado and is the county seat of Las Animas county. It is on the eastern side of the Continental Divide that here runs along the crest of the Sangre De Cristo Range. It is situated on the headwaters of the Purgatoire River (Picket-wire in cowboy parlance) where the old Santa Fe Trail crossed that stream. Trinidad was served by four rail lines at that time and had a population over five thousand in the 1900 census. In the surrounding mountains were numerous small mining towns for which Trinidad was a main trade center.

4. The Dry Cimmaron in extreme northeastern New Mexico is "a wonderful place for cattle—the flat at the bottom not very wide, but the sides gradually spreading out as they rise to the level of the mesa country lying north and south more than a thousand feet above the creek bed. Canyons cleave its side walls, deep and rugged in their upper portions, where cattle were hard to reach, and many a steer grew to be an outlaw" (Culley, *Cattle, Horses, & Men of the Western Range*, 199).

5. In his introduction to *Rhymes of the Ranges and Other Poems*, Kiskaddon dates his cowboy work from 1898 when he would have been about nineteen years old, but it seems from his description of youthful jobs with John, Johnson, Templin, and Gresham that he had significant experience in his earlier teen years. Perhaps he dated the beginning of his ranch work from a final leaving of the family home in town.

6. Deer Trail and Limon are far north of Trinidad in east-central Colorado, about fifty to seventy miles southeast of Denver.

7. Rincon is Spanish for a corner or a remote place.

8. The JJ was a large and well-known ranch on the Picket-wire. Culley, *Cattle, Horses & Men of the Western Range*.

9. The flash flood on the Picket-wire probably occurred in 1904, and Kiskaddon encountered the grown Tommy Carter some time after he came to Los Angeles in 1924 and moved to the Hollywood area.

10. Kiskaddon here states his preferences on three controversial points of cowboy gear and practice: he uses a short rope made of hemp or other fiber rather than a long, rawhide riata; he ties the rope fast to the saddle horn rather than using the quick temporary wraps ("dallies") which can save a busted cinch but also can cost a finger or thumb; and his preferred saddle has two cinches ("double rig") rather than one ("center fire").

11. This is the only mention in Kiskaddon's writings of his having a crippling accident in 1906; see "Bell-hop Succeeds as Poet," *Los Angeles Times* 11 January 1932, section II, 1.

12. About 1912.

13. August 1914.

14. The dude ranch successor to the Diamond Bar claims on its website that Kiskaddon worked on the ranch and wrote poetry there in 1915; see www.grandcanyonwestranch.com.

15. Kiskaddon would have been thirty-eight when he enlisted in 1917.

16. In 1919.

17. In his introduction to *Rhymes of the Ranges and Other Poems*, Kiskaddon credits Duncan with encouraging him to write poetry.

18. Los Angeles.

Chapter 2

1. *WLJ* 11, no. 11 (1 June 1933): 6.

2. *WLJ* 10, no. 48 (20 October 1932): 10.

3. *WLJ* 11, no. 46 (12 October 1933): 6.

4. *WLJ* 11, no. 1 (24 November 1932): 28.

5. The use of the word "home" here is curious because the following sentences make it clear he does not mean his parents' home, and he would likely refer to a cow ranch or camp with some word other than "home." Possibly Kiskaddon was married at this time.

6. *WLJ* 11, no. 32 (6 July 1933): 6.

7. *WLJ* 11, no. 5 (22 December 1932): 10.

8. *WLJ* 11, no. 41 (7 September 1933): 6.

9. *WLJ* 10, no. 40 (25 August 1932): 13.

Chapter 3

1. *WLJ* 12, no. 9 (25 January 1934): 12.

2. *WLJ* 12, no. 13 (22 February 1934): 10.

3. *WLJ* 12, no. 17 (22 March 1934): 14, 16.

4. *WLJ* 12, no. 22 (26 April 1934): 14, 16.

5. Baile is Spanish for dance.

6. "Auger" is used to describe either a high-powered discussion or good-natured banter. It probably derives from "argue."

7. The "powders" are the boss's orders.

8. *WLJ* 12, no. 44 (27 September 1934): 16.

9. *WLJ* 12, no. 26 (24 May 1934): 14.

10. A "hoggin' string" is a short length of flexible rope used to immobilize a thrown animal by tying its legs together, and "whangs" are leather tie-downs attached to a saddle.

Chapter 4

1. *WLJ* 12, no. 31 (28 June 1934): 16.
2. The original article has "Lige" in this place, an obvious error.
3. *WLJ* 12, no. 35 (26 July 1934): 18.
4. "Leaks out from" is one of Shorty's favorite synonyms for "leave."
5. *WLJ* 12, no. 40 (30 August 1934): 16.
6. *WLJ* 12, no. 48 (25 October 1934): 32.
7. To "cold jaw" is to refuse to be guided by the reins.
8. *WLJ* 13, no. 1 (29 November 1934): 20.
9. This incident is a good example of the down side of tie-fast roping.
10. *WLJ* 13, no. 5 (27 December 1934): 14.
11. *WLJ* 13, no. 10 (31 January 1935): 20.

Chapter 5

1. *WLJ* 13, no. 18 (28 March 1935): 27.
2. *WLJ* 13, no. 22 (25 April 1935): 20.
3. This seems to refer to a story that was never published.
4. *WLJ* 13, no. 27 (30 May 1935): 22.
5. Riding boots are built to slide easily from stirrups, partially to avoid grave injury or death that can come to a thrown rider snared by one foot in a stirrup and dragged by a runaway horse.
6. *WLJ* 13, no. 31 (25 June 1935): 18.
7. Bill is describing the ruin of a fine old piece of professional gear, Ed's double-rigged saddle ("hull"), which has had its rear ("flank") cinch and leather tie-downs ("whangs") removed. It is covered with chicken dung and is also lacking the rope, slicker, and saddle blankets that would be standard accessories on a working saddle.
8. In other words, a formerly stylish cowboy has turned into a frump.
9. To cowboys who hate any work that cannot be done on horseback, Ed appears totally debased, working from before dawn until after dark, digging with an irrigating shovel, milking cows, and slopping hogs.
10. Chopping wood is, of course, another job that cannot be done on horseback.
11. "Lietige" is probably a spelling of latigo, a stout leather strap used to connect a cinch to rigging rings of a saddle.
12. Shorty asks how Bill could have had his reins swiped by Homer, since he can see Bill's horse has a fine headstall and good quality split leather reins. Bill explains that even though he had told Ed he would use two hoggin' strings for reins, he had gotten even with Homer, and then some, by swiping Homer's headstall, leaving Homer his old headstall in return, and cutting himself new reins from the rear latigos of Homer's saddle, the good saddle that he had seen the night before near Ed's old wreck.
13. The "night hawk" tends the remuda (horse herd) through the night.
14. *WLJ* 13, no. 36 (30 July 1935): 18.
15. A "rep" (representative) for a brand travels to distant roundups to gather cattle that have wandered from the home range. Because of the responsibility the position has high status. A "nester" is a homesteader.
16. The "throw back" are cattle with brands belonging to the rep that have been gathered aside to be driven back to their home range.

17. *WLJ* 13, no. 40 (27 August 1935): 35, 38.
18. "Drag it" is another synonym for leave.
19. *WLJ* 13, no. 44 (24 September 1935): 30–31.
20. *WLJ* 13, no. 49 (29 October 1935): 59–60.
21. *WLJ* 14, no. 6 (31 December 1935): 25–26.
22. Of course the court clerk is writing in shorthand.

Chapter 6

1. *WLJ* 14, no. 10 (28 January 1936): 47–48.
2. *WLJ* 14, no. 14 (25 February 1936): 36.
3. Dinner is the noon meal.
4. In other words, Rildy's description of local geologic strata is borne out by the professor's reference material.
5. The hot, dry desert climate is responsible for the skin irritation, aggravated by repeated wetting and drying cycles that afflict horses and men.
6. Rildy has gotten back at Eph for his verbal attacks of the night before and for his jealousy of her attentions to the professor.
7. Typewriter.
8. The professor probably has ridden thoroughly trained saddle horses in the east, but he is unprepared for a less docile range horse, even one as accustomed to human handling as Old Barney. But he redeems himself in Shorty's eyes by analyzing his mistakes in what follows.
9. *WLJ* 14, no. 19 (31 March 1936): 54–55.
10. These are English riding saddles, lacking a saddle horn as well as the swell fork and high cantle which help a rider keep his seat on a bucker or while working cattle.
11. This is a safety razor with replaceable blades.
12. The professors are apparently liberals, favoring women's suffrage, which was certainly a hot issue in the 1900 time frame of the story. The west, then as now, was much controlled by government policies and bureaucracy, and the suffrage issue opens the door for Zeb to get off a salvo both at women and the absurdities of "the real government idee."
13. Zeb is taking a swing here at some of the crazy theories of dry farming, widely held in the early years of the century and originating from purportedly scientific authorities, like the notion that deep plowing preserved soil moisture. Such ideas played a key role in the genesis of the Dust Bowl experiences of the 1930s, events which Kiskaddon is letting Zeb predict in this passage.
14. That is, Eph has been bucked off when he first tries to ride the newly caught Chunky, and this creates an opportunity to bemuse the professors with some of the vast array of synonyms for being bucked off—Chunky "sunned [Eph's] moccasins," "broke in two," "swallowed his head," and so on.
15. Horses are social animals with a strong tendency to form a herd, but a "hoss fool" is a horse with an extreme case of this characteristic.
16. The first professor intends to catch a mount for the second professor from the herd in the large pasture. Because Gander is a hoss fool who likes to run long and hard (a "coon tailer"), the potential for disaster is great and leads to Shorty's offer to wrangle the pasture himself for more suitable horses for the professors. Of course both professors are smug and too busy making jokes and puns over Shorty's western speech to heed his warning.
17. The first professor has gathered a group of horses and is coming up toward the corral, but this herd spooks, perhaps as a result of the ruckus the professor is making with his riding crop and little spurs, and this causes the runaway and wreck that follow.

18. *WLJ* 14, no. 23 (28 April 1936): 39–40.
19. To "set up" is to rein a horse to a quick stop.
20. *WLJ* 14, no. 27 (26 May 1936): 35–36.
21. *WLJ* 14, no. 32 (30 June 1936): 47.
22. *WLJ* 14, no. 36 (28 July 1936): 41.
23. "Pirootin'" probably comes from pirouetting.
24. The spiritual heirs of Lem Sikes still deal in worthless and ill-assorted livestock, such as this elderly pacing horse in cow country, but their trading stock has expanded to include acres of rusted vehicles and machinery.
25. The professor is getting a low mark in horsemanship from Shorty. His tight rein on the old pacer is a pain-inflicting style of horsemanship that can produce such a "star gazer," a horse that habitually holds its head cocked back to escape pressure on the bit. A gentle snaffle bit might barely be noticed by a horse with a mouth as tough as the pacer's probably is, accounting for its wide turns. The loose reins, sensitive mouth, and abrupt turns the professor refers to negatively would in fact indicate a well-trained cow horse with a skillful rider.
26. Shorty is keenly aware of the absurdity of this hound ever being able to catch a coyote.
27. *WLJ* 14, no. 40 (25 August 1936): 50-52.
28. *WLJ* 14, no. 45 (29 September 1936): 29-31.
29. The cook's move gives him the high trump in the irrigation game, probably to the consternation of Rildy's uncle.
30. *WLJ* 14, no. 49 (27 October 1936): 33–35.

Chapter 7

1. *WLJ* 15, no. 2 (1 December 1936): 56–57, 60.
2. Between 1899 and 1902.
3. The William McKinley vs. William Jennings Bryan election was held in 1896.
4. November 11.
5. This is probably a reference to the soil erosion associated with the 1930s dust storms.
6. It was Bill, not Shorty, who tied his horse to the Indian in "Bill's Injun Trouble."
7. The captain was apparently insulting Bill for lacking the wrangler's cleverness.
8. White wine.
9. A soldier from the regular ranks who has been detailed into an easy duty, and who is thus able to stay clean.
10. A demi-liter would be a half liter.
11. *WLJ* 15, no. 6 (29 December 1936): 30–32.
12. The global influenza epidemic of 1918 caused 20 million deaths.

Chapter 8

1. *WLJ* 15, no. 10 (26 January 1937): 52.
2. An unemployed cowhand who rides from ranch to ranch, counting on western hospitality for his food, is said to "ride the grub line."
3. *WLJ* 15, no. 15 (2 March 1937): 35–36.
4. *WLJ* 15, no. 19 (30 March 1937): 41–43.
5. *WLJ* 15, no. 27 (25 May 1937): 37–38.
6. The incident referred to does not appear in any story that was found.

7.   *WLJ* 15, no. 36 (27 July 1937): 24–25.
8.   The roadrunner discussion had appeared in one of Frank M. King's Mavericks gossip columns.
9.   *WLJ* 15, no. 41 (31 August 1937) 26–27.

Chapter 9

1.   *WLJ* 15, no. 23 (27 April 1937): 31–33. "Shorty Corrects a Mistake" originally appeared between "Shorty Hears Ike Analyze Words" and "The Boss Buys a Mare," but it has been placed here because it begins the story that "The Fortune Teller Sends Ike Fishing" and "Ike Has Trouble with His Hat" continue. The order of the latter two stories has also been reversed to follow the temporal progression of the events of the narrative.
2.   The "mistake" Shorty has corrected is no mistake at all, but Spud's attempt to frame Ike for stealing a calf. Particularly in open range country, an unweaned calf having brand and ear marks different from its mother is strong evidence that the owner of that brand was attempting to steal the calf. Ike participates in the marking and branding because Spud claims he is replacing an animal of the Boss's "beefed" (killed and eaten) by Spud's crew. By using a brand and ear marks similar to the Boss's, Spud has been setting himself up for large-scale rustling of the Boss's stock, but Shorty cleverly turns the trick around by changing the Boss's brand and marks into Spud's.
3.   *WLJ* 16, no. 2 (30 November 1937): 60–62.
4.   Much of what Madame Egypta says in this paragraph is descriptive of Kiskaddon's life.
5.   The original mistakenly has "Bill" here.
6.   The chore man has now done a double back flip and is again in allegiance with Spud. It is not clear how Ike deduces their responsibility for the holdup and murder, nor does Shorty mention that he and Ike are expecting to encounter Spud at the work to which they are heading, and that they must try not to arouse his suspicion as they arrange his undoing.
7.   The deputy probably wants the buckboard for Spud's remains.
8.   *WLJ* 15, no. 49 (26 October 1937): 42–44.
9.   *WLJ* 16, no. 6 (28 December 1937): 26–28.
10. *WLJ* 16, no. 10 (25 January 1938): 62–64.
11. *WLJ* 16, no. 14 (22 February 1938): 21–22.

Chapter 10

1.   *WLJ* 16, no. 19 (29 March 1938): 24–27.
2.   *WLJ* 16, no. 32 (28 June 1938): 18–19.
3.   *WLJ* 16, no. 41 (30 August 1938): 38–40.
4.   *WLJ* 16, no. 47 (11 October 1938): 27–28.
5.   *WLJ* 16, no. 51 (8 November 1938): 47–48.
6.   *WLJ* 17, no. 8 (10 January 1939): 23–25.
7.   Relations have become so strained that Ike has not only threatened Cap and the boss, but Shorty is armed and ready to pull his revolver.
8.   "Hell among the Yearlin's" is a well-known old fiddle tune, and its title is emblematic of the hired hands' refusal to be cowed by the boss and Cap.
9.   While it is clear that Ike, along with the Tingles and the Blacks, is trying to finesse Cap and the boss out of the winter range in Middle Valley, it is not yet clear to Shorty how he plans to do it.
10. Big ranch operators in the 1900 era frequently used the homestead rights of their hired hands to gain control of public land. Each person had a one-time right to claim 160 acres of public land for a homestead

and could gain outright ownership by meeting requirements for residence and improvement of the land. Once employees had achieved ownership, the rancher would purchase the land from them. Control over large areas of unowned public land could result from ownership of key parcels, especially those with significant water rights.

11. By going into partnership with the two Tingles, and using their and his own homestead rights, Ike has beaten Cap and the boss to the key land parcels in Middle Valley, a scheme Ike has clearly been hatching for some time.

12. As yet Ike has no stock in Middle Valley, and Cap and the boss have tried to grab the winter feed by pushing in their cattle, in spite of the dangers posed by lack of water and green alfalfa, which causes cattle to bloat. The only cure for alfalfa bloat was to puncture an afflicted cow like a balloon, and Ike and his partners have declined to save the afflicted animals belonging to Cap and the boss.

13. If there is not enough grass for the cattle on the winter range, they must be fed hay, which of course must have been grown the previous season or be purchased.

14. *WLJ* 17, no. 13 (14 February 1939): 19, 45–46.

15. While the boss and Cap have been focused on Middle Valley, Ike has gotten control of feed that Cap and Morton on the South Ranch had thought they could count on.

Chapter 11

1. *WLJ* 17, no. 49 (24 October 1939): 46, 48.

2. *WLJ* 17, no. 28 (30 May 1939): 21–23.

3. The original article concludes, "The Mohave Livestock Growers are a mighty fine bunch of folks and no doubt you know some of them. Lisle Henifin is president; John Neal, vice president; Mrs. John Neal, treasurer; and A. J. Mullen, secretary. The directors are Wm. Epperson, Clyde Cofer, Tommy Walker, Miner Bishop, Curtis Neal, E. M. Garrow, Aubrey Gist, B. S. Fox, E. L. Jameson, C. L. Cornwall and T. G. Walker."